INTERNATIONAL HUMAN RIGHTS, SOCIAL POLICY AND GLOBAL DEVELOPMENT

Critical Perspectives

Edited by
Gerard McCann and Féilim Ó hAdhmaill

Foreword by Albie Sachs

First published in Great Britain in 2020 by

Policy Press
University of Bristol
1-9 Old Park Hill
Bristol
BS2 8BB
UK
t: +44 (0)117 954 5940
pp-info@bristol.ac.uk
www.policypress.co.uk

North America office:
Policy Press
c/o The University of Chicago Press
1427 East 60th Street
Chicago, IL 60637, USA
t: +1 773 702 7700
f: +1 773-702-9756
sales@press.uchicago.edu
www.press.uchicago.edu

British Library Cataloguing in Publication Data
A catalogue record for this book is available from the British Library

Library of Congress Cataloging-in-Publication Data
A catalog record for this book has been requested

ISBN 978-1-4473-4921-1 hardcover
ISBN 978-1-4473-4923-5 ePub
ISBN 978-1-4473-4922-8 ePdf

The right of Gerard McCann and Féilim Ó hAdhmaill to be identified as editors of this work has been asserted by them in accordance with the Copyright, Designs and Patents Act 1988.

The statements and opinions contained within this publication are solely those of the editors and contributors and not of the University of Bristol or Policy Press. The University of Bristol and Policy Press disclaim responsibility for any injury to persons or property resulting from any material published in this publication.

Policy Press works to counter discrimination on grounds of gender, race, disability, age and sexuality.

Cover design by Andrew Corbett
Front cover image: iStock-157327289 (1)
Printed and bound in Great Britain by CPI Group (UK) Ltd, Croydon, CR0 4YY
Policy Press uses environmentally responsible print partners

Contents

Notes on contributors

Margaret Buckley is Senior Tutor in the School of Applied Social Studies, University College Cork. She teaches a diverse range of topics which include politics, Irish social policy and social research methods. In 2014, she was awarded an Irish Research Council Postgraduate Scholarship. Her doctoral research examines life expectancy and mortality rates in relation to changing social policy measures.

Diana Buttu is a lawyer based in Palestine and an instructor at Harvard's Extension School. She teaches conflict resolution, negotiation and international law. Ms Buttu's areas of practice and research are in international human rights law, and international humanitarian law. Ms Buttu previously served as a legal advisor to the Palestinian negotiating team in its negotiations with Israel.

Michal Cenker was a research associate at the Institute of International Relations in Prague and the UNIDEV academic coordinator at Pontis Foundation in Slovakia. He has coordinated projects in North Africa and Eastern Europe and has a number of publications on international migration and development, migrant rights and development education. He currently works with the Ministry of Interior of the Slovak Republic on the reform of public administration bodies. He co-edited *Development Education in Theory and Practice* (2016).

Peter Collins is Senior Lecturer in History at St Mary's University College, Belfast. He is a founder member and editorial board member of *History Ireland* magazine. He is the director of annual summer schools for US universities and colleges, including Minnesota, Carleton, Michigan, Wisconsin, Notre Dame, Old Dominion, Washington & Jefferson, UMASS and many others.

Dessie Donnelly is Director at the Belfast-based Participation and the Practice of Rights (PPR – www.pprproject.org) and has been with the organisation since its inception in 2006. PPR organises across a range of social and economic rights issues and jurisdictions, building power with marginalised communities to force accountability and transparency from the state, expand democratic participation and effect real change. Prior to PPR, Dessie was an organiser with both the Irish and North American labour union movements.

Fiona Donson is Senior Lecturer in Law and the Director of the Centre for Criminal Justice and Human Rights in the Law School, UCC. She researches in the areas of children's rights and criminal justice, administrative justice and free speech/political activism. Her current research primarily focuses on children's rights and the impact of parental imprisonment. Her book *Parental Imprisonment and Children's Rights*, which is co-edited with Dr Aisling Parkes, was published by Routledge in 2019. Fiona also has a human rights practice background. She was a human rights practitioner in Cambodia between 2002 and 2007 where she was responsible for projects on child rights, particularly working on child labour and juvenile justice.

Fiona Dukelow is Senior Lecturer in Social Policy at University College Cork. Her research interests include critical welfare theory and various aspects of historical and contemporary Irish social policy. She is co-author, with Mairéad Considine, of *Irish Social Policy: A Critical Introduction* (2017) and co-editor, with Mary P. Murphy, of *The Irish Welfare State in the Twenty-First Century, Challenges and Change* (2016).

Giovanni Farese is Associate Professor of Economic History at the European University of Rome. He is Managing Editor of *The Journal of European Economic History* and is a Marshall Memorial Fellow of the German Marshall Fund of the United States. He co-edited the first annotated edition of Keynes' *General Theory* (2019), and is co-author of *Il banchiere del mondo: Eugene R. Black e l'ascesa della cultura dello sviluppo* [*The World Banker: Eugene R. Black and the Rise of the Culture of Development*] (2014). He is writing a history of Mediobanca, an Italian merchant bank, and its activities in the Global South in the post-war years.

Joe Finnerty is Course Director of the Higher Diploma in Social Policy at University College Cork. His research and teaching interests focus on the evaluation of policies impacting on housing precarity and homelessness. He is a coordinator of the Welfare Policy, Homelessness and Social Exclusion working group of the European Network of Housing Research, and a member of the Cork-Kerry Youth out of Home Forum. His most recent research is *Last Resort: Vulnerabilities, Resilience and Quality of Life in a Homeless Population*, published by Cork Simon Community in 2018.

Ann Marie Gray is Professor of Social Policy in the School of Criminology, Politics and Social Policy, Ulster University. She is also co-director of the ARK project (www.ark.ac.uk). Publications include two co-authored books published by Policy Press: *Transforming Adult Social Care: Contemporary Policy and Practice* (2013) and *Delivering Social Welfare: Governance and Service Provision in the UK* (2016).

Liz Griffith is a policy officer at Law Centre (NI) where she works primarily on employment and immigration issues. She previously worked as a caseworker at Refugee Legal Centre in Birmingham. She plays an active role in the Refugee Action Group and is a Trustee of the Horn of Africa Project. She has an LLM in Human Rights Law. Liz recently travelled to observe rights issues in Sudan.

Peter Herrmann is currently Professor of the Law School of Central South University, Changsha, China. His career spans positions in the Max-Planck Institute for Social Law and Social Policy, Munich (Germany), Berlin School of Economics and Law (Germany), University of Eastern Finland (Finland), and universities in Poland, The Netherlands, Italy, Russia and Ireland. He is a member of the European Academy of Science and Arts. His latest publications include *Right to Stay – Right to Move* (2019); and *Is There Still Any Value in It? Revisiting Value and Valuation in a Globalising Digital World* (2019).

Daniel Holder is Deputy Director of the Committee on the Administration of Justice (CAJ), which lobbies and campaigns on a broad range of human rights issues. Prior to this, Daniel worked for the STEP programme advocating for the rights of refugees, asylum seekers and minority ethnic groups across Ireland and Britain.

Nadia Makaryshyn is a researcher and lecturer at Lviv National University of Ivan Franko, Ukraine. She specialises in the fields of socio-linguistics and variantology. In March 2019 she was one of the coordinators of an international student exchange programme between the UK and Ukraine. She has also coordinated student involvement at the International Youth Festival organised by Krosno State College, Poland.

Benjamin Mallon is Assistant Professor in Development and Intercultural Education in the School of STEM Education, Innovation & Global Studies in the Institute of Education, Dublin City University. He researches and teaches in the area of Global Citizenship Education. Ben is on the Editorial Board of *Policy and Practice: A Development Education Review*.

Gerard McCann is Senior Lecturer in International Studies and Head of International Programmes at St Mary's University College, a College of Queen's University Belfast. In 2017 he was awarded an Honorary Professorship by the Jagiellonian University in Kraków and is a Visiting Professor at the Università Europea di Roma. Books or co-edited books include the three-volume *From the Local to the Global* (2003, 2011, 2015), *Ireland's Economic History* (2011), *Issues in Economic Development in Sub-Saharan Africa* (2011) and *Lustration* (2016). He coordinates a number of African diaspora projects.

Stephen McCloskey is Director of the Centre for Global Education, based in Belfast, and editor of *Policy and Practice: A Development Education Review*. He is co-editor of the three-volume *From the Local to the Global: Key Issues in Development Studies* (2003, 2011, 2015) and editor of *Development Education in Policy and Practice* (2014). He is coordinator of an education partnership in Gaza and has worked extensively in the Middle East.

Adam Nowakowski is Associate Professor in the Institute of Philology at the Jagiellonian University in Kraków. He is author of *W kraju Tysiąca Jezior* (2019) on intercultural interpretation and is currently undertaking research on the international diaspora experience. He has recently been coordinating academic visits to border regions of the eastern European Union and Ukraine.

Féilim Ó hAdhmaill is Lecturer in the School of Applied Social Studies at University College Cork where he is Programme Director for the Masters in Voluntary Sector Management. He teaches Social Policy, Community Development and Peace and Conflict Studies and his academic research and publications have focused primarily on social exclusivity and inequality, the voluntary sector, community development, and conflict transformation. He has a background working in the community/voluntary sector in Ireland, north and south, over many years and is currently on the Editorial Board of the journal *Voluntary Sector Review*.

Cathal O'Connell, Professor, is Head of School of the School of Applied Social Studies, University College Cork, Ireland. His main teaching, research and publication interests lie in the areas of Irish social policy development, housing policy, housing management and urban regeneration. His recent research has focused on children and young people in housing regeneration and quality of life in social housing.

Charles O'Mahony is a Head of the School of Law at the National University of Ireland, Galway. Charles teaches in the areas of comparative disability law and health law and policy. His research is broadly in the field of disability law, examining the intersection of mental health law and policy with the criminal justice system. He completed a PhD at the Centre for Disability Law and Policy, NUI Galway entitled 'Diversion: A Comparative Study of Law and Policy Relating to Defendants and Offenders with Mental Health Problems and Intellectual Disability'.

Fred Powell is Professor of Social Policy at University College Cork–National University of Ireland. His most recent books include: *Youth Policy, Civil Society and the Modern Irish State* (2012); *The Politics of Civil Society* (2013); *Dark Secrets of Childhood: Media Power, Child Abuse and Public Scandal* (2015); and *The Political Economy of the Irish Welfare State* (2017), which won the Richard Titmuss Book Prize 2018. He is currently researching education and the working class in Ireland.

Shivaun Quinlivan is Law Lecturer at the National University of Ireland, Galway. She primarily teaches Constitutional Law and Inclusive Education Law and Policy which focuses on educational rights for children with disabilities. She is a founding member of the Centre for Disability Law and Policy at NUI Galway and is currently on its board of management. She is a co-editor of *The Right to Inclusive Education in International Human Rights Law*, published by Cambridge University Press in 2019.

Mike Ritchie has worked on human rights and transitional justice issues for the last 35 years. He helped establish the ICRC in the north of Ireland as well as acting variously as Director of the Committee on the Administration of Justice, the main human rights body in the north of Ireland and Coiste na nIarchimí, the coordinating organisation for IRA ex-prisoners. Currently he is Casework Manager with the Relatives for Justice.

Birgit Schippers is Senior Lecturer in Politics at St Mary's University College, a College of Queen's University Belfast, and a visiting research fellow at the Senator George J. Mitchell Institute at Queen's. Her book publications include *Julia Kristeva and Feminist Thought, The Political Philosophy of Judith Butler* (2014), *Critical Perspectives on Human Rights* (2019) and *The Routledge Handbook to Rethinking Ethics in International Relations* (2020).

Acknowledgements

This book is the product of an international and multidisciplinary conversation around the nature and development of human rights. There is the general belief among our authors that the discourse around human rights has to be essentially sociological and developmental in order to ensure the effective application of this crucial aspect of policy-making and human development. There is also the belief that our engagement with this topic should entail a critical position in order to fully interrogate oversights and deficiencies in state applications of human rights in an increasingly hostile, truth-averse and sceptical geo-political environment. In order to get some appreciation of the complexities of this dialogue between social policy, international development and human rights, the authors have trawled through primary and secondary documents, laws and international agreements which have marked the formation of this topic. This research is built upon a platform created by a long list of critical theorists and hopefully a clearer overview of human rights as a developmental process has resulted. In terms of acknowledgements, we would like to thank Policy Press for encouraging the initial idea and having the patience to undertake such a task. Likewise, we would like to offer our appreciation to all the contributors, the Policy Press staff and associates for their understanding throughout what has been long and engaging process. For comments on the points made or reading drafts, we would like to acknowledge the help of Stephen McCloskey, Birgit Schippers, Angela Vaupel, Colin Harvey, Ciaran Crossey, Eoin Ó Broin, Chris Brighton, Liz Griffith, Peter Collins, Denis O'Hearn and Paul Hainsworth. Ba mhaith linn buíochas a ghabháil lenár gcomhghleacaithe agus lena gcairde i gColáiste na hOllscoile, Corcaigh agus i gColáiste Ollscoile Naomh Muire as a dtacaíocht agus a spreagadh le linn an tionscadail seo. Ba mhaith linn an deis seo a thapú freisin chun buíochas a ghabháil, le Máiréad agus le Karen go háirithe as a dtuiscint agus a dtacaíocht thar na hamanna deacra go léir agus an leabhar seo á chur le chéile. Finally, thanks are also due to the helpful librarians and colleagues in St Mary's University College, Queen's University, University College, Cork, Trinity College, Dublin, the Jagiellonian University, Kraków and Lviv University, Ukraine. While opinions are those of the authors, faults and flaws, neglect and oversights are due, in total, to the editors.

Foreword

Albie Sachs

What makes the human rights field so interesting is the constant battle between the general concepts and understandings, and their actual application in the lives of specific people on the ground. It is not difficult to set out certain general themes. We can state confidently that for decades now universal human rights and the international instruments which have been designed to promote and protect them, have been a source of hope for many in the world who have been denied freedom, equality and the basic means of survival. They have also provided a discourse and a set of tools for those seeking to end oppression. Ultimately, they show us a way to achieve global peace and solidarity.

Equally, the somewhat bolder ones among us can declare comfortably that as a general rule universal human rights are also a contested site, in terms of their articulation, interpretation and implementation. Universal human rights are not simply something handed down to us by the gods or nature; they are the creation of human agency, imagination, creativity, humanity and above all struggle. The universal human rights – civil, political, social, economic, cultural, environmental, developmental, individual and collective – which we know today, have had a long history in their making; one of protest, revolt, revolution and suffering. As the famous Irish poet, Seamus Heaney, so eloquently wrote:

> History says, don't hope,
> On this side of the grave.
> But then, once in a lifetime
> The longed-for tidal wave
> Of Justice can rise up,
> And hope and history rhyme
> (from the play *The Cure at Troy*)
> *Seamus Heaney, 1990*

An associate of my late colleague and comrade Professor Kader Asmal, who was Dean of Trinity College Law School, head of the Irish Anti-Apartheid movement and a great exponent of universal human rights, Heaney could have been thinking about the struggle against apartheid.

He knew in his bones that it was in those moments of upheaval that the greatest advances had occurred in the development of human rights around the world. The campaigns for workers and female suffrage, the campaigns by labour unions for workers social and economic rights, the struggles for self-determination against colonialism and neo-colonialism, the campaigns to abolish slavery in all its forms, the civil rights movements, the campaign to end homosexual oppression, all have contributed to the development of recognisable and accepted concepts of universal human rights.

And who would doubt that it was the world-wide death and destruction caused by World War II, including the Holocaust, which was to spur the world into action in trying to develop an International Bill of Human Rights? This, in turn, led first to the United Nations Universal Declaration of Human Rights in 1948, and then the two Covenants on civil and political rights, and on social, economic and cultural rights in 1966; the raft of subject-specific United Nations Conventions, particularly since the end of the Cold War; and a range of regional rights mechanisms such as the European Convention on Human Rights, the American Convention on Human Rights, the African Charter on Human and Peoples' Rights and the Arab Charter on Human Rights.

Similarly, it is widely accepted that human rights and the instruments created to promote and protect them are continually developing; changing with political and economic shifts in the world and our understanding of it. The struggle to develop and implement them is also a continuing process. What is not so well known is the detail of actual people struggling in specific situations to test the strength and adaptability on the ground of these generally accepted notions.

It is precisely this focus that makes this book so trenchant and timely. These are thoughtful and intense despatches from the frontline of the human rights struggle. *International Human Rights, Social Policy and Global Development*, in its twenty-one chapters (including the Introduction), attempts to describe, critique and add to our understanding of both the history of human rights developments, the strengths and weaknesses of existing international human rights instruments, and their potential application by citizens, NGOs, voluntary organisations and communities to advance social policy, global development and global welfare. The book argues that both the concept of universal human rights and the international instruments developed to promote them are sites of continuing struggle. So it has been historically and so it will be into the future. Despite their obvious weaknesses and failings and their abuse by the powerful, such international instruments can be part of the armoury to fight oppression, inequality and injustice 'if', in the words of John Lennon, 'we choose it'.

Thus, this book provides an important tool for any of us wishing not only to understand universal human rights and protect, promote and develop them, but also to use human rights-based approaches to social policy and global development. With twenty-four authors from different parts of the world and with different life experiences, backgrounds and opinions, the book provides a wide range of thoughts, ideas and views on international human rights today. Written from an unperfumed, critical perspective, it raises questions about human rights and challenges *common-sense* beliefs. While the different views expressed in the chapters may not be shared by all, the challenges they raise are something that we all should recognise and seek to address.

Lamentations and denunciations have their place in human rights activity, but they are not enough. Rolled up sleeves and positive, affirmative energy are required. The main message flowing through the pages of this book is one of gutsy determination and hope: the hope which concepts of universal human rights can bring to a world filled with inequality, injustice, suffering and poverty amidst plenty. The candle on the cover of this book is particularly significant. A candle flickering in the wind of adversity can be strong, a beacon of light, but it can also be fragile and blown out if we are not careful. It can also light other candles all over the world without diminishing its strength in any way and create new patterns of light with each new flame – an important message for all of us.

This is a stimulating book written by people with courage, humanity and integrity. It can open minds, provoke debate and prompt greater action and energy among academics, NGOs, activists and citizens to strive for a better world. In keeping with its own critical spirit, its findings and recommendations should be thought about and where necessary challenged by other equally keen-minded and committed scholar-activists. But, above all, it should be read, engaged with and acted upon.

Albie Sachs
Activist, lawyer, Professor *Extraordinaire*, University of Pretoria, former Constitutional Court Judge (South Africa) and National Executive member of the African National Congress
Cape Town, January 2020

Introduction

Gerard McCann and Féilim Ó hAdhmaill

Much has been written about the development of international human rights, the concepts, mechanisms and their implementation, from legal and institutional perspectives. Arguably, however, there has been a paucity of literature on the subject from a critical social policy-based perspective and hesitancy by policy-makers and analysts alike to challenge threats to a rights-based approach to human development. In an increasingly challenging geo-political context, with various state attempts to reverse even the most basic of rights, many communities have been left to deal with contradictions between the aspirations of the 1948 Universal Declaration of Human Rights and the systemic abuses that are so prevalent across the world today. Indeed, given the current diverging trajectories of inter-state governance, there is an urgent need to revisit the very concept of the universality of human rights, the processes that led to their development and the factors that could ensure the implementation of an internationally accepted rights-based policy framework.

In the volatility of the post-Cold War international order, there has been a drive to recognise the contribution of a rights-based philosophical discourse on equality, democracy and social justice, as well as ongoing dialogue on the impact of human agency itself in securing human rights (Alston and Goodman, 2013: 3–57; Donnelly, 2013: 7–23; Weissbrodt et al, 2009; Gearty and Douzinas, 2012; Morris, 2006). This discourse has not taken place in a vacuum. Ideology, cultural formation, geo-political considerations and combative power relations have all meant that universal human rights are being increasingly contested at a macro-level, in the development of policies to support them, and in the establishment of oversight mechanisms. They are also increasingly being contested and defended at a micro-level, by civil society for example, when it comes to the justiciability, realisability and enforceability of rights. Human rights are, essentially, about how humans interact with each other, how we view each other, and how our governments are obliged to protect citizens and others. As Mark

Frezzo highlights in *The Sociology of Human Rights*, rights relate to social cohesion and interdependence:

> our understanding of human rights has a great effect on our capacity to feel empathy for human beings experiencing interstate war, civil strife, forced migration, human trafficking, violent crime, extreme poverty, religious persecution, cultural exclusion, environmental destruction, and other social problems. The capacity for empathy provides an important basis for human rights. (Frezzo, 2015: viii)

The development of the concept of universal human rights and the international oversight of such rights since World War II has led to profound global changes in thinking about humanity, welfare provision and human development in general. Geo-political tensions, concerns about post-COVID-19 mitigation, continuing global inequalities and poverty, and the struggles of individuals and groups around the world whose rights have been denied, have all influenced our understanding of rights, entitlements and state responsibilities. These processes – leading to the application of rights and responsibilities – have not been without discord, controversy or debate (Donnelly, 2013: 107; Sen, 1999: 229–231; Pogge, 2002: 27–34). Indeed, such processes have generated conflict around what should be defined as 'universal' and what *human* rights should actually entail. For example, issues of universality and cultural relativism, ideological differences over civil and political rights, socio-economic rights, and individual versus collective rights, are all under scrutiny and open to interpretation.

Debates have often been framed in terms of the 'West versus the Rest', or perceptions of cultural or ideological 'imperialism'. Indeed, even where rights have been conventionally agreed and codified, issues may arise when one set infringes another, leading to what can best be termed a 'clash of rights'. Then there are issues around sovereignty, exclusivity, or negative communitarianism, which can result in the denial of rights to others. These can, if not politically engaged, bring into question the very validity of universality and leave us with a paradox, as we often have with the ideal of sovereignty and as noted by Kerri Woods in *Human Rights*:

> the principle that a single standard of justice is universally valid, and that the violation of that standard anywhere is a legitimate concern of any citizen of the world – and

at the same time, human rights affirm the right to self-determination, which the sovereignty-based international order is conceived to realize [creates] the 'sovereignty paradox'. (Woods, 2014: 9)

The realisability of rights in the most meaningful sense requires inclusiveness, mechanisms and supports that involve not just legislation but attendant social policy provision. Thus, the bestowal of rights has often led to the introduction or adaptation of social policy and welfare provision. Rights and their implementation have also resulted from developments in social policy and welfare provision in themselves, with rights to parental leave, pensions, healthcare and education being pertinent examples. Arguably, societies develop through such interventions and, indeed, the formative nature of human development is reliant on such policy-making interconnectivity (Oestreich, 2017: 3–23; Chomsky, 2003: 236; Uvin, 2004: 195–201; Hoover, 2016). The development of rights is contingent on a complex interplay of different pressures, such as the role of civil society, critical voices, protest, or the flexibility of the state itself. As a political process, rights have invariably emerged as a result of human agency influencing and being influenced by social, economic and cultural factors, and thus their evolution continues to be a process in flux. Notwithstanding this, in the new millennium a dominant discourse has evolved around a definable culture of human rights driven by activists, academic and legal specialists, together with governmental influences that have been receptive to a rights-based approach to human development. This agency is mostly change driven, as Jack Donnelly noted in *Universal Human Rights in Theory and Practice*: 'Human rights claims characteristically seek to challenge or change existing institutions, practices, or norms, especially legal practices' (Donnelly, 2003: 12).

Since the end of the Cold War, United Nations' (UN) rights oversight, though strengthened now by periodic monitoring reports relating to state adherence to covenants and conventions, remains limited to international peer pressure, and is often hindered by political and state intervention – or more recently by blatant political disregard. Essentially, state cooperation and compliance is central to international rights protection. As Julie Mertus commented in *The United Nations and Human Rights*: 'The variety of actors involved in UN human rights practice *has* expanded tremendously. States still remain central to the human rights system. Without state commitment to the domestic implementation of human rights, the system will fail' (Mertus, 2005: 4–5; also see Schippers, 2019: 63–82). For the most vulnerable within society, state intervention is essential, while systemic failure can be catastrophic.

State compliance with human rights standards has been particularly challenging during wars and armed conflicts. Attempts to intervene, enforce and enhance universal rights during warfare, in particular through international humanitarian law and a range of treaties banning certain types of weaponry and activities, for example, have often been frustrated by warring parties. Indeed, the changing nature of global conflict has had a profound effect on the content of the rights discourse and the authoritative ability to implement rights – with the use of armed drone technology and artificially intelligent weaponry being a case in point. Furthermore, violent conflict today usually takes the form of intra-state rather than inter-state conflict, involving non-state as well as state forces and non-conventional acts, such as torture, 'terrorism', extra-judicial executions, or deliberate attacks on civilians.

With the horrendous conflicts in Syria, Libya, Palestine, Sudan, Congo, Yemen, Iraq and elsewhere, the use of the United Nations Security Council (UNSC) to impose economic or military sanctions has remained linked more to geo-political pressures than to universal human rights concerns. In an early analysis of this emerging new world order, Tony Evans, in *The Politics of Human Rights,* anticipated the problems: 'This differential reach and impact reflects structural asymmetries in the geometry of global power relations' (Evans, 2001: 3). Arguably, this disparate application of international human rights, subject to erratic power imbalances, has created an atmosphere of cynicism as conflict and its repercussions – genocide, torture, millions of stateless refugees, human trafficking, the withdrawal of civil and political liberties, widespread insecurity and fear – have become normalised.

Disagreement over the articulation, interpretation and implementation of universal human rights has led to attempts to develop regional (as opposed to global) human rights mechanisms among states holding similar approaches, as a way of building human rights architecture. Examples of these include the European Convention on Human Rights, the American Convention on Human Rights, the African Charter on Human and Peoples' Rights and the Arab Charter on Human Rights (Donnelly, 2013: 161–196). Each express often diverging interpretations.

Within a European context, the two main international institutions concerned with the oversight of human rights and protection therein remain the Council of Europe with its European Convention on Human Rights (ECHR) (1953) and European Social Charter (1961), and the European Union (EU) which has promoted concepts of human rights via policy directives, the Charter of Fundamental Rights and more recent attempts to develop the European Pillar of Social Rights. Both have enforcement mechanisms which appear far stronger than the UN, with the power to direct penalties against states and to enforce changes in nation-state legislation. Indeed, many European states have EU human rights-linked directives and the ECHR incorporated within domestic (national) law. This has ensured that national courts, in this context, can rule on what were originally EU and ECHR rights (Alston and Goodman, 2013: 891–977). The weakness of both the EU and ECHR in relation to the articulation of social, economic and cultural rights, and their emphasis on civil and political rights, reflect the dominance of area-specific ideological considerations, while enforcement has at times appeared to be more concerned with political pragmatism among states rather than upholding the rights of individuals and groups within society. More specifically, the lack of ability by the European Court of Human Rights (ECtHR) to intervene proactively to investigate potential rights violations prior to a complaint being received – unlike the UN rights monitoring committees – may be viewed as a systemic weakness (and a strength for the UN monitoring process). The fact that cases taken to the ECtHR may wait many years to be heard, entail great financial costs, and that decisions made not be implemented for years, are also disadvantages. Nevertheless, the incorporation of the ECHR into domestic law in many European states means that domestic (national) courts can at least now consider ECHR rights in their rulings, with the ECtHR emerging as a court of last resort.

In recent years the 'universal rights' debate has faced substantial additional challenges. Universality of human rights relates to: 'the principle that a single standard of justice is universally valid, and that the violation of that standard anywhere is a legitimate concern of any citizen of the world' (Woods, 2014: 9). Yet it is clear that promoting and implementing such a principle in a diverse world is very difficult. Notwithstanding relativism, systemic failure, the sovereignty paradox, institutional weakness and the fog of war, there is also the more recent obstruction of ethno-populist opposition. Since the financial crash of 2008 there have emerged political voices which are sceptical of international solidarity and rights per se, as seen with the debate around the UK withdrawing from both the EU and the ECHR, and the return to bespoke/selective adherences to international law. The debate within Britain in recent years around rejecting ECHR 'interference' in British sovereignty has raised questions about international oversight and the protection of human rights within this context. In the USA, the Trump presidency has challenged the very rationale for universal human rights in relation to gender, disability, race, religion, torture, international relations and the conduct of war. In Turkey, after the coup attempt of 2016, there was a wholesale attempt to suppress political opposition, even by moderate lobbies – with limited concerns raised by the international community. In China, the government's use of 're-education camps' to target ethnic minorities has drawn limited global attention. In the Ukraine, the conflict between pro-Western and pro-Russian perspectives led to the annexation of Crimea in 2014 by Russia, and a protracted conflict in eastern Ukraine that has cost upwards of 15,000 lives with muted international discussion about human rights. In Spain, the central government's imprisonment of elected politicians making peaceful demands for self-determination for Catalonia was greeted with messages of solidarity with that government from fellow EU member state governments, rather than concerns for freedom of speech or support for democratic elections. With the emergence of 'democratic dictatorship', a new idea of international relations has forcefully arrived.

In the aftermath of the global refugee crisis of 2015–16, an apparent shift towards ethno-populism in many states across the globe presented fundamental challenges to both the nature of state intervention and international human rights oversight. In Poland, for example, the Law and Justice Party sought to overturn the separation of powers between the government and the judiciary, undermining an independent judiciary as well as working to dismantle an independent media. In Hungary, the Orbán administration set in train a series of policies that deliberately targeted the rights of third country nationals, establishing what his ministers called 'detention centres'. The approach of global powers such as the USA, China and Russia to international security leaves a further unknown in the global rights agenda. Conflict in Syria, Iraq, Afghanistan, Pakistan and Yemen, involving directly and indirectly UN Security Council permanent member states (with civilians representing up to 75 per cent of all casualties), has exposed the vulnerability of international humanitarian action and international human rights law. The list goes on and exposes the ideological debilitation that mixes the economic shock therapy of the post-Crash world with states actively undermining institutions that were established to protect rights. Ultimately, what this recent scenario has exposed has been the lack of commitment by powerful political and economic interests – alongside a creeping authoritarianism – to deliver on the protection of rights or the development of attendant social and economic policies (Chomsky, 2004: 234).

With the 70-year centenary of the United Nations Universal Declaration of Human Rights passing in 2018, one might have thought that at this stage in human development the global rights architecture would have been significantly embedded, robust, unquestioningly accepted and universally applied. However, numerous issues have emerged which could not have been foreseen by the original drafters. New demands for new rights have emerged to be fought over and these in turn have impinged on other existing rights. The struggles over climate change, COVID-19 pandemic mitigation, greenhouse gases, sustainable (and 'clean') energy sources, sustainable communities, employment, health and social service provision (in the face of demographic changes and migration fuelled by globalisation and war), together with concerns about safety and security, all impact on other rights. They all invariably have implications for social and economic rights, such as the right to health; or on civil and political rights, such as the right to do what we want with private property, businesses and land; or rights to free movement, privacy and speech. It is clear that rights are interdependent and necessarily inclusive. Indeed, civil and political rights are dependent on social and economic rights being realisable. Rights to security may not only impinge on individual rights in order to protect the rights of the collective, but also on cultural rights, rights to freedom from discrimination, and so on, although it may also be the case that we cannot have security without an end to discrimination and the promotion of cultural rights.

Ultimately, we live in a changing world with evolving struggles over rights and differing circumstances in which those struggles take place. Struggles around rights can also lead to changes in direction – denial or curtailment as well as the expansion of rights. Social policy, as with international development policy, has had to adapt to global patterns of change, often shifting from state-focused interpretations to global interpretations and vice versa, with more fluid and protean applications of policy and practice. Despite the challenges, innovation around universal rights and the mechanisms to oversee them, in support of social cohesion, remain salient. Critically, human agency is central to all of this. Around the world non-governmental organisations (NGOs) in particular use human rights-based approaches in their campaigning work and in spite of the defaulters already mentioned, many governments strive to show that they are human rights upholders rather than human rights abusers. Ultimately, as this book will show, the emergence of human rights as social development has revealed a process which has been, and will continue to be, hard fought for.

Human rights would not have succeeded in the way they have (as concrete rights; as central to discourse; as shapers of culture) if all that they were was the law and practice of niceness ... The human rights story is not all about givers, it is about takers, too: there is a large-scale subaltern tradition to take into account, a tradition of solidarity, of resistance to the abuse of power and to the assertion of right in the face of immoral might. (Gearty, 2014: 37)

This book

Through the lens of critical social science, the various chapters in this book analyse the form and development of concepts of universal rights and existing international human rights mechanisms, their strengths and weaknesses, and their impact on social policy, human welfare and international development. A critical perspective in social science involves a questioning, reflective approach towards knowledge and the research process in the study of society. It includes a recognition of the implicit assumptions and ideology which underlie, reinforce and reproduce existing power structures, social relations and inequalities and which often appear hidden in social, economic, political and cultural relationships (Lukes, 1974). It also involves a recognition of the role of social science both in revealing these underlying assumptions, ideology and power relations in the pursuit of knowledge and in challenging (rather than simply accepting or supporting, implicitly or explicitly) the inequalities and social injustices which exist in society. While recognising the importance of concepts of universal human rights for humanity, this collection contextualises the reality of their formulation, enforcement and realisability within wider geo-political shifts, and attempts to assess the social impact of this change. While pointing out the benefits of both the discourse and the practical 'tools' provided for social policy and global development it also aims to highlight the deficiencies of a universally attuned and inclusive rights architecture that has led to the accentuation of inequality in human relationships, while delineating power, wealth and status, on a global basis.

The book is innovative in that it takes a policy-based approach to universal human rights and the structures that oversee international rights. It engages with the opinion held by many that mainstream international human rights initiatives can often be viewed as akin to Western cultural imperialism – or other forms of neo-colonialism – in developing world cultures. Taking the perspective that human rights are being continually contested, the authors concede that there are processional, systemic policy failings and weaknesses, but acknowledge that they nevertheless do provide benchmarks and standards for the world to follow. The book borrows from and adds to existing academic literature. It provides a description and critical analysis of the historical development of concepts of human rights and the major international human rights mechanisms which operate today in peacetime and during war. It shows how such mechanisms evolve and are changed by changing circumstances and human agency. It discusses the wide range of internationally bestowed rights – including social, economic, cultural, developmental and environmental rights. It covers rights of specific groups in society, including people with disabilities, children, migrants and rights relating to gender. It looks at specific rights such as rights to health, housing and education. It also looks at what happens to rights in times of conflict and war – and analyses the effects of these rights on social policy, global development and welfare.

The aims of the text are as follows:

- To provide an introductory critical social science perspective on concepts of universal human rights and the international human rights mechanisms developed to deliver them.
- To critically analyse key issues pertaining to rights, the universality of rights, their formulation, enforcement and realisability.
- To highlight the deficit in the enforcement of human rights and the causal relationship between conflict, uneven development, sectoral differentiation and human rights abuses.
- To critically assess the links between human rights developments and social policy, social welfare and global development.
- To discuss a range of key human rights issues and their links to poverty, inequality and injustice, including policy-making, sustainability, interdependence, conflict and reconciliation, and intercultural dialogue.
- To discuss key trends in international human rights that impact on social policy and practice at local, national and international levels.
- To provide a reference in the catalogue of social policy and development studies material, a resource that can be utilised by NGO activists, academics and students, and practitioners of human rights.

The book aims to provide an accessible and comprehensive critical analysis of the concept of human rights and human rights-based approaches to social policy issues and global development. It argues that, despite its deficiencies, existing and developing international human rights frameworks provide important tools for engaging with policy development and implementation, and help promote understanding about the causes of poverty and inequality.

The 25 contributors to this book are drawn from a wide range of countries and from across a range of academic disciplines, NGOs and legal sectors. Each has a specialist interest in this subject. While the book covers a series of important issues and interdisciplinary, interrelated themes relating to human rights, it is important to acknowledge that other equally important issues and themes have had to be left out due to space limitations. These include, for example, the right to employment, rest and leisure, privacy and religion, the rights of indigenous peoples, rural communities, older people and carers, rights relating to language, self-determination, and the environment. Separate chapters could also have been devoted to other (than the European) regional human mechanisms such as the American Convention on Human Rights, the African Charter on Human and Peoples' Rights and the Arab Charter on Human Rights. All of these could be included in an additional volume and might provide scope in the future for a further publication.

The book is divided into three parts. The first part, 'International human rights: context', discusses the background to the development of international rights mechanisms, describing them and analysing their respective strengths and weaknesses. It also provides various examples of how the development of such international rights mechanisms has impacted (or not) on social policy and social welfare around the globe. It includes six chapters: 'The historical development of the concept of rights'; 'The United Nations and international oversight of human rights'; 'The Council of Europe, the European Convention on Human Rights and the Social Charter'; 'The European Union and human rights'; 'Human rights and the USA'; and 'International Humanitarian Law: protecting rights and promoting welfare during war?'

The second part, 'Key issues for universal human rights-based approaches', looks at some of the issues pertaining to the development of 'universality' of rights in diverse and disparate policy environments, influenced by competing ideological, cultural, social, economic, political, historical and geographical tensions. This includes the difficulty of promoting universal rights in a political context framed by insecurity, rights denial and persistent conflict where 'normal rules' relating to the protection and promotion of human rights no longer seem to apply. This part includes six chapters: 'The European Union, human rights and international development policy'; 'Socio-economic rights'; 'Cultural rights'; 'Migration and refugees: applying human rights to "everyone"'; 'Conflict, "terrorism" and non-state actors'; and 'Gender and human rights'. The third part, 'Human rights approaches to social policy development', looks at how both the discourse of international human rights and the international human rights instruments and processes may be used as tools to promote social policy development. It includes chapters which discuss a number of specific areas of social policy (education, healthcare, housing, and so on). It has seven chapters: 'Human rights-based approaches to social policy development'; 'The right to education'; 'The right to healthcare'; 'The right to housing'; 'Children's rights and social policy'; 'The rights of people with disabilities'; and 'The right to development'. The book ends with a concluding chapter looking at current international human rights concerns, protest and potential developments into the future – 'Human rights in a brave new world: the shape of things to come?'

Overall, this book is an attempt to integrate our understanding of social policy, global development and human rights policy and practice. It is polemical in that it asserts the interdependency of human welfare and the protection of rights in the broadest sense. While the contributors approach the subject from a range of different opinions and widely differing contexts, the consensus is drawn on the need to assert the importance of a global discourse on rights and the obligations of the state and international institutions to protect and enhance rights in the interests of an equitable and just process of human development.

References

Alston, P. and Goodman, R. (2013) *International Human Rights*, Oxford: Oxford University Press.

Chomsky, N. (2004) *Hegemony or Survival*, London: Penguin Books.

Donnelly, J. (2013) *Universal Human Rights in Theory and Practice*, Ithaca, NY: Cornell University Press.

Evans, T. (2001) *The Politics of Human Rights*, London: Pluto Press.

Frezzo, M. (2015) *The Sociology of Human Rights*, Cambridge: Polity Press.

Gearty, C. (2014) 'Human rights: The necessary quest for foundations', in C. Douzinas and C. Gearty (eds) *The Meanings of Rights*, Cambridge: Cambridge University Press, pp 21–38.

Gearty, C. and Douzinas, C. (2012) *Human Rights Law*, Cambridge: Cambridge University Press.

Hoover, J. (2016) *Reconstructing Human Rights*, Oxford: Oxford University Press.

Lukes, S. (1974) *Power: A Radical View*, London: Macmillan.

Mertus, J.A. (2005) *The United Nations and Human Rights: A Guide for a New Era*, London: Routledge.

Morris, L. (ed) (2006) *Rights: Sociological Perspectives*, London: Routledge.

Oestreich, J. (2017) *Development and Human Rights*, Oxford: Oxford University Press.

Pogge, T. (2002) *World Poverty and Human Rights*, Cambridge: Polity Press.

Schippers, B. (2019) *Critical Perspectives on Human Rights*, London: Rowman and Littlefield.

Sen, A. (1999) *Development as Freedom*, Oxford: Oxford University Press.

Uvin, P. (2004) *Human Rights and Development*, Bloomfield, CT: Kumarian Press.

Weissbrodt, D., Ni Aolain, F., Newman, C. and Fitzpatrick, J. (2009) *International Human Rights: Law, Policy and Process*, 4th edition. New Providence, NJ: Imprint.

Woods, K. (2012) *Human Rights*, Basingstoke: Palgrave Macmillan.

PART I

International human rights: context

1

The historical development of the concept of rights

Peter Herrmann and Féilim Ó hAdhmaill

> I sit on a man's back, choking him and making him carry me, and yet assure myself and others that I am very sorry for him and wish to ease his lot by all possible means – except by getting off his back. (Leo Tolstoy, 1882, *What Then Must We Do?*)

We live in a world where the discourse on universal human rights – rights bestowed on all of us equally by virtue of the fact that we are humans – is now predominant. Yet it is also a world which is ill-divided in the realisation of such rights; a world where a lack of basic socio-economic rights condemns millions to hunger, thirst, ill-health and limited access to shelter, healthcare and education – in a world of plenty (UNICEF, 2018). It is a world where a lack of civil and political rights denies many the right to self-determination or control over their government, or to freedom of speech or cultural expression, or to freedom from arbitrary arrest, torture and even death (Amnesty, 2019). It is clear that the realisability of human rights is directly related to access to power and resources, and inextricably linked to relationships between human beings – all subject to the outcome of human agency and constant struggles on a daily basis by communities around the world.

This chapter discusses the historical development of 'rights' and how these transformed into ideas about 'universal human rights'. It shows how the concept of rights developed historically from notions of legal through to political, social/economic and cultural rights, and has involved both individual and group rights. It describes how thinking about rights has developed from identifying rights solely with clans, tribes, communities, ethnic groups and then nation-states, to linking them to all humanity – including minorities – through concepts of universal human rights. It recognises the contribution of philosophical ideas about humanity, equality, democracy and social justice, as well as the impact of human agency on the development of a range of rights, and argues that such developments do not take place in a vacuum (Donnelly, 2013: 75–92). Social, economic, ideological, cultural and geo-political influences affect our power to change society and ensure that human rights are a contested site. Rights are contested in their conceptualisation and in the development of oversight mechanisms. They are also contested in their implementation, enforceability and realisability on the ground (Freeman, 2017). In essence, it is argued that humans make human rights. As Karl Marx wrote in *The Eighteenth Brumaire*: 'Men make their own history, but they do not make it as they please; they do not make it under self-selected circumstances, but under circumstances directly encountered, given and transmitted from the past' (Marx, 1851: 103).

The rights we have today are different from the rights people struggled for in the past and potentially different from those that people will have in the future. Thus, rights and our understanding of rights continually change and adapt. Since humans are influenced by a wide range of factors, so too are the rights they create. Rights also influence politics and culture, how we live socially, how we organise the economy, and how we organise social policy and provide for social welfare. Thus national and international human rights mechanisms have been shaped and influenced by developments in thinking and practice in relation to social policy and global development. Indeed, rights to social protection and provision have moved social policy away from notions of charity or residual provision to a position where nation-states and the international community have legal responsibilities for all people in society; what Frezzo (2015: viii) refers to as the link between concepts of human rights and 'our capacity to feel empathy for human beings' is important in this regard.

A long history of 'rights' development

Rights and ideas about them have been constantly evolving throughout human history. Rights, along with responsibilities, were often attached to communitarian structures, groups or society in general, linked to membership of, first, extended families, then tribes and wider communities. They provided protection and strengthened bonds creating a 'social contract' which reinforced the concept of a shared community identity. Rights were limited to group members and, in different societies, different types of member – for example men, women and children – enjoyed different sets of rights. As city-states and then nation-states developed, citizenship rights developed. For a nation-state to exist, a sense of imagined community or solidarity must also exist (Anderson, 1983). A sense of difference from other imagined communities or nation-states was also important. The conferring of certain rights on the citizens of a particular state thus enhanced the ideal of a shared community and difference from those in other imagined communities or nation-states.

One early example of the codification of laws for such a 'state' which included individual rights was the code of Hammurabi in ancient Mesopotamia, dating back to the 1700s BC. In principle, it gave protection from arbitrary persecution. In the sixth century BC, Cyrus the Great in Persia issued a series of decrees bestowing rights on subjects. The Cyrus Cylinder was probably the first charter of rights known in history. However, such rights were bestowed by rulers who also had the power to remove or deny rights. Notions that human rights should be viewed as distinct from rulers began to develop in ancient Greece, where the concept of human rights became synonymous with 'natural rights', rights that were derived from 'natural law'. According to Socrates and Plato, natural law reflected the natural order of the universe and the will of the gods who control nature. Plato believed in universal truth and virtue – ideas which were to influence the development of notions of universalism, universal human rights which superseded the laws of individual states. Of course natural rights in ancient Greece and later ancient Rome did not bestow the same rights on everyone (and thus were not universal). For example, Roman citizens enjoyed the right to vote in assemblies and the right to a fair hearing if accused of an offence. Although these rights were later extended to citizens of the Roman Empire, they were denied to women and slaves. The crucial importance, however, of these early philosophical ideas was that they introduced the concept of universalism linked to universal truth and virtue, as well as the notion of 'natural rights' beyond the laws of individual rulers or states. Such ideas were to influence the development of ideas about universal rights in later years.

Thomas Hobbes (1588–1679) was to challenge the notion that natural law provided human rights. He contended, instead, that rights come from the state in what he called 'positive law' and as such could be modified and taken away to suit state needs (Hobbes, 1651). John Locke (1632–1704), conversely, argued that state law comes from natural law. Thus, the state must uphold the human rights bestowed on people by natural law and if it does not then people have a right to revolt against it. In many respects such views provided the philosophical justification for the American and French Revolutions. Jean-Jacques Rousseau

(1712–78) stated that rights emerged because people had entered into a social contract to form society in exchange for being treated equally. Then there was the utilitarian Jeremy Bentham (1748–1832), who argued that the most important rights were those which allowed the greatest happiness for the greatest number (Boucher and Kelly, 2009). This was echoed by another utilitarian, John Stuart Mill (1806–1873), who in *On Liberty* (1869) presented the case that while actions which promoted the greatest good should be supported, individual rights to 'liberty' against the tyranny of the majority were also important. The only time such rights should be curtailed by the state was when they deprived others of their ability to achieve their own liberty.

These philosophers were obviously influenced by their own positionality within society as well as by the dominant discourse of the day on social, economic and cultural structures, and norms. As such, Mill presented a classical liberal perspective on the concept of rights and the primacy of freedom of the individual (Mill, 1869). Alternatively, Karl Marx (1818–83) and Friedrich Engels (1820–95) saw rights in an entirely different way. For them, it was equality and collective human purpose that was important. Liberty was linked to democratic control over all aspects of life – including the economy (Marx and Engels, 2002).

With the development of nation-states, rights were initially limited to legal rights; rights before the law – limited to members of the particular state. Among the earliest legal rights in the West were those granted by the Magna Carta, a charter of liberties signed by King John in England in 1215 and similar to other charters defining people's rights granted around the same time by other rulers in Europe. This aimed to regulate relations between the monarch and the people. Clauses 39 and 40, for example, state that: 'no freeman should be imprisoned or dispossessed except by the lawful judgement of his peers or by the law of the land' (Magna Carta, 1215). This has since been acknowledged as the origin of 'trial by jury' and *habeas corpus*, the legal remedy against unlawful imprisonment.

Notions of political rights had initially developed with concepts of democracy in the city-states of Greece in the fifth century BC. At that time, this meant simply 'rule by the citizens' (the *demos*). This right was exercised at mass meetings in a form of direct democracy. However, not everyone had a vote and it could only work as long as the citizen body remained relatively small and homogenous. In fact this system only operated for about 200 years. What are called today liberal democracies are very different from this ancient Greek model. Representative democracy in a modern sense was established in seventeenth century England with the Cromwellian Revolution, which challenged the 'natural law' of the 'divine right of kings' and led to further extensions of political rights to citizens. This eventually became the model adopted by much of the world. Politicians were elected to represent the interests of voters in debates, with decisions taking place in a parliament (Donnelly, 1999). There was still no concept of democracy for all citizens. 'Democracy' was to lie in the hands of the nobility and represented a change in control over political power from the monarch to the nobility rather than to all the people equally.

Enlightenment thinking in the eighteenth century heralded in new ways of looking at the world, based on scientific discovery and reasoning. It marked a shift in thinking about rights. Dependence on notions of morality and, indeed, acceptance of divine laws justifying existing power elites – such as the divine right of kings – were to be challenged. The new thinking posited that rights should be based on reason, that people make history in a rational way and that there should be, at least in a formal sense, equal rights (Herrmann, 2012a, 2012b).

Inspired by the ideas of the Enlightenment, both the US (1776–83) and French Revolutions (1798–99) extended the right to political power to a new emerging group; the business/bourgeois class. Only later was this extended to un-propertied men and later still to women. These revolutions led to an increasing democratisation of these societies and the legitimisation and proliferation of the ideas of equality, liberty and citizenship. 'We hold these truths to be self-evident, that all men are created equal' announced the United States Declaration of Independence (1776). However, the notion of equality was limited to equality of treatment of individuals *by* governments, partly because the leaders of these revolutions, reflecting classical liberal views, focused on the need to protect citizens from oppressive government. They had no notion that governments could intervene in positive ways to promote a better society. The concept of equality also did not extend to slaves, Native Americans or women. Indeed, women did not get the vote in the US until 1920. Both George Washington and Thomas Jefferson (the main writer of the Declaration of Independence) were themselves slave owners, the White House itself built by slave labour. Slavery was not finally abolished until 1865 and after a bloody civil war.

Article 1, section 2, of the US Constitution (1787) stated that for the purposes of representation and taxation all 'free persons' – excluding Indians – and three-fifths of slaves were to be counted. In other words, slaves were valued as equivalent to three-fifths of a 'free person'. This classification of slaves lasted nearly 100 years, being ended by the 13th (1865) and 14th (1868) amendments to the Constitution. The ending of slavery in 1865 did not lead to equal political rights for Whites and Blacks however. Even Abraham Lincoln made it clear that he believed 'the White race' to be superior to 'the Black race' (Lincoln, 1858). While the 15th amendment to the Constitution (1870) stated that the vote could not be denied on grounds of race, colour or previous slavery, many states developed poll taxes and literacy tests to deny the vote to Black people. It was not until 1965 that the Voting Rights Act prohibited such tests. Today in the USA former prisoners are denied voting rights in most states and since Black people are five times more likely to be imprisoned than are Whites, this has had a major impact on group voting (NAACP, nd).

The French Revolution also promoted ideas of equal rights: 'Men are born and remain free and equal in rights' (Declaration of the Rights of Man and of the Citizen, 1789). Such ideas, and the revolution which accompanied them, provoked a massive reaction from conservatism throughout Europe, both violently in the form of a counter-revolution by Britain and other European powers against the new revolutionary government, and philosophically. Edmund Burke, for example, declared that: 'Political equality is against nature. Social equality is against nature. Economic equality is against nature' (quoted in Freeman, 1980: 21). Thomas Paine set out to refute such views in his *Rights of Man* in 1791, legitimising the French Revolution and developing ideas about citizenship rights. In his 1792 *Rights of Man, Part Two*, he went further, arguing for government programmes to relieve poverty through progressive taxation (Paine, 1985). Meanwhile, Mary Wollstonecraft (1792) was pioneering the case for equal rights for women in *The Vindication of the Rights of Woman*. While the French Jacobins, the most radical of the revolutionaries, wanted political power to reside with the masses, not just the middle classes, they were resisted by more conservative elements. Thus, when the vote was extended to all French males in 1792 it was restricted to tax payers in 1795 and it wasn't until 1848 that full male suffrage was introduced. Despite the efforts of Mary Wollstonecraft, women did not get the vote in France until 1944, while many women in French colonies had to wait until the 1960s. Notwithstanding such restrictions, the revolution was to inspire many future generations of socialists, feminists and democrats whose notions of rights extended to all.

In the nineteenth century, political power remained concentrated in the hands of powerful groups in society across most of the world. In 1801, less than 3 per cent of people in Britain and Ireland had the right to vote. Voting was controlled by the rich. By the middle of the twentieth century political struggles for rights by Chartists,

Suffragettes and others meant that the vote had been extended to all men and women in most Western European states. Struggles in the West's colonies, especially after 1945, meant that voting rights were also eventually extended to most of their colonies. Thus, while the UN estimated that in 1900 more than half the world's people lived under colonial rule, no country gave all its citizens the right to vote, by the end of the century 'some three-quarters of the world lived under democratic regimes' (UNDP, 2000: 1).

Throughout the nineteenth century increasing demands for social and economic rights were being made by workers in the new industries in Europe as well as by tenant farmers. Marx, in *The Communist Manifesto* (1848) and later *Das Kapital* (1867), argued that scientific study showed that societies progressed through struggle in every epoch against the contradictions of the exploitation of labour for the profit of the few. As he saw it, class conflict would continue until capitalism, an economic system based on the pursuit of private profit, was replaced by socialism – an economic system based on the maxim 'from each according to their ability to each according to their needs', and a classless society. Since the holders of power would not relinquish it easily, revolution would be necessary. Marx lived in a rapidly industrialising Europe, with limited democratic rights, where attempts to bring about social change were obstructed and suppressed. However, as states, particularly in the West, became more democratic, alternative opportunities for organising collectively emerged. Working-class movements began to use the machinery of the state, elections and government to introduce reform.

Fear of the growing workers' movement and the potential overthrow of capitalism – and its replacement by socialism – led some governments to introduce welfare reform. For example, Bismarck pioneered a number of national insurance schemes in Germany from 1883–89. Similar schemes were introduced in other countries, including Britain where the first social insurance-based pensions, sickness and unemployment benefits were brought in by the Liberal government from 1906 to 1911. Legislative health and safety provisions in factories, a shortened working week and the provision of education and training all served to ameliorate increasingly vocal demands for change by trade unionists and their political representatives, while also maintaining the smooth working of capitalism. By the twentieth century, most states in the West allowed the population to engage in oppositional activity through social movements, albeit within strictly defined legal guidelines and with limited rights. In turn, working-class movements began to use the machinery of the state, elections and government to introduce reforms themselves. In the West, reformist approaches to address some of the worst symptoms of capitalism began to replace demands for its destruction and the creation of a new system based on social need (Gough, 1979; Mishra, 1981). Indeed, when revolutions did occur in the twentieth and twenty-first centuries, they almost always took place in developing, unindustrialised countries ruled by political elites, with limited political freedom.

Rights after World War II

In the post-World War II era citizenship rights had extended to include social and economic rights in most Western European countries – rights to education, healthcare, social security benefits and social services. These types of rights were embodied in what came to be known as welfare states, whereby society as a whole took responsibility through a principle of solidarity to provide welfare support for its population 'from the cradle to the grave', albeit attached to a capitalist market economy. In Western Europe this type of socio-economic model became the norm in opposition to the system of communism being advocated in the Eastern bloc countries.

According to T.H. Marshall, the British welfare state was the culmination of a historical evolution of rights from civil rights in the eighteenth century, through political rights in the nineteenth, to social and economic rights in the twentieth. Together they composed a 'three-legged stool', representing the three pillars of democracy: civil rights providing individual freedom; political rights and participation in the decision-making process; while social and economic rights allowed people to exercise these rights (Marshall, 1950). The extension of rights to minorities *within* states was slower in coming however. By the 1960s campaigns by and in support of minorities began to lead to anti-discrimination and equality measures. Globalisation and increased migration also led to debates around multiculturalism and minority cultural rights (Kymlicka, 2011; Levrau and Loobuyck, 2018). New social movements emerged espousing rights relating to gender, environmentalism and global development.

The post- World War II period saw the development of the UN with its array of universal rights and international oversight mechanisms, and a number of regional rights mechanisms such as the European Convention of Human Rights (1953) and the European Union's Charter of Fundamental Rights (2000). Karel Vasak, writing specifically about developments in human rights within international law, argued that there were three generations of such rights. First, civil and political rights, which were rights contained in the International Covenant on Civil and Political Rights (ICCPR) (1966). Second, social, economic and cultural rights, which were contained in the International Covenant on Economic Social and Cultural Rights (ICESCR) (1966). And third, the generation of collective rights linked to international solidarity and providing for rights to development, self-determination, a healthy environment and minority rights (Macklem, 2015; Vasak, 1977: 29).

By the 1980s, the emergence of neoliberalism as the dominant global ideological force along with the collapse of the Eastern bloc led to a retrenchment of rights, particularly social and economic rights; a retrenchment reinforced during the 'austerity' years in the West after the great financial crash in 2008–10. The refugee crisis in the aftermath of the wars in Syria and elsewhere influenced the development of populist right-wing governments in Europe, the USA and Latin America, further challenging existing rights – not just social and economic, but civil, cultural and minority rights. Such factors, combined with continuing armed conflict globally, seem to make *universal human rights* more elusive than ever.

It has also long been argued in the context of the nation-state that it is difficult to realise any rights that are not underpinned by social and economic rights and a redistribution of resources (Deacon, 2007). In the global context, the question must be raised; whether it is possible to have universal human rights, including the right to self-determination and development, in a world fuelled by an economic system which reinforces and reproduces vast global inequalities in wealth and power. Is it possible to promote global solidarity and cooperation around protecting the environment and the satisfaction of need, when the global economy is geared towards competition, the pursuit of personal profit and perpetually increasing economic growth? Therefore, maybe the focus for international human rights into the future should be on how we collectively organise society and the economy to promote genuine and aspirational universal human rights.

Conclusion

Today, a whole host of rights mechanisms exist at national, regional and global levels, outlining quite comprehensive collections of rights, protections and responsibilities, with the obligation on states to uphold them. Different countries will value civil and political rights over social, economic and cultural rights, as well as individual as opposed to group or collective rights (Evans, 2001). Thus, some countries, especially in Western Europe, have highly developed public welfare systems with strong welfare rights and entitlements – such as rights to healthcare, education and social security – whereas the vast majority of countries around the world do not. Even within Western Europe, however, rights to welfare will be different between states and even within regions of states (Esping-Andersen, 1990). Ultimately, societies decide *who* will have rights and who will not. Societies also decide *what* rights people or certain groups will have and *how* they will be delivered. Such decisions will no doubt remain sites of struggle into the future.

References

Amnesty (2019) *The State of the Worlds Human Rights: Global Annual Report, 2017/18*, Amnesty International. Available from: www.amnesty.ie/who-we-are/global-annual-report-201718/

Anderson, B. (1983) *Imagined Communities: Reflections on the Origin and Spread of Nationalism*, London: Verso.

Boucher, D. and Kelly, P.J. (2009) *Political Thinkers: From Socrates to the Present*, Oxford: Oxford University Press.

Deacon, B. (2007) *Global Social Policy and Governance*, London: Sage.

Declaration of the Rights of Man and the Citizen (1989) Approved by the National Assembly of France, 26 August 1789. Available from: www.bl.uk/collection-items/the-declaration-of-the-rights-of-man-and-of-the-citizen

Donnelly, J. (1999) 'Human rights, democracy, and development', *Human Rights Quarterly*, 21(3): 608–632.

Donnelly, J. (2013) *Universal Human Rights in Theory and Practice*, Ithaca, NY: Cornell University Press.

Esping-Andersen, G. (1990) *The Three Worlds of Welfare Capitalism*, Cambridge: Polity Press.

Evans, T. (2001) *The Politics of Human Rights*, London: Pluto Press.

Freeman, M. (2017) *Human Rights*, Cambridge: Polity Press.

Freeman, M. (1980) *Edmund Burke and the Critique of Political Radicalism*, Oxford: Blackwell.

Frezzo, M. (2015) *The Sociology of Human Rights*, Cambridge: Polity Press.

Gough, I. (1979) *The Political Economy of the Welfare State*, London: Macmillan.

Herrmann, P. (2012a) *God, Rights, Law and a Good Society. Writings on Philosophy and Economy of Power, Two*, Bremen: EHV Academic Press.

Herrmann, P. (2012b) *Rights – Developing Ownership by Linking Control over Space and Time. Writings on Philosophy and Economy of Power, Three*, Bremen: EHV Academic Press.

Hobbes, T. (1651) *Leviathan*, Reprinted 1965, Oxford: Clarendon Press.

Kymlicka, W. (2011) 'Multicultural citizenship within multination states', *Ethnicities*, 3: 281–302.

Levrau, F. and Loobuyck, P. (2018) 'Introduction: mapping the multiculturalism-interculturalism debate', *Comparative Migration Studies*, 6(1): 13.

Lincoln, A. (1858) Abraham Lincoln, 18 September 1858 – Fourth Debate with Stephen A. Douglas at Charleston, Illinois. Available from: https://www.nps.gov/liho/learn/historyculture/debate4.htm

Macklem, P. (2015) 'Human rights in international law: three generations or one?', *London Review of International Law*, 3(1): 61–92. Available from: https://doi.org/10.1093/lril/lrv001

Magna Carta (1215) Available from: www.bl.uk/magna-carta/articles/magna-carta-english-translation

Marshall, T.H. (1950) *Citizenship and Social Class: And Other Essays*, Cambridge: Cambridge University Press.

Marx, K. (1851) *The Eighteenth Brumaire of Louis Bonaparte*, in K. Marx and F. Engels (2010), *Collected Works, Volume 11, Marx and Engels: 1851–53*, London: Lawrence and Wishart, pp 99–197.

Marx, K. and Engels, F. (2002) *The Communist Manifesto*, London: Penguin.

Mill, J.S. (1869) *On Liberty* (1999 edition), London: Longman, Roberts and Green.

Mishra, R. (1981) *Society and Social Policy: Theories and Practice of Welfare*, London: Macmillan.

NAACP (nd) *Criminal Justice Fact Sheet*. Available from: www.naacp.org/criminal-justice-fact-sheet/

National Archives (nd) Available from: www.nationalarchives.gov.uk/pathways/citizenship/struggle_democracy/getting_vote.htm

Paine, T. (1985) *Rights of Man*, Harmondsworth: Penguin Classic.

United Nations Development Programme (UNDP) (2000) *Human Development Report 2000: Human Rights and Human Development*, New York: Oxford University Press.

UNICEF (2018) Press release. Available from: www.unicef.org/press-releases/child-under-15-dies-every-five-seconds-around-world-un-report

US Constitution (1787) Available from: https://constitutioncenter.org/media/files/constitution.pdf

US Declaration of Independence (1776) Available from: https://history.state.gov/milestones/1776-1783/declaration

Vasak, K. (1977) 'Human rights: a thirty-year struggle: the sustained efforts to give force of law to the Universal Declaration of Human Rights', *UNESCO Courier*, 30(11): 29–30. Available from: https://unesdoc.unesco.org/ark:/48223/pf0000048063

Wollstonecraft, M. (1792) *The Vindication of the Rights of Woman with Strictures on Political and Moral Subjects*, London: J. Johnson.

2

The United Nations and international oversight of human rights

Féilim Ó hAdhmaill and Gerard McCann

Up until the end of World War II it was almost universally accepted by the major powers that how a state treated its citizens and those of its colonies was a matter for itself and not a legitimate concern of states outside its frontiers. The widespread persecution and extermination of minorities culminating in the industrial scale slaughter of the Holocaust, along with the wholesale targeting of civilian populations in bombing and reprisal attacks during that War, led to a complete reappraisal of this. In the aftermath of World War II, the demand arose for a new international body that would help resolve future disputes between nation-states and prevent tensions developing into war. There was also a contemporaneous demand to establish a set of universally accepted and respected human rights which would be the same for all human beings and based on universality. Linked to this was a view that the international community has responsibility to ensure that such rights are protected, particularly for vulnerable people and minorities living within states. Thus, an international human rights oversight framework was demanded that could police and enforce agreed rights. A transnational consensus appeared to be emerging that such a body could underpin a new world order and address the causes of armed conflict.

The idea of an international human rights body was not new of course. Attempts had been made after World War I to establish the League of Nations. However, this failed to get the necessary political support from world powers and eventually collapsed with the growth of fascism. While attempts were made to develop some form of international human rights framework, via the International Labour Organization (ILO) set up after the Treaty of Versailles (1919), this lacked international oversight. Workers' rights, where granted, were provided by governments for their own citizens and in their own interests, often to provide for the needs of their economies or for reasons of political expediency, to placate workers' demands and to stall the growth of socialism (Clapham, 2007; Mishra, 1981).

The Treaty of Versailles did lead to some limited international commitment to the right of national self-determination, but this mainly applied to those peoples formerly ruled by the Austro-Hungarian, Germany and Ottoman Empires that had lost the war. The colonies of the victorious powers – Britain, France and Belgium – were not compromised (Throntveit, 2011: 445–450). In Ireland, the December 1918 election returned an overwhelming majority of elected representatives demanding independence from Britain and led to the establishment of their own independent Parliament. Under British pressure the Irish parliamentary representatives were refused a hearing at the treaty talks and Britain set about militarily crushing what it saw as a 'rebellion'. Similar expressions of dissent were also crushed in Egypt and at Amritsar in India, both in the spring of 1919. The right to self-determination related only to some nationalities and, indeed, by the end of the inter-war period 75 per cent of the world's currently recognised nation-states still remained under the control of colonial powers. Where new states with new borders were created as a result of Versailles, civil and political rights' protections for minorities within those states were included in the international treaties. This seemed to challenge the argument that 'the way a state treats its inhabitants is not a subject of legitimate international concern' (Clapham, 2007: 26). However, such protections and limited international oversight only applied to select states and specific minorities. The notion of *universal human rights*, applicable to all, remained unrealised. The new world order was more about the winners of the war consolidating power and exerting authority than an example of international oversight by a body representing all humanity on the basis of equality.

Before World War II had ended, the Allies' political leaders had begun to plan for 'peace'. Geo-politics and national self-interest remained major drivers influencing the development and use of international human rights and oversight mechanisms. On 25 April 1945 delegates from 50 nations met in San Francisco, USA, to set up what was to become the United Nations (UN). The UN Charter was drafted, adopted unanimously, and signed on 26 June 1945 by all 50 states present. A 51st state – Poland – signed it later in October 1945. These 51 became the founding member states of the UN. That there were only 51 at that point (out of the currently recognised 193 member states), reflected the colonised nature of the world at that time.

The UN Charter

The UN Charter outlined the four main aims of the UN: to maintain international peace and security; to develop friendly relations among nations; to cooperate in solving international problems and in promoting respect for human rights; and to be a centre for harmonising the actions of nations (UN, 1945). Article 55 further highlighted the interrelationship between 'war prevention' and 'fundamental human rights', an important point to consider when thinking about why violent conflict happens in the first place, as well as the human rights violated through war.

> With a view to the creation of conditions of stability and well-being which are necessary for peaceful and friendly relations among nations based on respect for the principle of equal rights and self-determination of peoples, the United Nations shall promote:
>
> a. higher standards of living, full employment, and conditions of economic and social progress and development;
> b. solutions of international economic, social, health, and related problems; and international cultural and educational cooperation; and
> c. universal respect for, and observance of, human rights and fundamental freedoms for all without distinction as to race, sex, language, or religion. (UN, 1945: Chapter 1X, Article 55)

The Charter also established the six main organs of the UN, including the UN General Assembly (UNGA), the UN Security Council (UNSC) and the International Court of Justice (ICJ) at The Hague, which was set up to interpret international law. Each recognised member state can send representatives to the UNGA sitting in New York, which drafts resolutions and can make recommendations on issues of relevance to the international community. By 2020 there were 193 UN member states and two non-member observer states – Palestine and the Vatican. Many groups of people around the world have made unfulfilled political claims for recognition as nation-states (e.g. Kurds, Catalans, Basques) while a number of established states (for example, Kosovo, which declared independence from Serbia in 2008, or South Ossetia, which declared independence in 1991) are recognised as states by some countries but not by the UN. Membership status applications must be supported by the UNGA and the UNSC.

All member states agree to abide by the decisions of the UNSC, whose main role it is to promote global security, prevent wars and protect rights in wartime. While other organs of the UN make recommendations to governments, only the UNSC has the power to take decisions which are binding on all member states under the Charter. It is the only UN body which can order UN policing measures against member states (or individuals, or private, or voluntary organisations) including economic sanctions, trade embargoes and war. This is important when it comes to the enforcement of human rights. However, more often than not it is geo-politics and self-interest rather than a desire to uphold human rights that dictates many UNSC decisions. Under the UN Charter each member state is still allowed to engage in warfare for the purposes of self-defence, the protection of the national interest or citizens.

The UNSC has 15 members (since 1965 – prior to that there were only 11). These include five permanent members: USA, UK, France, USSR/Russia and China – the 'winners' of World War II, and subsequently the 'big' global powers. They each have a veto over UNSC decisions, any changes to the UN Charter and new member state membership applications. Ireland, for example, did not join the UN until 1955 despite being recognised as an independent state by legislation in both Ireland (1948) and the UK (1949). This was partly due to Cold War politics and opposition from the USSR which viewed Ireland as an ally of the West, despite its declared 'neutrality'. Attempts by Palestine to be recognised as a full member state were vetoed by the USA in 2011.

The other ten members of the UNSC are elected by the General Assembly for a two-year period, with five elected each year. UNSC decisions need 9 out of 15 votes, including support or acquiescence of the five permanent members. In practice, it is the UNSC that holds the real power in the UN, especially the five permanent members with the veto. There were 241 UNSC resolutions vetoed from 16 February 1946 until 28 March 2019 (USSR/Russia 141, USA 85, UK 32, France 18 and China 14[1]), mainly to oppose UNSC decisions which affected geo-political self-interest. Russia/USSR has used it the most, especially during the Cold War, when it had no allies amongst the other permanent members (the People's Republic of China's membership was only recognised in 1971). In recent years it used it 12 times (from 2011 to 2018) to prevent UN intervention against the Assad government in Syria. The USA first used it in 1970 and since then has used it primarily to prevent UNSC decisions against Israel (UN, nd). With this in mind it is clear that the notion of equal *universal* rights for all member states is a misnomer when it comes to the structures of the UN. However, undemocratic as it is, the UN has represented a pragmatic approach to the realities of global power, especially in the immediate aftermath of World War II, with Cold War positioning, a politically divided world and the rapid acquisition of nuclear weapons by each of the five permanent members. With the USA, UK, France, West Germany and other Western European capitalist countries aligned against Eastern bloc 'communist' countries led by the USSR, there was constant fear of nuclear war up until the fall of the Eastern bloc in the late 1980s, and constant geo-political manoeuvring in the UN. When China became 'communist' in 1949, the West, viewing it as a threat, vetoed its claim to replace Chiang Kai-Shek's old Chinese nationalist government (in exile in Taiwan) as China's legitimate representative in the UNGA and the UNSC until 1971. The USSR boycotted the UN in protest against this exclusion in January 1950 and in its absence the Western-controlled UNSC took the opportunity to vote for UN troops to be deployed against North Korea, which was supported by China and the USSR in the Korean War. By returning to the UN in August 1950 the USSR was able to ensure that such UN action against its strategic interests could be vetoed in future. The veto ensures the necessity for agreement and unanimity among these powers in any international disputes before any action can be taken by the UN, and is viewed as important in maintaining the UN structures and, indeed, peace between these powers. However, now that they have been joined as nuclear powers by at least four other countries – North Korea, Pakistan, India and Israel – and some of the permanent members appear less powerful today than in the past (France and Britain), there has been increasing pressure for UN reform (Butler, 2012: 23–39; Gould and Rablen, 2017: 145).

UN Universal Declaration of Human Rights (UDHR) (1948)

The UN Charter had declared in Article 55 that the UN should promote 'universal respect for, and observance of, human rights and fundamental freedoms for all without distinction as to race, sex, language, or religion'. Article 56 bound its member states to take action to achieve that purpose. At that stage it was not clear exactly what these rights and freedoms were, although one of the UN's first tasks was to try and define them. The UN Commission on Human Rights

(UNCHR), established in 1946 and chaired by Eleanor Roosevelt, the widow of President Franklin D., set about this task. Early disagreements led to the abandonment of a plan for an international bill of rights and instead a voluntary human rights declaration, the Universal Declaration of Human Rights (UDHR), was proposed. It took a further three years to develop the Declaration and what resulted was primarily a resolution adopted by the UNGA that was considered non-binding and aspirational. Even then 8 of the then 58 UN members abstained from voting due to differences – six communist members (including the USSR), Saudi Arabia, South Africa – while two others neither voted nor abstained (Donnelly, 2013).

The UDHR, adopted on 10 December 1948 by the UNGA, echoes Franklin D. Roosevelt's 'four essential freedoms': freedom of expression, freedom of belief, freedom from want and freedom from fear (FDR Library, 2019). Its 30 Articles outline a set of civil, political, economic, social and cultural rights for all (universal rights). Article 1 declares that: 'All human beings are born free and equal in dignity and rights. They are endowed with reason and conscience and should act towards one another in a spirit of brotherhood'. Article 2 states that: 'All people are entitled to these rights regardless of race, colour, sex, language, religion, opinion, origin, property, birth or residency'. Articles 3 to 21 outline civil and political rights, which include the right to life, not to be tortured or unfairly persecuted, to an effective remedy for human rights violations, and to take part in government. Interestingly, in relation to political rights, the right to self-determination is absent in the UDHR. Articles 22 to 27 detail economic, social and cultural rights, such as the right to work, to form and to join trade unions, to marriage, to education, and to participate freely in the cultural life of the community (UN, 1948).

While the UDHR was heralded as a landmark in the promotion of universal human rights, a number of questions remained unanswered about what in practice such rights should look like and how they could be realised. *Universal* human rights for all in a culturally and ideologically diverse world, with people experiencing different socio-economic, political, geographical and environmental conditions and different levels of peace, stability, governmental organisation and conflict, has proven difficult. Invariably, different countries have different 'abilities' and/or desires to implement certain rights and enforce them. As a consequence, the UNHRC set about trying to develop the legal instruments that would define and realise the general rights of the UDHR. It was to take another 18 years before some level of agreement was reached. Disagreement existed especially around negative rights (what states *should not do* to infringe the rights of people) and positive rights (what states *should do* to promote rights such as education, welfare, healthcare) as well as around enforceability and to what extent states should be made accountable to bodies outside the state to promote rights.

Ideological disagreement and geo-political manoeuvring led Western bloc states to emphasise liberal individual rights, such as religious and civil liberties, political rights to vote, individual freedoms of expression/behaviour, rights to private property and protection from government actions (negative rights) rather than rights requiring governments to take action (positive rights). Alternatively, Eastern bloc states emphasised community rights provided by government action and intervention, such as social and economic rights, rights to education, healthcare, housing, employment and welfare (Weiss, 2012). These disagreements were not straightforward in ideological terms. For example, many Western European states developed comprehensive welfare states in the post-war period. Even the USA (with the New Deal under Franklin D. Roosevelt and later the 'War on Poverty', Medicare and Medicaid under President Johnson) provided some level of welfare provision. Indeed, it could be argued that the level of socio-economic rights provided in some Western states was superior to that in the 'socialist' East, although differences in economic growth also need to be considered here. As for individual rights, much has been written about the denial of such rights in the Eastern bloc with the suppression of religion and political dissent. However, the extent to which Western states upheld these rights is also open to question. For example, political censorship was practised in the USA against alleged 'communist' sympathisers during the McCarthy 'witch-hunts' of the 1950s. In the UK and Ireland political censorship alongside internment without trial were introduced at various times to deal with political 'emergencies'. In the north of Ireland, the promotion of religious discrimination by the government (1921–72) is well documented (Farrell, 1987). The denial of political rights and torture was also widely practised by Western states in many of the colonies (Cobain, 2012, 2016).

Different ideas about rights have also been associated with cultural differences, with some developing world countries suggesting that Western views on rights reflect Westernisation and cultural imperialism, linking colonial domination and notions of Western superiority in the past to cultural domination today (Jacobsen and Bruun, 2000). In this view, cultural traditions (Asian values, for example) on respect for leaders and hierarchies, and the importance of 'the community', outweigh notions of individual rights (Jenco, 2013: 237–258; Mahathir, 1996). Such challenges to universalism have been noted by others (eg Sen, 1997: 33–40; Donnelly, 2013; Freeman, 2017) arguing that these views are often aimed at preserving hierarchical ideas about power and denying democracy. In reaffirming the UN's commitment to the universality of human rights, the Vienna Conference in 1993 acknowledged that: 'the significance of national and regional particularities and various historical, cultural and religious backgrounds must be borne in mind' (UN, 1993: 3).

Despite this, challenges to universality remain. For some political leaders in the Global South, the interest by Western states in individual rights seems to smack of hypocrisy given the West's historic and contemporary interference in the political rights of others, first through colonisation, then through the imposition of and support for dictators friendly to the West, and the neo-colonial control of the global economy (Nkrumah, 1965). The result has often meant instability, conflict, absolute poverty and the denial of basic rights to life for many people throughout the world. By 2018 the UN was estimating that 815 million – one in nine of the global population – were undernourished, including 13 per cent of the people in developing countries and 23 per cent in Sub-Saharan Africa. Poor nutrition causes nearly half (45 per cent) of deaths in children under five – 3.1 million children – each year, 8,500 children per day, including a third of all childhood deaths in Sub-Saharan Africa. According to UNICEF (2018) an estimated 6.3 million children under 15 years of age died in 2017, or one every 5 seconds, mostly of preventable causes. It is difficult to argue about other human rights if the basic right to life is denied to so many people. No wonder that Léopold Senghor (Former President of Senegal, 1960–80) famously argued at the UN that "Human rights begin with breakfast".

UN human rights covenants and conventions

Eventually the UN gave up trying to develop one set of legally binding universal human rights for member states and in 1966, 18 years after the UDHR, it produced instead two separate legal covenants. It took a further ten years, until 1976, for enough states (35) to ratify them before they could come into force. The International Covenant on Civil and Political Rights (ICCPR) and the International Covenant of Economic, Social and Cultural Rights (ICESCR) are the only genuinely global and general human rights treaties. Having two covenants gave states options to ratify the rights they wanted to promote and those they did not. Not all UN states have ratified both covenants and some have not ratified either. Also, some have ratified with reservation, thus derogating from some elements. For example, the USA included reservations allowing it to keep the death penalty when it ratified the ICCPR (which includes the right to life). By 2018 the ICCPR had been ratified by 172 member states (including the UK in 1976, Ireland in 1989, and the USA in 1992). The ICESCR has been ratified by 169 (including the UK in 1976, Ireland in 1989, and China in 2001). Four states had signed but not ratified it up to 2018 (including the USA and Cuba) and 22 had not signed or ratified it by 2018 (for example, Saudi Arabia, United Arab Emirates, Oman) (UN Treaties, nd).

From 1966 on there followed a series of UN conventions on specific subjects – children, disability, discrimination against women, torture – designed to allow different states to pick and choose which rights they wished to ratify. In particular, the break-up of the Soviet Union and end of the Cold War led to a flurry of international human rights activity as geo-political disputes amongst the big powers appeared to diminish for a period with increased détente between the USA, USSR and China. Besides the two covenants, there are now seven other major UN human rights conventions:

- Convention on the Elimination of Racial Discrimination (CERD) (1966)
- Convention on the Elimination of All Forms of Discrimination against Women (CEDAW) (1979)
- Convention Against Torture and Other Cruel, Inhuman or Degrading Treatment or Punishment (CAT) (1984)
- Convention on the Rights of the Child (CRC) (1989)
- Convention on the Protection of the Rights of All Migrant Workers and Their Families (CRMW) (1990)
- Convention on the Rights of Persons with Disabilities (CRPD) (2006)
- Convention on Enforced Disappearances (CED) (2010)

The CRC is the most ratified convention. Since Somalia ratified it in 2015 the USA remains the only country yet to do so, though it has signed it, indicating support. The CRMW is the least ratified. By January 2020 only 55, mainly Global South states, had ratified it – with none from the industrialised West. These covenants and conventions, along with the UDHR, constitute the core of international human rights law. Some have also developed additional optional protocols providing more precise or progressive interpretations of covenants or conventions, giving them more substance and which member states can ratify if they wish. For example, the Second Optional Protocol to the ICCPR (1989) relates to the abolition of the death penalty. By 2018, 86 states had ratified it. The Optional Protocol on the Convention Against Torture (CAT) (2002) allows closer monitoring of states by its specific UN monitoring committee and by 2018 this had been ratified by 88 states. One of the Optional Protocols on the CRC relates to the prevention of children being involved in armed conflicts and by 2018 this had been ratified by 168 states.

Since the UDHR in 1948, all UN member states have ratified at least one core international human rights treaty, and 80 per cent have ratified four or more. There are also many other UN treaties relating directly or indirectly to human rights, including the 17 UN Sustainable Development Goals (SDGs), adopted by all UN member states in 2015, which aim to tackle issues including poverty, hunger, disease, inequality, education, healthcare, climate change and ecological degradation on a global basis. A number of regional rights mechanisms have also been developed outside of the UN as states with similar ideas on rights have decided to go ahead and promote their own more comprehensive and enforceable rights mechanisms through, for example, the Council of Europe (European Convention on Human Rights, 1953) and the European Union (Charter of Fundamental Rights, 2009).

International human rights enforcement

International human rights emerge from voluntary agreements made by nation-states when they ratify covenants or conventions. States agree to accept responsibility to protect and provide certain rights relating to their citizens and other citizens on their territory. Everyone has a responsibility for human rights. However, usually only states can provide complaints and redress mechanisms for citizens and enforce them through policy, practice, legislation and their own courts by imposing fines or imprisonment for infringement. States can also establish independent national human rights bodies to scrutinise legislation and advise the government involved on human rights adherence (for example, there are separate human rights and equality commissions for Ireland, North and South, and one for England, Scotland and Wales).

There are also international mechanisms which hold states accountable for defending rights. They tend to be weak and dependent on the support, compliance and power of the state. Each covenant or convention has its own UN reporting committee, as does the Optional Protocol on the CAT. These monitor on a regular basis each ratifying state's adherence to the rights mechanisms. They can make recommendations, use persuasion, or indeed embarrass states. Under certain conditions, including the agreement of the state concerned, most can receive and consider complaints or communications from individuals, although, by January 2020, the complaints mechanism under the CRMW had not yet entered force. The reporting process also provides opportunities for NGOs to mobilise and lobby nationally and internationally to promote particular human rights, policies and practice during the reporting process, while the signing and ratifying process facilitates means by which NGOs can raise awareness about rights and lobby for ratification by states.

On 15 March 2006 the UN Commission on Human Rights (UNCHR) was replaced by the UN Human Rights Council (UNHRC) which acquired more powers, including the power to introduce its own human rights investigations with the appointment of Special Rapporteurs. A new Universal Periodic Review (UPR) was introduced to report every four or five years on every member state's compliance with all the human rights treaties they have ratified (www.ohchr.org). The UN International Court of Justice (ICJ) also exists. Based in The Hague since 1946, it adjudicates on international law, mainly giving advice or opinions. Matters can only be raised by member states or UN bodies, and the Court's judgements do not necessarily have to be acted on. For example, in 1986 the USA government refused to accept the Court's ruling against American support for the use of force by the Contras against the Nicaraguan government. In 2004 it gave an opinion that the Israeli 'Partition Wall' was illegal under international law. Israel refused to accept it (ICJ, nd).

The UN General Assembly can pass resolutions against violations of human rights but other than moral pressure these have limited enforcement. Only the UNSC can employ enforcement measures – impose sanctions, trade embargoes, establish special investigative tribunals, or launch wars – on member states (or indeed on individuals, private or voluntary organisations) and has done so against some states deemed by the UNSC to be violating international human rights. However, that rarely happens solely as a result of human rights violations. When it does happen, geo-political factors are usually involved. The UNSC is greatly influenced by major powers, leading former UN Secretary-General Boutros Boutros-Ghali to argue that: 'the UN is now the sole property of a single power – the US – which through intimidation, threats and the use of its veto, manipulates the world body for the benefit of its own interest' (Boutros-Ghali, 1999).

Conclusion

Attempts to develop and promote universal human rights and universal oversight have met with many difficulties. Differences exist in defining, interpreting, policing and realising universal human rights. There are often different cultural or ideological views on what should be a right as well as different levels of priority and ability to police rights. The role of power in 'who decides' what is a right and where and when rights should be enforced is also an issue. Debates exist around the importance of civil and political rights versus social, economic and cultural rights; individual versus collective/community rights; and majority versus minority rights. There may also be clashes of rights, such as the right to freedom of speech versus the right to be protected from abuse or incitement to hatred. Difficulties in reaching agreement on rights have led to the development of different sets of rights mechanisms that states can choose to ratify or not and which allow for derogations in different circumstances. Even then, differences may exist on interpretations of agreed rights – the right to adequate shelter, healthcare and education may mean different things in different societies, for example. Crucially, the influence of geo-political or national self-interest concerns in international oversight by the UNSC has meant that such oversight is usually skewed by factors other than universal human rights concerns. Thus the oversight of rights is usually dependent on the voluntary compliance of states themselves. In many poorer states in the developing world, with weaker less well-resourced systems, the enforceability of rights may be limited. The realisability of rights may require awareness of rights, confidence in demanding them, empowerment to challenge for them and the availability of legal advice and representation. Indeed, the realisation of one right (for example, the right to vote) may be dependent on the realisation of a wide range of other rights (for example, food, education, healthcare, housing, transportation). The question arises whether it is possible to have civil and political rights without also having social and economic rights.

Despite such issues, UN Human Rights instruments have made human rights part of the contemporary political discourse (Forsythe, 2012) and created a climate of empathy for 'the other' (Frezzo, 2015). They have led to improvements in the human rights records of states across the world and provided tools for NGOs and other activists to campaign and lobby for change. They have also been used as a benchmark to develop policy and practice. Ultimately, however, human rights are about change. They have been historically and they will continue to be.

Note

[1] Sometimes two or more countries will have used the veto on the same resolution, which is why the number of vetoes exceeds the number of vetoed resolutions.

References

Boutros Boutros-Ghali (1999) *Unvanquished: A US–UN Saga*, New York: Random House.

Butler, R. (2012) 'Reform of the United Nations Security Council', *Journal of Law and International Affairs*, 1(1): 23–39. Available from: http://elibrary.law.psu.edu/jlia/vol1/iss1/2

Clapham, A. (2007) *Human Rights: A Very Short Introduction*, Oxford: Oxford University Press.

Cobain, I. (2012) *Cruel Britannia: A Secret History of Torture*, London: Portobello Books.

Cobain, I. (2016) *The History Thieves: Secrets, Lies and the Shaping of a Modern Nation*, London: Portobello Books.

Donnelly, J. (2013) *Universal Human Rights in Theory and Practice*, London: Cornell University Press.

Farrell, M. (1987) *Northern Ireland: The Orange State*, London: Pluto Press.

FDR Library (2019) *The Four Freedoms*. Available from: https://www.fdrlibrary.org/four-freedoms

Forsyth, D.P. (2012) *Human Rights in International Relations*, 3rd edition (Themes in International Relations), Cambridge: Cambridge University Press.

Freeman, M. (2017) *Human Rights*, Cambridge: Polity Press.

Frezzo, M. (2015) *The Sociology of Human Rights: An Introduction*, Cambridge: Polity Press.

Gould, M. and Rablen, M.D. (2017) 'Reform of the United Nations Security Council: equity and efficiency', *Public Choice*, 173: 145–168. Available from: https://doi.org/10.1007/s11127-017-0468-2

ICJ (nd) International Court of Justice Decisions. Available from: www.icj-cij.org/en/decisions

Jacobsen, M. and Bruun, O. (2000) *Human Rights and Asian Values: Contesting National Identities and Cultural Representations in Asia*, London: Routledge/Curzon.

Jenco, L. (2013) 'Revisiting Asian values', *Journal of the History of Ideas*, 74(2): 237–258. Available from: www.jstor.org.ucc.idm.oclc.org/stable/43291300

Mahathir, M. (1996) 'Asian values debate', Speech at the Twenty-Ninth International General Meeting of the Pacific Basin Economic Council, Washington, 21 May. Available from: www.mahathir.com/malaysia/speeches/1996/1996-05-21.php

Mishra, R. (1981) *Society and Social Policy: Theories and Practice of Welfare* London: Macmillan.

Nkrumah, K. (1965) *Neo-Colonialism: The Last Stage of Imperialism,* London: Thomas Nelson and Sons.

Sen, A. (1997) 'Human rights and Asian values: what Lee Kuan Yew and Le Peng don't understand about Asia', *The New Republic,* 217(2–3): 33–40.

Throntveit, T. (2011) *Diplomatic History,* 35(3): 445–481. Available from: www.jstor.org/stable/pdf/24916429.pdf?refreqid=excelsior%3A5cf79c684ce1b1d7680e2f1f01574971

UN (1945) *United Nations Charter,* New York: United Nations. Available from: www.un.org/en/charter-united-nations/index.html

UN (1948) *Universal Declaration of Human Rights.* Available from: www.un.org/en/universal-declaration-human-rights/

UN (nd) Security Council Report. Available from: www.securitycouncilreport.org/un-security-council-working-methods/the-veto.php

UN Treaties (nd) UN Treaties website. Available from: https://treaties.un.org/

UN (1993) *Vienna Declaration and Programme of Action. Adopted by the World Conference on Human Rights in Vienna on 25 June 1993,* New York: United Nations. Available from: https://www.ohchr.org/EN/ProfessionalInterest/Pages/Vienna.aspx

UNICEF (2018) Press Release. Available from: https://www.unicef.org/press-releases/child-under-15-dies-every-five-seconds-around-world-un-report

Weiss, T. (2012) *What's Wrong with the United Nations and How to Fix it,* Cambridge: Polity Press.

3

The Council of Europe, the European Convention on Human Rights and the Social Charter

Liz Griffith

The end of World War II left Europe in mourning for its 60 million dead and reeling as the atrocities perpetrated by the Nazi regime came to light. Europe was divided between the Western and Eastern blocs, economies lay in tatters and the United States and the Soviet Union emerged as new global superpowers. In Western Europe a priority for political leaders was to get the economies working again and to defend against the spread of communism from the East. Within the context of the Cold War, the solution appeared to lie in greater Western European unity, with recovery possible through the pooling of Europe's economic resources and with new, jointly run institutions. Linked to the promotion of Western values and concepts of human rights, this model could provide a contrast to the lack of civil and political freedoms in the East. The concept of European unification, while not new, gained traction in the post-war years with a proliferation of congresses, conferences and declarations exploring the topic. Enthusiasm for European unity was shared by the United States, which saw an integrated Western Europe as a potential bulwark against the spread of Soviet communism and a constraint upon a resurgent German nationalism (Greer, 2018: 13).

The Hague Congress of Europe paved the way for the founding of the Council of Europe in May 1949 with ten members (there are now 47). It immediately set about drafting the European Convention on Human Rights (ECHR) – which was adopted in 1950 – and establishing its oversight body, the European Court of Human Rights (ECtHR). Despite the UN having adopted the Universal Declaration of Human Rights (UDHR) in 1948, disagreements between East and West at United Nations (UN) level were preventing the development of legally binding rights mechanisms. Crucially, the ECHR allowed Western European states to develop their own set of rights for their citizens with which they could all agree and which could be used to promote the benefits of living in Western liberal democracies to those living in the East.

Given the British government's recent scepticism of the ECHR, it is perhaps surprising to note that British establishment figures – including the former Prime Minister Winston Churchill and lawyer David Maxwell-Fyfe – played a prominent role in initiating and developing the Convention. In November 1950, the UK was the first country in Europe to sign the ECHR, although it resolutely rejected the Optional Protocol that would permit individuals to pursue a complaint, known as 'individual petition'. The Secretary of State for Foreign Affairs, Ernest Bevin, informed parliament that the UK was 'not prepared ... to hand over' its highest appeals to the Strasbourg court (HC Deb, 13 November 1950). That the UK was so quick to sign the ECHR is curious. A generous interpretation is that the UK was proud to showcase its perceived commitment to human rights. More cynically, we might interpret the UK's prompt response as a means of throwing its weight behind the full convention while undermining the Optional Protocol. It would take a further 16 years before the UK agreed to accept individual petitions (Beddard, 1993: 29).

The concern of an 'unwelcome judicial authority' taking precedence over British law is therefore nothing new (Simpson, 2001). So vehement was the British Conservative Party's distaste for the ECtHR that its 2015 manifesto committed to repeal the Human Rights Act itself – the central plank in human rights legislation in the UK. This would free the UK from the influence of the ECtHR and would restore the Supreme Court as the ultimate arbiter of human rights matters in the UK (Jay, 2017). That the UK had somehow been emasculated by Europe's institutions became a key point in the 2016 Brexit Vote Leave campaign, which described the 'loss of control' as deeply 'damaging and undemocratic' (VoteLeave, 2016). There is an irony in the UK citing democracy as a reason for turning its back on Europe, when the desire to protect democracy and promote peace was a driving factor in developing Europe's human rights system.

The ECHR came only two years after the UDHR and yet the two instruments are quite different. An immediate textual difference is size: the ECHR has only half the number of rights of the UDHR. The reason for this is relatively simple. The ECHR focuses primarily on civil and political rights, and largely excludes social and economic rights, whereas the UDHR incorporates both. While advocates of human rights ostensibly talked of the interdependency and interconnectedness of rights, in the 1940s human rights had become a politicised issue divided between the two camps of (Soviet) socialism and (Western) capitalism. Soviet states championed a state-centred system and the cause of economic, social and cultural rights, whereas Western states asserted the priority of private initiative, civil and political rights (Morsink, 1999).

The UDHR drafting committee included representatives from both camps and the process proved fraught. Eventually a compromise was reached: a non-binding universal declaration that included both sets of rights. It would take a further two decades for the UN to commit to legal obligations in the form of two separate covenants adopted in 1966. In contrast, the architects of the ECHR all hailed from Western Europe and could focus on civil and political rights without objection from Soviet states. While the ECHR's text makes no explicit reference to trying to counter the might of the USSR, this sentiment was not far away. Luzius Wildhaber, the first President of the ECtHR, spoke of 'a need, for protective purposes, after the iron curtain had come down, to make a pre-emptive strike against the menace of new tyrants' (Bates, 2010). So, although the ECHR formed part of Europe's new peace apparatus, its focus on civil and political rights was a pointed attempt to articulate a statement of common values that contrasted sharply with communism.

Cold War ideology led to civil and political rights being viewed as inherently different to social, economic and cultural rights. Over the years, theorists have highlighted perceived differences between the two sets of rights: whereas civil and political are considered *negative* rights and economic and social rights place *positive* duties on states (Bouandel, 1997). Also civil and political rights are costless, whereas economic and social rights are resource dependent (Cranston, 1973). Civil and political rights are easily justiciable, whereas economic, social and cultural rights are more difficult to manage solely through judicial processes (Sunstein, 1993). The idea that rights are inherently different has not gone unchallenged. Back in 1944, US President Franklin Roosevelt proclaimed that 'necessitous men are not free men', thereby acknowledging that civil and political freedoms – such as the right to liberty and security – cannot be fully enjoyed by persons who have no shelter, food or income. This vision was shared by Eleanor Roosevelt, who was tenacious in her insistence that economic and social rights should be part of the UDHR's catalogue of rights. Further, the UN has consistently rejected the classification of rights as 'artificial and even self-defeating' (OHCHR, 2008) and warns that such an approach is 'arbitrary and incompatible with the principle that the two sets of human rights are indivisible and interdependent' (CESCR, 1998). Many academics have also criticised the classification of rights, describing it as a 'fallacy' (An-Na'im, 2004), a 'common mistake' (O'Cinneide and Lester, 2004) and 'ill conceived' (Nolan et al, 2009).

Nevertheless, given the lesser status afforded to economic and social rights in the West, it is unsurprising that the European Social Charter was not adopted until a decade after the European Convention on Human Rights. Often referred to as Europe's 'social constitution', the European Social Charter of 1961 focuses on economic, social and cultural rights and aimed to carry Europe a 'big step forward' by giving its citizens the legal right to work, social security, social and medical assistance, maternity protections, and so on (Tomuschat, 2014: 35). Although intended to be the ECHR's counterpart, for many years the Charter remained overshadowed by the Convention and under-utilised by potential litigants. The fall of the Berlin Wall gave a renewed urgency to improve the protection of economic and social rights across Europe, and with it an attempt to revitalise the Charter and address its shortcomings through the Revised Social Charter of 1996. Table 3.1 compares the Convention with the Charter.

The European Charter differs from the European Convention in a number of ways. States must abide by the entirety of the Convention but can pick and choose which Charter provisions they wish to be bound by – although they must accept a minimum number of 'core' rights (the right to work, organise, bargain collectively, social security, social and medical assistance, protection for families and protection of migrant workers). The rationale for permitting states to choose from a menu of rights was that they would gradually agree to opt in to more and more rights (Giacca et al, 2014). Critics have variously applauded this approach as 'innovative and exciting' (Beddard, 1993: 32), or criticised it as failing to establish a 'firm guarantee' of economic and social rights (Tomuschat, 2014).

The Convention applies to *everyone* within a state's territory and indeed can have 'extraterritorial' effect by applying outside the national territory at times. In contrast, the Charter is limited to nationals who are 'lawfully present' or 'working regularly' in the territory of the host state. Despite this restrictive language, the Charter's Committee insisted that it protects a 'minimum core' of social rights for all persons – regardless of their immigration status (Cholewinski, 2005). The Convention is governed by its court (ECtHR), which receives individual complaints and inter-state disputes. Individual petition has had an enormous uptake and to date the Court has dealt with over 780,000 cases. Inter-state disputes have proved much less common, with only 23 cases. For example, the 'hooded men' case involving the treatment of terror suspects by British forces in the north of Ireland

Table 3.1: Comparison of European Convention on Human Rights and European Social Charter

	European Convention on Human Rights (ECHR) 1950	European Social Charter (Charter) 1961 and the Revised Social Charter 1996
States parties	All 47 Council of Europe countries have ratified ECHR. New Council of Europe members must accept ECHR before they may join EU.	43 member states of Council of Europe have ratified ESC and 34 have ratified the Revised Charter.
Contents	States are bound by the entirety of ECHR and must comply with all 14 substantive rights. States can opt into the Optional Protocols.	ESC contains 19 guarantees and Revised ESC brings an additional 8 guarantees. States can choose which provisions they are bound by but must accept at least 5 of the 7 'core' rights.
Supervisory mechanism	ECHR is governed by the European Court of Human Rights. The Court rules on complaints through individual petition and on inter-state disputes.	ESC is monitored by the Committee on Economic and Social Rights, which has a dual function: - It scrutinises regular reports submitted by member states (reporting process) - It assesses collective complaints (only 15 member states have accepted this).
Recent activity	In 2016, the Court dealt with 38,505 applications and delivered 993 judgements. As of July 2018, 54,350 applications are pending.	In 2016, the Committee received 21 new collective complaints and handed down 11 decisions. It examined reports by 34 states parties. As of July 2018, 50 collective complaints were pending.
Remedies and implementation	The Convention is directly enforceable in domestic legal systems. Rulings issued by the Court *must* be adhered to and implemented. In practice, implementation is a problem, with nearly 10,000 cases still awaiting execution. The Court can award compensation.	The Charter is not directly enforceable in domestic legal systems. The Committee cannot award compensation.
Derogations	Article 15 permits derogation. Eight states parties – Albania, Armenia, France, Georgia, Greece, Ireland, Turkey and the United Kingdom – have relied on their right of derogation.	There is a derogation clause in both the Charter (Article 30.1) and Revised ESC (F.1). No state has ever sought to derogate.

is a famous example (*Ireland v UK*, 1978). The Charter is monitored by a Committee which has a dual function. First, through the regular reporting process, the Committee enters into a social policy dialogue with each member state with the aim of identifying any violations of the Charter and then encourages the state to rectify it. Second, through the collective complaints procedure, the Committee determines complaints submitted by specified NGOs on behalf of a group of people. As of July 2018, only 15 countries had accepted the collective complaints procedure.

The ECtHR's inability to intervene proactively and investigate potential rights violations prior to a complaint being received – unlike the UN human rights treaty bodies – may be viewed as a weakness. Long delays in cases being heard and decisions being implemented by states, and the great financial cost involved, are other disadvantages. The incorporation of the ECHR into domestic law in EU states has streamlined this process to some extent. Now non-compliance of states with the ECHR can be heard in domestic courts, although appeals to the ECtHR can still be made once redress through domestic courts is exhausted.

The derogation from rights during periods of war, conflict, or 'emergency', has also further weakened ECHR enforcement mechanisms in times of insecurity and uncertainty, while enforcement has at times appeared to be more concerned with political pragmatism among allies rather than upholding the rights of individuals and groups within society. The first case taken by an individual to the ECtHR, for example, was by a man who had been interned without trial by the Irish government in the 1950s (*Lawless v Ireland*). In 1960, the ECtHR accepted the government's defence under Article 15 that the conditions laid down for a valid derogation had been satisfied and that internment in Ireland was necessary to deal with the emergency situation. Governments can derogate from any of the ECHR rights (except torture) in an emergency situation. Governments may decide to ignore ECtHR decisions. Despite rulings by the ECtHR (in 2010 and 2014) that a blanket ban on prisoners having the right to vote contravened Article 3 of Protocol 1 of the ECHR, the UK government has refused to change its policy regarding this as too much ECtHR interference in UK policy-making. Indeed, such rulings have spurred on further demands that British sovereignty needs to be protected by withdrawing from such institutions. Nevertheless, it should be added that these rulings did lead to other states (for example, France and Ireland) legislating to allow some short-term prisoners the vote.

The EU itself has acceded to the ECHR through the Treaty of Lisbon. This makes the EU the 48th contracting party to the Convention. Work continues on accession and eventually the EU and all its institutions will be directly bound by the Convention. However, there are no plans for the EU to accede to the Charter.

Described as 'the most successful human rights instrument in the world today', there is no shortage of literature waxing lyrical about the achievements of the Convention (Beddard, 1993; Dickson, 1997; Greer, 2006). Finding comparable praise for the European Charter is more difficult. Indeed, finding *any* literature on the Charter is a challenge: its neglect in scholarship makes it something of an 'orphan' in human rights literature (Sant'ana and De Schutter, 2012). While a buoyant appraisal of the Charter can be found on the Council of Europe website – 'no other legal instrument at pan-European level can provide such an extensive and complete protection of social rights' (CoE, 2018) – it is clear that this enthusiasm is not readily shared by critics, who point to a number of weaknesses. These include the opinion that the Charter's menu approach has resulted in 'patchwork ratification practice'; the majority of states' parties have tended to reject important rights; its procedures are 'long, drawn out and scarcely effective'; and ratification of the Revised Social Charter has taken too long (Beddard, 1993). Furthermore, the reporting process is complicated and the social dialogue process is slow. For example, in 2017 the Committee examined the UK's compliance with the Charter during the preceding four-year period. The Committee's report honed in on restrictions on European nationals in the UK accessing social security benefits. Rather than make a finding, the Committee chose to defer its conclusions pending further information from the UK government. By the time the Committee makes its finding, the UK context is likely to have been changed irrevocably by Brexit.

An oft-cited weakness of the Charter is that the last stage of its monitoring mechanism involves the Committee of Ministers, which is essentially a political entity. In practice, this can mean that Ministers avoid voting to issue recommendations against a particular member state if it means condemning a political ally. In consequence, even where a state repeatedly fails to comply with the Charter – such as the UK's ongoing failure to provide an adequate level of social security benefits – the state can expect little in the way of sanction. Critics suggest that the Committee's dual function is problematic and risks undermining the credibility of the Charter system: 'it is a hard assignment for one body, first to engage a state party in constructive, fruitful dialogue ... and then to behave as a quasi-judicial investigative and settlement body. It should opt for one or the other' (Churchill and Khaliq, 2007: 230). One critic concluded that the European Social Charter has 'hardly ruffled' the status quo in relation to economic and social rights in Europe (Giacca et al, 2014) and a similarly damning assessment was offered by Catherine Lalumière, a former Council of Europe Secretary-General, who describes the Charter as the 'poor relation' to the Convention, a mere 'paper tiger' (Akandji-Kombe, 2006). Certainly, Table 3.1 shows that relatively few victims of violations of social and economic rights seek a remedy from the Charter.

Despite general criticism of the Charter and its reporting process, its collective complaints procedure merits attention as it has clearly brought about progressive change in some instances (De Schutter, 2013; Harris, 2009). For example, the NGO Association for the Protection of All Children (APPROACH) lodged a complaint against Ireland in 2012, alleging that the Irish common law of 'reasonable chastisement' allowed parents to commit common assault against children with impunity and thus violated the Charter. The complaint was upheld. The Irish government accepted the Committee's decision and amended legislation to include an explicit prohibition of all forms of corporal punishment. Given the usual slow speed of government machinery, the speed in which this violation was identified and rectified, is quite remarkable. By the end of 2017, all children in Ireland enjoyed new protections. APPROACH's complaint against Ireland was one of a series of complaints made against the remaining EU member states bound by the collective complaint procedure that do not explicitly prohibit all forms of corporal punishment. Like Ireland, Slovenia also promptly changed legislation to implement the Committee's findings. Other countries – Belgium, the Czech Republic, Italy and France – have still not introduced reforms.

Another NGO that has made extensive use of the European Social Charter is the European Roma Rights Centre (ERRC). Established in 1996, ERRC has made a series of collective complaints against Italy, Bulgaria, Portugal and Greece. In doing so, ERRC has successfully exposed racial segregation and discriminatory practices in provision of medical services and education, the forced evictions of Roma, and the systematic destruction of Roma property. A collective complaint against the Czech Republic for placing a disproportionate number of young Roma children and children with disabilities in medical institutions remains pending. A successful collective complaint by a Croatian NGO led to Croatia withdrawing a school biology textbook that contained materials held to be biased, discriminatory and degrading towards LGBT (lesbian, gay, bisexual, and transgender) communities.

As a result of the Committee's findings, Croatia agreed to remove the homophobic content of its 'Clean Start' educational programme. The Committee's findings in this case continue to be cited: homophobia veiled as education clearly violates the Charter. These are just some examples of how the Charter has resulted in progressive change.

Meanwhile, ECtHR cases, which tend to be given a higher profile in the media, also effect social change. Landmark cases in the ECtHR include *Norris v Ireland* (1988), which led to the decriminalisation of homosexuality in Ireland in 1993, and the *Oliari and Others v Italy* (2015) case, which led to the provision for same-sex civil union legislation in Italy. In 2018, the ECtHR ruled that the UK's mass surveillance practices revealed by Edward Snowdon's release of documents in 2013 violates privacy and the freedom of expression, with implications for security policy and the right to privacy.

Among the ECtHR's more controversial decisions was a ruling in favour of France, in *S.A.S. v France* (2014), when it upheld a ban on full-face coverings in public. The legislation, which had been introduced in 2010, had been criticised as targeting Muslim women. In the aftermath of the ruling a number of other European states (including Belgium and Denmark) also banned the wearing of full-face covering veils in public, with implications for more traditional Muslim women and the notion of inclusion and interculturalism.

Conclusion

Post-war Europe has generally seen progress in civil and political rights, for example with increased electoral rights, improved political participation, advances in equality for LGBT persons, developments in the rights of persons with disabilities, protections of privacy and personal data, and so on (Ghai, 2001). That is not to say that all civil and political rights have flourished. Some countries have seen a decline in the freedom of the press and a rise in intolerance towards people of religious belief (Freedom House, 2017). When it comes to social and economic rights, Europe has seen a widening of socio-economic divides which intensified with the onset of the global financial crisis (OECD, 2017). While health and life expectancy have generally improved, health inequalities persist and are particularly marked among ethnic minorities, as are inequalities in educational outcomes, housing standards and so forth (FRA, 2018).

With racist politics on the rise across Europe, ongoing neoliberal austerity measures and a populist disdain for social protections and racial equality, there is an urgent need to keep economic and social rights in focus. Multiple measures are necessary. It is also critical that *existing* legal protections – such as the European Social Charter – are fully utilised. There is a role for different parts of society to improve the Charter's effectiveness. At the level of Strasbourg, the Turin Process offers a blueprint for strengthening enforcement of the Charter (CoE, 2014). There is a role for NGOs and the trade union movement in lobbying governments such as the UK that have hitherto failed to sign up to the collective complaints system. Civil society could also engage more with the ECSR. Whereas it is common practice for NGOs to submit shadow reports to treaty bodies such as the Committee Against Torture, the Committee on the Rights of the Child, and so forth, this author is not aware of a single NGO in Northern Ireland that has submitted information to the Committee on Economic and Social Rights about compliance with the Charter. What is the reason for this? Is it due to the relative obscurity and complexity of the Charter's reporting process? Or is it that NGOs 'doth protest too much'? While we scold government for not taking social and economic rights seriously, we afford little attention to the Charter. Certainly, there is a lot to be done if the paper tiger that is the European Social Charter is to roar.

Acknowledgements

With thanks to my colleague Dr Ciara Fitzpatrick.

References

Akandji-Kombe, J. (2006) *The European Social Charter and European Convention on Human Rights: Prospects for the Next 10 Years.* Available from: https://rm.coe.int/1680490830

An-Na'im, A. (2004) 'To affirm the full human rights standing of economic, social and cultural rights', in J. Cottrell and J. Ghai (eds) *Economic, Social and Cultural Rights in Practice*, London: Interights, pp 7–17.

Bates, E. (2010) *The Evolution of the ECHR*, Oxford: Oxford University Press.

Beddard, R. (1993) *Human Rights and Europe*, 3rd edition, Cambridge: Cambridge University Press.

Bouandel, P. (1997) *Human Rights and Comparative Politics*, Aldershot: Dartmouth Publishing.

CESCR (1998) Available from: https://www.escr-net.org/resources/general-comment-9

Cholewinski, R. (2005) *Study on Obstacles to Effective Access of Irregular Migrants to Minimum Social Rights*, Strasbourg: Council of Europe Publishing.

Churchill, R. and Khaliq, U. (2007) 'Violations of economic, social and cultural rights: the current use and future potential of the collective complaints mechanism of the European Social Charter', in M. Baderin and R. McCorquodale (eds) *Economic, Social and Cultural Rights in Action*, Oxford: Oxford University Press, pp 105–241.

CoE (2014) *High Level Conference on the European Social Charter.* Available from: www.coe.int/en/web/turin-european-social-charter/conference-turin

CoE (2018) *European Social Charter.* Available from: www.coe.int/en/web/turin-european-social-charter

Cranston, M. (1973) *What Are Human Rights?*, London: Bodley Head.

De Schutter, O. (ed) (2013) *Economic, Social and Cultural Rights as Human Rights*, Cheltenham: Edward Elgar.

Dickson, B. (1997) *Human Rights and the European Convention*, London: Sweet and Maxwell.

Freedom House (2018) *Freedom of the Press Annual Report 2017*, New York: Freedom House Press.

Ghai, Y. (2001) *Human Rights and Social Development: Toward Democratization and Social Justice*, Geneva: UN Research Institute for Social Development.

Giacca, G., Golay, C. and Riedel, E. (2014) 'The development of economic, social and cultural rights in international law', in E. Riedel, G. Giacca and C. Golay, *Economic, Social and Cultural Rights in International Law*, Oxford: Oxford University Press, pp 3–48.

Greer, S. (2006) *The European Convention on Human Rights*, Cambridge: Cambridge University Press.

Greer, S. (2018) 'Europe', in D. Moeckli, S. Shah and S. Sivakumaran, *International Human Rights Law*, Oxford: Oxford University Press, pp 416–40.

Harris, D. (2009) 'Collective complaints under the European Social Charter: encouraging progress?', in K.H. Kaikobad and M. Bohlander (eds) *International Law and Power: Perspectives on Legal Order and Justice*, Brill: Nijhoff, pp 3–24.

Jay, Z. (2017) 'Keeping rights at home: British conceptions of rights and compliance with the European Court of Human Rights', *British Journal of Politics and International Relations*, 19(4): 842–860.

Morsink, J. (1999) *The Universal Declaration of Human Rights: Origins, Drafting and Intent*, Philadelphia: University of Pennsylvania Press.

Nolan, A., Porter, B. and Langford, M. (2009) 'The justiciability of social and economic rights: an updated appraisal', *CHRG Working Paper*, 15: 1–34.

O'Cinneide, C. and Lester, L. (2004) 'The effective protection of socio-economic rights', in J. Cottrell and J. Ghai (eds) *Economic, Social and Cultural Rights in Practice*, London: Interights, pp 7–17.

OECD (2017) 'Understanding the socio-economic divide in Europe', Paris: OECD Centre for Opportunity and Equality.

OHCHR (2008) *Fact Sheet No 33: Frequently Asked Questions on Economic, Social and Cultural Rights*. Available from: https://www.refworld.org/docid/499176e62.html

Sant'ana, M. and De Schutter, O. (2012) 'The European Committee of Social Rights', in G. de Beco (ed) *Human Rights Monitoring Mechanisms of the Council of Europe*, London: Routledge, pp 71–99.

Simpson, B.A.W. (2001) *Human Rights and the End of Empire – Britain and the Genesis of the European Convention*, Oxford: Oxford University Press.

Sunstein, C. (1993) 'Against positive rights', *East European Constitutional Review*, 35(2): 35–38.

Tomuschat, C. (2014) *Human Rights Between Idealism and Realism*, 3rd edition, Oxford: Oxford University Press.

VoteLeave (2016) *Briefing: Taking Back Control from Brussels*. Available from: www.voteleavetakecontrol.org/briefing_control.html

Speeches

House of Commons Debate (13 November 1950) volume 480, column 1499.

4

The European Union and human rights

Gerard McCann and Nadia Makaryshyn

This chapter discusses how the European Union (EU) has developed a range of human rights-based policies, measures and instruments, and surveys this influence on social and welfare policies in member states. It starts by outlining the ideological tensions and practical difficulties in post-war Western Europe which influenced the establishment of what was to become the EU during the Cold War period. It then looks at how an increasingly centralising political and economic union began to adopt and promote concepts of human rights in principle and policy, culminating in the 2000 Charter of Fundamental Rights (the Social Charter). The discussion considers the tension between notions of 'pooled sovereignty' and the impact this has had on concepts of national sovereignty, workers' rights and equality. It also explores the implications that EU oversight and enforcement of socio-economic policy may have for the development – or otherwise – of rights and social development at member state level. In doing this it considers how an economic union of some of the richest countries in the world, which is primarily focused on protecting economic growth for its own member states, can adhere to its stated commitments to universal human rights. It assesses the impact of an exclusive 'Fortress Europe', which maintains the market and wealth of the member states and their citizens, but paradoxically denies rights to vulnerable migrants. Finally, the chapter looks at the challenges facing EU human rights commitments as a result of rapidly shifting geo-political circumstances – refugees fleeing ongoing conflicts, COVID-19 mitigation, neoliberal globalisation, wealth inequality and global insecurity (Craig and de Búrca, 2015: 380–428; Buonanno and Nugent, 2013: 246–250).

The context

Today's European Union developed from a series of common economic agreements among six Western European states, beginning with the Treaty of Paris creating the European Coal and Steel Community (ECSC) on 18 April 1951. In the 1950s Europe was still recovering from war and was engulfed in a Cold War between the West's market-based model of economic development and the command economies of the Soviet Union. Western European leaders – including Jean Monnet, Robert Schuman and Joseph Adenauer, the first post-war Chancellor of the Federal Republic of Germany (West Germany) – had agreed on the need to unite Western European states and bring together, where possible, the former warring states of Germany and France to promote economic growth. The ECSC enabled the six founding countries (France, West Germany, Italy and the three Benelux countries, Belgium, Luxembourg, and the Netherlands) to develop closer working and trading relationships (Gillingham, 2003: 53–67; McCormick, 2014: 47–71; Eichengreen, 2007: 163–197). This partnership was consolidated on 25 March 1957 by the Treaty of Rome and the creation of the European Economic Community (EEC) or 'Common Market' – later called the European Community (EC). On 1 November 1993, this took a further step into becoming fully integrated with the establishment of the European Union itself and its introduction of European citizenship, institutional alignment and increased competences such as foreign and security policy, economic and monetary union. It aimed to promote trade, economic growth, solidarity and peace between old enemies who were now committed to working in solidarity in face of external economic and political threats. Robert Marjolin, one of the first French representatives on the European Commission in the early years, commented that this community was:

> one of the greatest moments in Europe's history. Who would have thought during the 1930s, and even during the ten years that followed the war, that European states which had been tearing one another apart for so many centuries and some of which, like France and Italy, still had very closed economies, would form a common market intended eventually to become an economic area that could be linked to one great dynamic market? (Marjolin, 1989: 284; Dinan, 2010: 26)

From its earliest association, the European Community's objective was to show the citizens of both the West and the East that Western notions of social democracy and a common market economy were more attractive than what existed in Eastern command economies. Consequently, notions of rights and freedoms were central to this pan-European project. A rights-based understanding became enshrined in the treaty-base and was, subsequently, reinforced in its citizenship-focused agreements: the Single European Act (1986), the Maastricht Treaty (1992) and the Lisbon Treaty (2007). The 'conscience' of the organisation had particular resonance for those states which had committed early to this process and the evolving belief in a European *demos*. This can be seen from this European Commission statement on rights from its *Declaration on the European Identity*, dated 14 December 1973. It stipulated that those committed to this process of European integration:

> wish to ensure that the cherished values of their legal, political and moral order are respected, and to preserve the rich variety of their national cultures. Sharing as they do the same attitudes to life, based on a determination to build a society which measures up to the needs of the individual, they are determined to defend the principles of representative democracy, of the rule of law, of social justice – which is the ultimate goal of economic progress – and of respect for human rights. All of these are fundamental elements of the European Identity. (European Communities, 1973; cited in Buonanno and Nugent, 2013: 246)

Attached to the rights focus in policy formation were what were termed the 'four freedoms': the free movement of goods, services, capital and labour. Carried through from the EEC treaty in 1957, this framework for integration represented not only a structure for economic activity but also a platform for socio-economic rights. 'Freedoms', such as the right to work or study in other member states, were gradually expanded to include additional rights for citizens to promote greater equality of opportunity in the workplace, labour market and society in general, with particular focus being given to gender, disability, age and nationality. As the treaties were amended and extended, human rights became increasingly central to the rationale for the integration process. By the time of the Maastricht Treaty and the introduction of EU citizenship, the *acquis communautaire* – the repository of all Community law – had the purpose of enhancing 'the protection of the rights and interests of the nationals of its Member States' (Article 3). Article 17 set out the absolute nature of citizenship rights: 'Citizenship of the Union is hereby established. Every person holding the nationality of a Member State shall be a citizen of the Union … Citizens of the Union shall enjoy the rights conferred by this Treaty and shall be subject to the duties imposed thereby' (https://eur-lex.europa.eu; also cited in Shaw et al, 2007: 283).

Integration and the development of human rights mechanisms

Until the 1970s, responsibility for proposing legislation and implementing decisions lay with the European Commission, the Brussels based institution overseeing the management of policies (Dinan, 2010: 171–203). By then EEC regional policy was transferring large financial incentives to promote job creation and infrastructural support in disadvantaged areas across the Community. Criticisms of a democratic deficit and lack of oversight led, in June 1979, to the expansion of democratic rights with the first direct election of Members of the European Parliament (MEPs) representing national constituencies. Complementing this, the Schengen Agreement, signed by most member states on 14 June 1985, permitted people the right to travel within the zone without having their passports or vehicles checked. EU states became very protective of this right to free movement, with two notable opt-outs – the UK and Ireland (Shaw et al, 2007: 283–294). EU support also enabled students and academics to study or teach/research across different member states, changing the nature and form of the university system in Europe. Hand in hand with a liberalisation of trade and free movement came demands for equality and anti-discrimination legislation, shaped through a series of directives and regulations which promoted the equality of opportunity and the protection of minorities in employment and in service provision. This was by and large achieved at the application of Maastricht, as can be seen in Article 39: 'Freedom of movement for workers shall be secured within the Community … Such freedom of movement shall entail the abolition of any discrimination based on nationality between the workers of Member States' (https://eur-lex.europa.eu; Church and Phinnemore, 2002: 249).

The European Council (the highest authority in the institutional triangle of the Community) Summit's Copenhagen Criteria of 1993 significantly augmented the development of the rights base.

With this, for accession to Community membership, it would now mean expansion of equality and anti-discrimination legislation. The accumulated body of legislation that was rolling out across Europe changed the nature of workers' relationships and socio-economic life for member states. With rights on Equal Pay (1975), Work Conditions (1976) and Parental Leave (1996), directives and regulations continued to promote gender equality affecting working time, part-time work, adoptive leave, maternity pay, leave, health and safety, and so on. Anti-discrimination directives also *promoted* equal treatment in housing, education, the provision of goods and services, and in relation to racial or ethnic origin, religion, disability, sexual orientation and age. Socio-economic supports through regional funds for under-developed regions, anti-poverty programmes, and indeed peace programmes informed social policy initiatives often linked to concepts of social, economic and cultural rights (Craig and de Búrca, 2015: 380–428). Furthermore, the role and powers of the European Court of Justice (CJEU), the enforcing body on EU law, gradually moved centre stage in the administration of the rights of EU citizens. T.C. Hartley noted of its evolution: 'it is probably fair to say that the conversion of the European court to a specific doctrine of human rights has been as much a matter of expediency as conviction' (Hartley, 1994: 139). More assertively, in *Ever Closer Union*, Desmond Dinan presented the Court as being central to the whole European project: 'the Court not only defined and shaped a new legal order but also contributed to the revival of European integration' (Dinan, 2010: 265).

In the context of such policy expansion and spatial reach (28 members by 2013), the ratification of the Lisbon Treaty, signed on 13 December 2007 (in force 1 December 2009) brought with it a series of changes that confirmed human rights provisions. The treaty led to the removal of member state vetoes and the introduction of qualified majority voting in at least 45 policy areas, resulting in the situation where the unanimous agreement of all individual member states was no longer required to pass EU legislation. It had its complications. The partial removal of the national veto from member states gave much more leverage to power brokers on the Council – Germany and France in particular. The removal of the veto meant that national sovereignty was in question, with the result that other states would have to accept measures with which they may have disagreed in order to remain in the EU. Later, the UK Parliament was to link the loss of the veto to its withdrawal from the EU. Importantly for the development of a rights-based architecture within the EU, the Lisbon Treaty made the EU's Charter of Fundamental Rights, signed in 2000, legally binding on EU member states from 1 December 2009. Resisting this, the UK and Poland negotiated the UK–Poland Protocol – in effect an opt-out of the Charter. At the time, it was clear that the UK did not want an EU court to supersede its own domestic courts through cases brought to the CJEU over non-compliance with the Charter. Indeed, the UK was already raising concerns about decisions made by the Court and challenging its authority (Dinan, 2010: 265–277; Craig and de Búrca, 2015: 380–393). As with the veto, the role of the Court of Justice was to emerge as a central bone of contention across the range of European 'exit' debates from 2016 onwards.

The Charter of Fundamental Rights

While all EU member states must ratify the (quite separate) Council of Europe's European Convention on Human Rights (ECHR) and most have incorporated it into their domestic law, the EU has also developed its own rights mechanisms, initially through directives and legislation, the Charter of Fundamental Social Rights of Workers (CFSRW) (2000), and then with the Charter of Fundamental Rights and Freedoms which was made legally binding on member states by the Lisbon Treaty (Zetterquist, 2011: 4; Craig and de Búrca, 2015: 394–399). The 54 Articles of this Charter list the political, social and economic rights for EU citizens under six titles – Dignity, Freedoms, Equality, Solidarity, Citizens' Rights and Justice – and are broadly in line with both the United Nations Declaration on Human Rights (UNDHR) and the ECHR. There are also specific principles which apply to targeted demographic groups, such as older people, children and people with disabilities. Notable are: Article 2, which outlines the rights to life and prohibits the death penalty; Article 3, which prohibits the cloning of humans, the sale of body parts, or using eugenics to select types of people; Article 4, which prohibits torture; Article 5, which prohibits slavery and forced labour; and Article 22, which enforces respect for cultural, religious and linguistic diversity. Other rights relate to healthcare, education and so on. The Charter is notable as an ideological interpretation of rights, as can be seen in the Preamble, which states that: 'it is necessary to strengthen the protection of fundamental rights in the light of changes in society, social progress and scientific and technological developments by making those rights more visible' (CFREU, 2009: Preamble; Di Frederico, 2011).

As with other international rights mechanisms at transnational level, the Charter faces similar issues in relation to the interpretation of rights. For example, what does 'respect' for 'cultural and religious and linguistic diversity' actually mean in policy-making across different EU states and, indeed, are such rights realisable and enforceable? Rights are also contingent on the means of enforcement and the resources available to make such rights reality (for example, a right to healthcare) (Foster, 2018: 124–130). This is particularly pertinent in light of neoliberal policies which specifically aim to assimilate public resources into private enterprise – which is *market* and not *rights* driven. Complementing the Charter, the EU Agency for Fundamental Rights (FRA) was established to carry out research, produce evidence-based publications and raise awareness on what citizens can expect from the EU (www.fra.europa. eu). It also provides advice to EU institutions and member states on the enforcement of the rights set out in the Charter. The Agency, however, has no mandate to examine legislation adopted by member states or to investigate individual complaints, but rather its role is to look at trends and general issues relating to rights. Its existence has been criticised by right-wing politicians as an unnecessary addition to EU bureaucracy and expense. Indeed, the rights mechanisms of the EU have been criticised in general by populist politicians as duplicating work on rights already being carried out by the Council of Europe (COE) through the ECHR and the European Social Chapter.

EU law, including the Charter of Fundamental Rights, is overseen by the EU Commission and the CJEU based in Luxembourg. Rulings are binding on member states and there can be penalties or fines for breaches. CJEU and EU Commission decisions are, in principle, to be immediately implemented within the EU and thus the system has the potential to offer very strong enforcement powers. However, decisions and their implementation are often affected by political and national considerations, with some states ignoring or bypassing decisions. Unlike UN covenants and conventions, which are overseen by specific monitoring committees with country-by-country reviews and reports for each rights instrument, the EU does not operate a regular reporting system for its rights. Cases need to be raised sequentially with the CJEU or the EU Commission to be addressed.

The main role of the CJEU is to interpret EU law to make sure it is applied in the same way in all EU countries and to settle legal disputes between member states and EU institutions. It can also be used by individuals, companies or organisations to take action against EU institutions or an EU state if they feel it has somehow infringed their rights. From its initial mandate the Court has been highly protective of the principle and law of EU citizenship and the rights therein (Dinan, 2010: 267–270). The Court is made up of one judge from each EU state and it can impose sanctions. Numerous cases have been brought to the CJEU in relation to breaches of EU directives and in many cases the decisions have forced member states to change policy and practice. It is important to note, however, that not all EU rights-related decisions have been met with compliance from member states. For example, a plan pushed through the EU Council in September 2015 to take in 120,000 Syrian refugees was met with opposition and non-compliance by some members. Romania, Poland, Hungary, Czechia and Slovakia are among those who voiced opposition to a mandatory refugee quota. In December 2015, Slovakia filed a case with the CJEU to oppose the plan, which was dismissed. Lower numbers were eventually allocated, while some states opted out – the UK included – causing further conflict with the European Commission and the Court. Decisions can also reflect political pragmatism and positioning, and invariably can get in the way of rights enforcement. For example, in September 2010, the EU Commission ruled that France had contravened EU anti-discrimination laws by rounding up and expelling Roma from its state, but it decided not to take any legal action through the Court or impose any sanctions.

The EU and its institutions have also been responsible for a number of contentious decisions which appeared to fan the flames of Islamophobia and denied Muslim people rights to practise their religion in public and the right of people to choose their own clothing. For example, in 2004 France banned the wearing of overt symbols of religious affiliation in state schools on the grounds of the government separation of Church and State. While the ban did not directly refer to the wearing of headscarves by Muslim women in public, it was interpreted by many as being directed against this particular community. Belgium, since 2010, and in 2011 France, have banned the wearing of face-covering veils (niqab, burqa) or masks in public, followed by other EU states (Netherlands, 2015; Germany, 2016: Austria, 2017). Attempts to raise the issue as a discriminatory policy and practice have failed in domestic courts, the Council of Europe and the EU. Indeed, a European Court of Human Rights (ECtHR) case in 2014 upheld the French ban on the burqa in public on the grounds that preservation of a certain idea of 'living together' is the 'legitimate aim'. It was deemed non-discriminatory and not in violation of human rights.

In March 2017, the CJEU went further by ruling that even private employers could introduce bans in the workplace on religious symbolism, as long as they applied to all religions. Such policies and practices raised a number of questions about the flexibility of fundamental rights. These include the right of people, and particularly women, to wear whatever clothes they choose to wear, the right of religious minorities to practise their religion in public, and indeed, the right of ethnic minorities to participate in public life. Ultimately, these types of judgements raise questions about the kind of society this model of European integration was creating and the form of diversification Europeans wanted in an increasingly complex and globalising world.

EU human rights law and emerging strains

Under provisions set out in the Treaty of Lisbon all EU member states were party to the ECHR *and have to be* to join the EU. The Treaty committed that the EU, as a collective body, should sign up to the ECHR so that all laws and directives would comply with it and as such could be scrutinised by an outside body, the ECtHR. Primacy in law was an immediate problem. Article 6 of the Treaty stipulates that: 'The Union recognises the rights, freedoms and principles set out in the Charter of Fundamental Rights of the European Union of 7 December 2000, as adapted at Strasbourg on 12 December 2007, which shall have the same legal value as the Treaties' (Treaty of Lisbon, 2007: Article 6). The human rights provisions were already under stress, with three states – namely Poland, Czechia and the UK – insisting that as a condition of signage the Charter could not introduce new rights for EU citizens. This commitment was included as Protocol 30 of the Lisbon Treaty. It meant that effective development of a human rights-based policy framework could be frustrated on this point (Buonanno and Nugent, 2013: 294). To complicate things further, in January 2015 the CJEU rejected ECHR inclusion on the basis that it would violate EU treaties. The existence of two separate European rights mechanisms were viewed by some states, the UK in particular, as problematic, especially if the institutions diverged on the interpretation, definition and implementation of law.

As EU political disintegration gathered pace there emerged highly combative challenges to the very nature of EU human rights provision, notably with recurring reference to rights. In the run-up to the Brexit referendum on 23 June 2016, the UK had a number of very public disagreements with both the ECtHR and the EU over issues of rights and decisions on rights being made outside the UK, its Parliament and its courts, which might be binding on the UK. Indeed, some of these disagreements emboldened the pro-Brexit campaigners to argue for withdrawal from the EU on the basis of retrieving national sovereignty, closing borders, restricting movement and 'taking back control'. Harold Clarke and colleagues, in the most authoritative text on the subject, *Brexit: Why Britain Voted to Leave the European*

Union, concluded that the question over the right of movement in particular was crucial:

> Although arguments about how exiting the EU would help to re-establish national sovereignty and invigorate democracy were prominent themes in the Leave campaign, our analyses indicate that strong public concern over the large number of migrants entering the country was front and central to Leave securing victory. (Clarke et al, 2017: 208)

Furthermore, during the negotiation process, UK Prime Minister Theresa May set out a plan that, as well as leaving the EU (and the CJEU's jurisdiction), the UK might also leave the ECHR. Unlike withdrawing from the EU, however, leaving the ECHR would pose severe problems for the UK in relation to many international commitments and, in particular, rights clauses included in the 1998 Good Friday/Belfast (Anglo-Irish intergovernmental) Agreement relating to the Irish peace process. That Agreement included both the UK and Ireland incorporating the ECHR into their respective domestic laws. It remains to be seen what impact Brexit will have on rights and social policy both in the EU and in the UK. Across the EU, the debate alone has been very damaging. Secessionist reaction to the historic rights-based agenda for European integration could invariably affect a range of social policies and rights – notably free movement, migration, trade, employment, rights to residency, education, healthcare, pensions and social benefits – for all member states. It also represents a closing of European states to external connectivity by applying isolationism, a practice understood by former colonies to be 'Fortress Europe'.

Conclusion

The discourse around rights and the European Union's policy base has largely been a compromise on legal precedents. In practice, the rights of citizens have extended well beyond this. The EU to its core remains an advanced market society gelled together by the coherence of member states in the interests of their respective citizenry. This has caused problems. In protecting this 'Community' it has also denied equal access to those who reside outside its borders, particularly those who are from former colonies of European powers or escaping wars on the periphery of the EU itself. The rights architecture of the EU promotes freedom of trade and movement within the EU, but actively denies this to people and goods from poorer regions, despite increasing migration linked to war, climate change, post-colonisation, globalisation and growing global inequalities. Since the Lisbon Treaty, and in part because of it, the EU has witnessed populism and xenophobia re-emerging as forces to reckon with. The upshot of this is that as the region moves into perhaps the most challenging political times since World War II, with many member states and significant political lobbies questioning the very nature of universal rights and European integration as a process, the effects will be widespread for those most in need of a sound rights-based approach to policy.

References

Buonanno, L. and Nugent, N. (2013) *Policies and Policy Processes of the European Union*, London: Palgrave Macmillan.

CFREU, Charter of Fundamental Rights of the European Union (2009) 2012/C 326/02. Available from: https://eur-lex.europa.eu/legal-content/EN/TXT/?uri=CELEX:12012P/TXT

Church, C.H. and Phinnemore, D. (2002) *The Penguin Guide to the European Treaties*, London: Penguin Books.

Clarke, H.D., Goodwin, M. and Whiteley, P. (2017) *Brexit: Why Britain Voted to Leave the European Union*, Cambridge: Cambridge University Press.

Craig, P. and de Búrca, G. (2015) *EU Law: Texts, Cases, and Materials*, 6th edition, Oxford: Oxford University Press.

Di Federico, G. (ed) (2011) *The EU Charter of Fundamental Rights: From Declaration to Binding Instrument*, New York: Springer.

Dinan, D. (2010) *Ever Closer Union*, London: Palgrave Macmillan.

Eichengreen, B. (2007) *The European Economy Since 1945*, Princeton, NJ: Princeton University Press.

European Communities (1973) *Document on the European Identity*, 14 December, Bonn: PEC. Available from: http://aei.pitt.edu/4545/1/epc_identity_doc.pdf

Foster, N. (2018) *EU Treaties and Legislation*, Oxford: Oxford University Press.

Gillingham, J. (2003) *European Integration 1950–2003*, Cambridge: Cambridge University Press.

Hartley, T.C. (1994) *The Foundation of European Community Law*, Oxford: Oxford University Press.

Marjolin, R. (1989) *Architect of Europe*, London: Weidenfeld and Nicolson.

McCormick, J. (2014) *Understanding the European Union*, London: Palgrave Macmillan.

Shaw, J., Hunt, J. and Wallace, C. (2007) *Economic and Social Law of the European Union*, London: Palgrave Macmillan.

Treaty of Lisbon (2007) Available from: https://eur-lex.europa.eu/legal-content/EN/TXT/?uri=CELEX%3A12016M006

Zetterquist, O. (2011) 'The Charter of Fundamental Rights and the European *res publica*', in G. Di Federico (ed) *The EU Charter of Fundamental Rights: From Declaration to Binding Instrument*, New York: Springer, pp 3–14.

5

Human rights and the USA

Peter Collins

> We hold these truths to be self-evident, that all men are
> created equal; that they are endowed by their Creator
> with inherent and unalienable Rights; that among these,
> are Life, Liberty, and the pursuit of Happiness. (United
> States Declaration of Independence, adopted by Congress,
> 4 July 1776)

The history of human rights in the United States has been a paradox.
Despite the theoretical adherence to equal human rights in the
foundation documents of the country itself, in practice they were not
extended to many sections of the population – in particular African
Americans and Native Americans. Indeed, George Washington and
Thomas Jefferson (the main author of the Declaration of Independence)
were themselves owners of black slaves and this activity remained
central to economic development until finally abolished in 1865 after
a protracted and bloody civil war. For a century after this abolition
many in the white population refused to see African Americans as
equal or, more alarmingly, even human. Crucially, despite bringing
an end to slavery, Abraham Lincoln is a part of this national paradox.

> I will say then that I am not, nor ever have been in favour of
> bringing about in any way the social and political equality of
> the white and black races ... nor ever have been in favour
> of making voters or jurors of negroes, nor of qualifying
> them to hold office, nor to intermarry with white people.
> (Abraham Lincoln, 18 September 1858 – Fourth Debate
> with Stephen A. Douglas at Charleston, Illinois)

After the Civil War and Reconstruction, the lot of African Americans
in the southern states was not much better than before 'emancipation'.
The initial rights granted to former slaves were gradually eroded in the
former Confederacy, enforced by the influence and violence of the Ku

Klux Klan through exclusions, imprisonment, beatings and lynchings. Indeed, systematic lynching of African Americans from 1890 to 1920 amounted to over 4,000 murders and major riots between white supremacists and African Americans were ongoing, with particularly heavy casualties in Memphis and New Orleans in 1866 (Zinn and Buhle, 2008: 158). Facing this history down was seen on occasion, with an early attempt coming from President Ulysses S. Grant, who took strong action via the Justice Department – which he set up in 1870 – and used troops against the Klan.

The 14th Amendment of the US Constitution in 1868 granted citizenship to all persons born or naturalised in the United States, including former slaves, and guaranteed all citizens 'equal protection of the laws'. In 1870, the 15th Amendment stated that the vote could not be denied on grounds of race, colour or previous slavery. Nevertheless, each state defined who could vote. Most had property restrictions limiting the vote to white men of property, with many states introducing poll taxes and literacy tests to deny the vote to African Americans. The prejudice also affected Native Americans and many poor whites such as the Okies during the 1930s. Structural obstructions to citizenship rights remain to this day in states across the US, with intimidation in some areas of the south preventing African Americans from attending polling stations. These obstacles hold as a legacy of the segregated system of the 1800s.

The 'Jim Crow' laws, so-called after a racist 'blackface comedy' theatre act, led to segregation in every aspect of American life. For African and Native Americans, inferior status and widespread discrimination in jobs, housing, education and human rights were rigidly enforced, often violently, and there was no legal redress. Segregation was codified and legitimised by the 1896 Supreme Court judgement in the case of *Plessy v Ferguson*. It declared that segregationist measures were constitutional so long as the facilities provided were equal in quality. In fact 'separate but equal' provision was rarely implemented. While the facilities were indeed separate, for the most part they were anything but equal – and not only in the southern states. When the Civil War ended, 19 northern states did not extend the vote to African Americans. A *New York Times* editorial at the time stated that: 'northern men ... no longer denounce the suppression of the Negro vote ... the necessity of it under the supreme law of self-preservation is candidly recognized' (www.historyisaweapon.com). Even in the military, segregated units were the rule until President Truman had to issue a decree on integration in 1948.

Women were denied the vote in most states (except New Jersey) until 1920, par for the course worldwide, while the government's treatment of Native Americans was a litany of broken treaties, land grabs, enforced moves to 'reservations' and the sustained denial of human rights. The worst incident of this maltreatment occurred in December 1890 at Wounded Knee, South Dakota, where an estimated 300 Lakota Sioux, mainly women and children, were massacred by soldiers of the US 7th Cavalry. Anger over this act of genocide has continued and it remains a fulcrum in Native American history to this day. In 1973, a shoot-out at Wounded Knee between Federal Marshals, the FBI and Native Americans arose from the ongoing poor state of indigenous rights (Brown, 1995).

The recurring fault-line in US society: racial discrimination

The migration of over a million African Americans to northern cities between the wars brought with it a deterioration of race relations in the north. Remarkably, *Plessy v Ferguson* remains to be repealed, although it has been largely mitigated by subsequent legislation and various Supreme Court rulings, such as *Brown v Board of Education of Topeka* (1954), which ruled that racial segregation in public schools – even with separate but equal provision – was unconstitutional. This resulted in a campaign of 'massive resistance' to school desegregation with white 'citizens committees' being set up to frustrate school integration. African American children wishing to enrol, often had to run a gauntlet of baying mobs, an issue brought to international attention at Little Rock Central High, Arkansas, in 1957. Here, the Arkansas National Guard, on the orders of the segregationist Governor Orval Faubus, barred entry to nine African American students. It was only resolved after federal troops were sent in by President Dwight Eisenhower to ensure the students' entry, with armed troops remaining to protect the African American students. It represented a sea-change, however, in demands for civil rights across US society. During the Eisenhower administration, the civil rights movement emerged, demanding equal rights and desegregation, involving non-violent protest, sit-ins, marches, bus boycotts and other actions. These were often met with repression by southern state authorities, involving violent attacks by police and white mobs on protestors, marchers and 'Freedom Riders' (the civil rights activists who travelled to support the protests). Irrespective, a Civil Rights Act was passed in 1957 to ensure African

American voting rights. It too faced stiff southern opposition, including filibustering by southern segregationist members of the Congress, in a campaign of intimidation that largely rendered the Act ineffective.

The Federal government intervened more proactively on civil rights during the Kennedy and Johnson administrations, with remedial and head-start programmes, such as the Great Society and War on Poverty, helping marginalised communities to challenge the discrimination and disadvantage. The Democratic Party drive on civil rights – seguing through the assassination of Kennedy – led to the Civil Rights and Labor Act of 1964, which outlawed discrimination on the grounds of race, colour, sex or national origin. It prohibited unequal voter registration requirements and segregation in schools, employment and public accommodation. In the same year the 24th Amendment prohibited use by state and federal government of poll or other taxes to impinge on voting rights. In 1965 the Voting Rights Act prohibited tests for voting. By 1968 a further enhancement of rights provision was achieved through a Civil Rights Act which aimed to rectify much of the ineffectiveness of the previous legislation (Riches, 1997: 76–88).

Workers' rights

During the late nineteenth and early twentieth centuries tremendous but largely unregulated industrial growth across the USA resulted in poor, often dangerous, working conditions and low wages. There were many industrial accidents and deaths due to neglectful employers. In New York City in 1911, a fire at the Triangle Shirtwaist Factory cost the lives of 146 workers, mainly Italian and Jewish immigrant women. Few escaped because the employers had illegally locked the exit doors. The employers got off lightly in subsequent judicial proceedings, but the disaster led to more workplace regulatory legislation and campaigning for rights in the workplace. At this period in the early twentieth century, there was a big increase in membership of trade unions and socialist organisations that sought to protect and promote the rights of American workers. This provoked a hostile response from employers, the authorities and much of an unsympathetic press. Company security and police were used to break strikes, often using violence which led to recurring gunfights.

In 1914, strikers at a Rockefeller-owned mine in Ludlow, Colorado, went on strike for better conditions and wages. They erected a tent encampment for their families. The company sent in the Colorado National Guard and private security gunmen to break up the striking miners. The attack started with the burning of the family tents, resulting in two women and 11 children being smothered by the smoke. The miners obtained guns and fought back. Twenty miners and family members were killed in the conflict. News of the Ludlow massacre spread around the world. Most of the miners and their families were immigrants from Southern Europe, providing easy scapegoats for the company and state to blame for the violence. Hostility to immigrants and left-wing activists created an atmosphere of intolerance which undoubtedly played a part in the judgement dispensed during the infamous trials and executions of Joe Hill, a Swedish socialist immigrant, in 1915 and Sacco and Vanzetti, Italian anarchists, in 1920. The authorities were unnerved by the impact of the 1917 Russian revolution and a global anarchist bombing campaign. Newspapers whipped up mass hysteria against immigrants and militants in what became known as the 'Red Scare'. The US Attorney General, A. Mitchell Palmer, organised raids to arrest suspected militants, many of whom – without trial – were randomly deported to Europe, including to the USSR. This was followed by the passing of the very restrictive Immigration Act of 1924, a precedent set then but current to this day.

During the 1930s President Roosevelt introduced the New Deal to mitigate mass unemployment during the Depression. Work programmes such as the Civilian Conservation Corps augmented labour law to put America back to work. In addition to this, the first ever Social Security Agency was set up (in 1935), which administered welfare and retirement benefits that would be drawn from taxable income. Each worker would be tracked in the system through their social security card, providing, in theory, a basic safety net against poverty. This initiative was almost revolutionary in American terms, given that it was far behind other developed nations in terms of welfare provision. During the Depression, labour relations remained problematic and potential conflict between the company owners, the state and workers was always just under the surface (Tindall and Shi, 1984: 908–926). In Chicago in 1937, police fired on striking steel workers, who were holding a peaceful picket and family picnic, killing ten and wounding many more. Despite having earlier personally given permission for the event, the Mayor of Chicago took no action against the police involved in the massacre.

The paranoia attending the Cold War era brought about a second 'Red Scare'. In 1947 President Truman introduced the Loyalty Order, a review by the FBI of federal employees, to detect and dismiss members of communist or fascist organisations. Though very few were dismissed, it engendered a climate of fear. The House Un-American Activities Committee (HUAC), chaired by Senator Joseph McCarthy, subpoenaed witnesses, who were pressured into outing suspected communists. This witch-hunt led to many public officials, theatre and movie actors, writers and directors – most of whom posed no threat – being blacklisted. The most notorious incident of this period was the execution of Soviet spies Julius and Ethel Rosenberg. As the Cold War era rolled out, the US government became much more authoritarian, showing a distinct lack of rights awareness towards its citizens. The Soviet Union, then justifiably criticised for its poor human rights record, was accordingly able to point to America's treatment of African and Native Americans, and the oppressive treatment of its dissidents.

The most cited disavowal of human rights by all US administrations has been the ongoing sequence of executions. Article 3 of the UDHR provides for the 'right to life'. Among Western countries, all European Union member states have abolished the death penalty, yet the US stands alone in the West for not abolishing it. Between 1 January 1976 and 31 May 2019, 1,499 prisoners were executed in the US (Death Penalty Info, 2019). In the US, 19 states have abolished the death penalty (seven since 2007), but it is retained in the Federal system. At the end of 2017, 106 countries (out of 193 globally) had abolished the death penalty in law for all crimes and 142 countries (more than two-thirds) – including Russia – had abolished the death penalty in law or practice (Amnesty International Report, 2018).

Foreign affairs

American foreign policy has, over the years, become a particularly difficult sphere of influence in relation to contested human rights protection. Its avowed commitment to human rights has often been set aside in favour of its geopolitical, economic and strategic interests, resulting in actions that were either illegal under international law, or morally reprehensible. Human rights violations in the perceived protection of the US state are not a recent problem. For example, following victory in the Spanish American War in 1898, the US took over the Spanish colonies Guam, Puerto Rico, Cuba and the Philippines. The peoples of these countries were expecting their independence. Indeed, in the case of Cuba, America had purportedly gone to war to help it win its independence. However, many in the American political, business and military establishment sought to annex Cuba and the Philippines for commercial or strategic exploitation. Having broken away from the British Empire, the idea of becoming an imperial power had long been anathema to most Americans. However, by the turn of the century, with American industrialisation resulting in the overproduction of goods, colonies would bring captive markets and raw materials. Thus Cuba was made a protectorate, against the wishes of its population. The Filipinos rose up against exchanging one colonial master for another. The result was an armed invasion by US forces who behaved with ferocity against both insurgents and unarmed civilians alike. At least 200,000 Filipinos died in the process, many from famine; 4,000 US soldiers were killed. The occupation set a pattern for future US overseas intervention (Zinn and Buhle, 2008: 74). William Blum lists 55 states where the USA has moved to overthrow governments since World War II. Thirty-four of these attempts were successful (Blum, 2019).

During the Cold War, the USA tended to support repressive or colonial regimes against independence movements which they feared were coming under communist influence. In 1953, a coup was orchestrated in Iran by the CIA and the UK to overthrow the democratically elected nationalist Prime Minister, Mohammad Mosaddegh, and install the Shah as dictator. This ensured that British and American companies could keep control of Iran's huge oil reserves which Mosaddegh was intent on nationalising. It was also intended to forestall any Soviet incursion into Iran. In 1973, the democratically elected socialist government of Salvador Allende was overthrown by the Chilean military with the support of the CIA. President Allende was killed, as were many others, by a usurper regime headed by General Pinochet. Historically, going back to the Mexican wars of 1846–48, and invoking the Monroe Doctrine, supposedly allowing the USA to do whatever was necessary to prevent outside powers taking over states in its 'sphere of influence' in the Americas, the US has interfered in many Latin American countries. Significant destabilising interventions came in Guatemala, Nicaragua and El Salvador. In Central America, right-wing military forces, abetted by death squads and the CIA, have been responsible for the massacre of countless innocent civilians, clergy, peasants and trade unionists. In Guatemala, General Rios Montt overthrew the government in a coup and subsequently, under the cover of fighting a Marxist insurgency, carried out the genocide of many thousands of indigenous Maya. President Ronald Reagan voiced his approval. After meeting Montt in 1982, he said the general was getting a 'bum rap on human rights' (*New York Times*, 1 April 2018). To put US foreign policy into context in regard to human rights violations, as a member of the United Nations Security Council, it has bombed the following countries since World War II: China 1945–46, Korea 1950–53, China 1950–53, Guatemala 1954, Indonesia 1958, Cuba 1959–60, Guatemala 1960, Belgian Congo 1964, Guatemala 1964,

Dominican Republic 1965–66, Peru 1965, Laos 1964–73,Vietnam 1961–73, Cambodia 1969–70, Guatemala 1967–69, Lebanon 1982–84, Grenada 1983–84, Libya 1986, El Salvador 1981–92, Nicaragua 1981–90, Iran 1987–88, Libya 1989, Panama 1989–90, Iraq 1991, Kuwait 1991, Somalia 1992–94, Bosnia 1995, Iran 1998, Sudan 1998, Afghanistan 1998, Yugoslavia–Serbia 1999, Afghanistan 2001, Libya 2011, Pakistan 2007–11, and Syria 2014–19 (www.globalresearch.ca, 6 June 2019; Blum, 2006).

In the late 1960s, facing a mass anti-war movement highlighting atrocities in Vietnam, the authorities used inordinate force against protestors. In 1968, Chicago Mayor Daley's police viciously attacked anti-war protestors outside the 1968 Democratic national convention. Witnesses described it as a 'police riot'. The worst incidence of this official violence occurred in 1970, when the Ohio National Guard fired on a peaceful protest at Kent State University, killing four students and wounding nine others. During the Vietnam War, between 20,000–30,000 'draft-resisters', political exiles, felt they had to flee to Canada.

In 2001, following a series of terrorist attacks on iconic US buildings, the Twin Towers and Pentagon, with al-Qaeda terrorists killing thousands of civilians, President George W. Bush implemented what he labelled the 'War on Terror'. The first major action of this was the invasion of Afghanistan in 2001, the most impoverished country on earth, which led to the overthrow of the Taliban government. It was followed by the second Gulf War in 2003, carried out without UN approval, and justified on the grounds that the President of Iraq, Saddam Hussein, was fomenting international terrorism, carrying out mass murder of his own people and being in possession of what the US and UK defined as 'weapons of mass destruction' (WMD). As it transpired, the WMD evidence was manufactured by Western intelligence agencies to justify an invasion that was primarily to the benefit of Western oil companies. After toppling Saddam, mismanagement and endless military operations led to years of civil war and culminated in the insidious Daesh's occupation of much of the region. This template for shock therapy regime change was attempted again in Libya and Syria with the encouragement, and participation, of the US. The intervention in Libya resulted in civil war and a humanitarian disaster affecting millions of Libyans with refugees fleeing in tens of thousands to get to the perceived safety of Europe.

A further paradox of the US's involvement in the evolution of human rights policies has been that the chief forum for international relations since 1945, the United Nations, was largely the brainchild of President Roosevelt. Indeed, the UN has initiated many agencies which are both arbiters and protectors of human rights. The USA has been a principal actor in setting these up, yet it has had an ambivalent relationship to many such bodies. Eleanor Roosevelt, seen by many as the conscience of her husband, was a member of the NAACP, an advocate for women's rights and for all marginalised Americans. She also served as US envoy to the UN General Assembly from 1945 to 1952, and as the first chair of the UN Commission on Human Rights, she oversaw the drafting of its Universal Declaration of Human Rights (UDHR). This is generally seen as the founding statement of international human rights law. In 1976, the UDHR was augmented with two new covenants on Civil and Political Rights (ICCPR) and on Economic, Social and Cultural Rights (ICESCR). The USA has still failed to ratify the ICESCR and when it ratified the ICCPR, it included a reservation to allow it to maintain the death penalty. This was to become the pattern for what Michael Ignatieff deemed 'American exceptionalism'.

> Since 1945 America has displayed exceptional leadership in promoting international rights. At the same time it has also resisted complying with human rights standards at home or aligning its foreign policy with these standards abroad. Under some administrations it has promoted human rights as if they were synonymous with American values, while under others, it has emphasized the superiority of American values over international standards. This combination of leadership is what defines American human rights behaviour as exceptional. (Ignatieff, 2005: 1)

The UN Charter allows member states to wage war for purposes of self-defence or protection of national interest or protection of their citizens. The UN Security Council (UNSC) can impose sanctions or wage war on members who flout these regulations. However, the decision to implement military or economic sanctions is usually more related to political considerations than legal or human rights. For instance, the UN General Assembly (UNGA) has consistently voted in opposition to the US's economic, commercial and financial blockade of Cuba and indeed the Israeli occupation of Palestinian Territories (since 1967), but the UNSC has never acted due to the veto wielded by the US as a permanent member. The US is not exceptional in this regard. Russia has also used the veto many times to frustrate resolutions of the UNGA. The veto was first used by the USA in 1970 and it has been the principal user since then (http://research.un.org/en/docs/sc/quick/veto). The International Criminal Court (ICC), based at The

Hague, was set up in 2002 by the UN in line with the Rome Statute (1998). It was constituted to try people for war crimes, genocide and crimes against humanity, where national courts are unwilling or unable to do this. However, only three people have been convicted to date. As of June 2018, it issued arrest warrants for 42 individuals, six of whom are in Court custody, with its main targets being obscure African leaders. Only 124 states (out of 193) have agreed to accept its rulings – the US is not one of them.

Another area of human rights in which the US has taken an exceptional path is in relation to torture, which is prohibited by the Universal Declaration of Human Rights (1948), Article 5. Torture is forbidden in war by international humanitarian law (the Geneva Conventions). The UN Convention Against Torture (CAT) and other cruel, inhuman or degrading treatment or punishment was ratified by more than 156 states out of 193 by March 2016. It outlaws torture or extradition to a state where torture may occur. Monitored by the UN CAT Committee, states agree to produce regular reports and let it investigate complaints. The US has come under criticism and scrutiny on a number of occasions over accusations of torture. Much of this relates to the war against Islamist terror in which the US has used torture in prisons, especially at Guantanamo Bay in Cuba and Abu Ghraib in Iraq. In the latter, 'waterboarding' and the sexual abuse of prisoners took place. Indeed, George W. Bush admitted, in November 2010, that he personally authorised the 'waterboarding' of al-Qaeda suspects in the aftermath of 9/11. 'Waterboarding' was first documented by the US in use, as torture, against Filipino insurgents in the early 1900s. Furthermore, 'extraordinary rendition', and lack of human rights protection, has meant that prisoners caught in Afghanistan and elsewhere (for example, Pakistan) could be subjected to torture with little recourse to courts and often families were left unaware of their whereabouts for long periods. Others were flown to friendly states, such as Jordan and Egypt, where they could be 'legally' subjected to torture (Centre for Constitutional Rights, 2017). The UNDHR articles in relation to the right to a fair trial have seemingly been set aside, notably Article 10 on the right to a fair public hearing by independent tribunal, and Article 11 on the right to presumption of innocence until proven guilty at public trial with all guarantees necessary for defence. America's exceptionalism springs from its perennial desire not to be bound by international treaties and from a distrust of the United Nations. One final example is where the US is the only country not to ratify the Convention on the Rights of the Child despite being heavily involved in the drafting process. Even

President Obama, who in 2008 had described the non-ratification as 'embarrassing', took no action.

Conclusion

There are many contradictions on human rights issues which deeply divide the people of the US. Invariably, President Trump has served to exacerbate these domestic issues for political gain, especially given his overt sexism and divisive comments about disability and race. On the international stage, he has reneged on vital agreements pertinent to human rights protection, such as the Paris Climate Agreement and the Iran Nuclear Deal. He has ended all US financial aid to the United Nations Relief and Works Agency (UNRWA), the UN body which for decades has supported Palestinians in refugee camps throughout the Middle East, and has persecuted Hispanic migrants. Such policies risk causing a massive humanitarian crisis across the Americas, the Middle East and Southern Europe. He provocatively moved the US embassy from Tel Aviv to Jerusalem, provoking political unrest in the region and has tightened sanctions on Cuba, Iran and Venezuela. Ironically, President Trump is comfortable meeting with the execrable Kim Jong-Un, and lauds populist politicians such as Viktor Orban in Hungary and Jair Bolsonaro in Brazil, who have openly denied human rights. Arguably, though, perhaps the biggest potential human rights disaster actioned by the current US President is in regard to climate change. The US, more than any other nation on earth, has the power to take remedial action, yet it refuses to act. With populism on the rise everywhere and the US reneging on fundamental rights that its founders would have taken for granted, the outlook for human rights globally remains decidedly bleak.

References
Amnesty International Report (2018) *Death Penalty Facts and Figures 2017*. Available from: www.amnesty.org/en/latest/news/2018/04/death-penalty-facts-and-figures-2017/
Blum, W. (2006) *Rogue State: A Guide to the World's Only Superpower*, London: Zed Books.
Blum, W. (2019) 'Overthrowing other people's governments: the master list'. Available from: http://williamblum.org/essays/read/overthrowing-other-peoples-governments-the-master-list
Brown, D. (1995) *Bury My Heart at Wounded Knee*, London: Vintage Books.

Centre for Constitutional Rights (2017) 'Torture and cruel, inhuman, and degrading treatment of prisoners at Guantanamo Bay'. Available from: http://ccrjustice.org/learn-more/reports/report%3A-torture-and-cruel,-inhuman,-and-degrading-treatment-prisoners-guantanamo-

Death Penalty Info (2019) Available from: https://deathpenaltyinfo.org/executions-year

Ignatieff, M. (ed) (2005) *American Exceptionalism and Human Rights*, Princeton, NJ: Princeton Press.

Riches, W.T.M. (1997) *The Civil Rights Movement: Struggle and Resistance*, London: Palgrave.

Tindall, G.B. and Shi, D. (1984) *America: A Narrative History*, New York: W.W. Norton and Company.

Zinn, H. and Buhle, P. (2008) *A People's History of American Empire*, New York: Metropolitan Books.

6

International Humanitarian Law: protecting rights and promoting welfare during war?

Diana Buttu and Féilim Ó hAdhmaill

And the rocket's red glare, the bombs bursting in air, Gave proof through the night that our flag was still there. (*The Star-Spangled Banner*)

World War I was supposed to be 'the war to end all wars'. With an estimated 9 million military deaths and up to 13 million civilian deaths caused directly and indirectly by the war, it was claimed at that point to have been the most destructive war in recorded history.[1] Despite attempts to outlaw war at the League of Nations in 1919, however, an even more destructive war was to follow. During World War II, 1939–45, an estimated 50–70 million were killed in six years, with far greater numbers of civilian deaths than recorded in any previous war – about 50 per cent of all deaths. By World War II the nature of war had changed profoundly, particularly with the aerial bombardment of cities and the dropping of two atomic bombs on Japan. Above all, the Holocaust, the deliberate attempt to wipe out whole groups of people, including an estimated 6 million Jewish people, left an indelible mark on the world (Jewell et al, 2018).

In the aftermath of World War II the United Nations (UN) was established with the expressed intent of preventing future wars between nation-states and to provide an international mechanism whereby future international disputes might be resolved peacefully. The UN Charter (1945) expressed the hope 'to save succeeding generations from the scourge of war' and ruled against 'wars of aggression'. It did not prohibit war however, but rather attempted to limit it to certain specific circumstances. States and, indeed, non-state groups can wage 'war' using the allowable criteria of 'self-defence', 'defence of national interests', 'citizens' protection' or by claiming that what they are doing is not 'war' but dealing with an 'emergency', 'criminality' or 'terrorism', etc. Indeed, the use of armed conflict to advance a range of different interests has continued into the twenty-first century. The Uppsala Conflict Data Programme (UCDP), for example, estimates that since World War II there have been 286 armed conflicts in 158 different locations globally – where an armed conflict is defined as involving a death rate of at least 25 people a year – with an estimated 179 conflicts in 96 locations since the end of the Cold War. In 2018 it was estimated that there were at least 76,000 deaths caused by armed conflict globally and 52 active state-based conflicts taking place (Pettersson et al, 2019: 2).

What happens to human rights in time of war/armed conflict, when the most basic of human rights, the right to life, can be denied legally? There are two main types of international human rights mechanisms: International Human Rights Law (IHRL), dealing with rights at all times, and International Humanitarian Law (IHL), dealing with rights during the special circumstances of war/armed conflict. The development of international mechanisms to promote rights and responsibilities of warring parties in times of war, in relation to the welfare of combatants and non-combatants, began to emerge in the late nineteenth century culminating in the 1949 Geneva Convention(s) after World War II. IHL was designed by states, established by states, ratified by states and enforced by states to serve the purposes of states. It developed historically in response to changes in the nature of war, weaponry, technology and medical advances. It also developed, if much more slowly, to try and cover the increasing involvement of 'non-state' forces in armed conflicts, particularly since World War II. However, the latter has posed a number of difficulties at a time when most wars/conflicts now involve non-state forces to some degree or another. While all combatants (state or non-state) have responsibilities to uphold IHL, it is usually only states, except in a few exceptional circumstances, which are allowed to sign the IHL treaties. It is also generally up to states themselves (or the UN Security Council (UNSC)) to decide whether non-state combatants are recognised as such under IHL and thus benefit from its protections – such as captured combatants being treated as prisoners of war (POWs). Most states are not prepared to offer such 'legitimacy' to non-state combatants however.

In the absence of a total prohibition on war, the main aim of IHL is to protect non-combatants in armed conflicts; civilians, including those living under occupation and soldiers no longer posing a threat because they are wounded or captured. It also aims to minimise unnecessary suffering to active soldiers who are being targeted. Thus the aim is to promote the conduct of warfare in as 'humane' a manner as possible. IHL provides both negative rights (what *should not* be done) and positive rights (what *should be* done). Thus it places prohibitions against the direct targeting of civilians as well as the killing of wounded or captured enemy soldiers. The methods used to kill and maim 'the enemy' are controlled and regulated. It also places responsibilities on those in control of a geographical area to care for the wounded, captured prisoners and for civilians living under occupation. IHL is also supposed to provide 'universal' rights to all in that it does not matter who the person is (race, colour, creed), they are supposed to be entitled to the same rights of equal protection. It also ostensibly applies to all types of conflict.

Today IHL comprises a range of international treaties on the conduct of war, including the weaponry, tactics and strategies permissible in war. It includes the Geneva Conventions, the Hague Conventions, customary international law (developed as a result of custom) and case law in relation to armed conflict which has built up over the years.

Historical background

Historically there have been two major points of discussion of particular relevance in relation to the use of armed conflict: when is it 'just' to engage in armed actions, *jus ad bellum*, and what methods are 'just' when war takes place, *jus in bello*. Different views on these have emerged amongst different groups of people living in different historical epochs and influenced by different cultural, ideological, religious, philosophical, political and socio-economic circumstances. Views about armed conflict have also been influenced by changes in weaponry, advances in medicine, governmental and policing developments at national and international level to regulate the use of armed conflict, and evolving views on human rights.

A variety of justifications have been made for wars historically based on religious belief, cultural tradition, rational self-interest, or claims of self-defence. Today the UN Charter allows self-defence as a cause for war while the pursuit of self-determination against colonial domination (in 1965) and apartheid (in 1966) have also been accepted by the UN General Assembly (in 1965) as a just cause. Two broad principles came to be associated with the 'right conduct in war' (*jus in bello*), the principles of discrimination and proportionality. The principle of discrimination concerns who are legitimate targets in war and primarily relates to the avoidance of targeting civilians. The principle of proportionality concerns how much force is morally appropriate or necessary to achieve a military objective and no more and avoiding acts that cause unnecessary harm and suffering. Thus, while it might be necessary to kill the enemy who is firing a weapon at you, it is unnecessary and inhumane to kill a person who has surrendered and no longer a threat. Such principles eventually became incorporated in what we know today as IHL.

One of the first codifications of humanitarian law, albeit for one army, was the US Army's Lieber code, drawn up by Francis Lieber in 1863 under President Abraham Lincoln in response to reports of atrocities committed during the American Civil War. The Lieber Code consisted of 157 articles defining how military personnel were to conduct themselves in war (Labuda, 2014). In the same year one of the most influential organisations in the development of IHL was established in Europe. Henry Dunant had been greatly affected by the suffering of the wounded he had seen on the battlefield after the Battle of Solferino in Italy. He began to lobby the European powers to agree to establish a mechanism whereby the wounded in battles would be cared for by all. In 1863 he established a committee to develop what was to become known as the Red Cross. In 1864, delegates from 16 countries travelled to Geneva to discuss the terms of a humanitarian agreement to allow care and treatment for wounded soldiers on the battlefield. Out of this emerged the first Geneva Convention in 1864 for the amelioration of the condition of the wounded in armies in the field. It involved agreement to provide care – without discrimination – to wounded and sick military personnel and to respect medical personnel (ICRC, nd a). This became particularly important as advances in scientific discovery and medical treatments/care meant that many more of the wounded could now be treated and returned to civilian life. The work of pioneers, such as Florence Nightingale, promoting improved sanitation, nutrition and efficient treatment procedures during the Crimean War showed that many unnecessary deaths among the wounded could be avoided. With proper care many could be saved. In 1906 a second Geneva Convention included an obligation to care for wounded naval armed forces, while a third Geneva Convention in 1929 agreed to a series of rights for POWs.

Furthermore, a number of parallel conventions were agreed to regulate the use of weaponry in response to rapid technological change and weaponry innovation. The 1868 St Petersburg Declaration banned the use of certain types of projectiles in war. The 1899 and 1907 Hague Conventions, which are referred to as Hague Law, developed rules and principles of war based on, or expanding upon, customary international law in relation to the conduct of war. World War I saw new methods of war such as poisonous gas, aerial bombardment, new and more powerful artillery, the capture of an estimated 8 to 9 million prisoners, and a range of new conventions developed in response. These included the 1925 Geneva Protocol banning the use of poisonous gas in warfare. In many ways the great (mainly European) powers were reacting to changing circumstances in their own interests and in the interests of their own soldiers. Most of the world's population did not factor into such considerations – they were ruled by the imperial powers and in the main were not covered by such conventions. Also, despite these conventions there was no agreed mechanism for the enforcement of any breaches and the whole issue of enforcement is one that has continued to affect IHL to the present day. Enforcement mechanisms do exist, but their use is often dictated by political expediency, geopolitics and power or lack of it.

After World War II the Allies decided to put a number of German and Japanese soldiers on trial for war crimes. Two International Military Tribunals were established and subsequent trials took place at Nuremberg in Germany and Tokyo in Japan. Two hundred German and 29 Japanese officers and politicians were put on trial. Twelve were sentenced to death at Nuremburg and seven at Tokyo for 'war crimes', 'crimes against humanity' and 'crimes of aggression'. Others were sentenced to long prison terms. No Allied troops, however, were put on trial, raising a perennial problem about the issue of enforcement of IHL. Few victorious powers are prepared to admit that their soldiers have done wrong, or try them for wrongdoing while acting under orders. The Allies' bombing of Hamburg and Dresden, as part of the strategy to break German morale and resistance, was not deemed a war crime. In Hamburg 43,000 were killed in one week, about the same number as were killed in whole of the Blitz on British cities during World War II. In Dresden, a refugee centre at the time, 25,000 were killed in three days. Likewise, the deliberate killing of civilians with the dropping of two atom bombs on Hiroshima (135,000 killed) and Nagasaki (75,000 killed) were not deemed war crimes. Besides this, many who had assisted the Nazis in their war effort were not charged with war crimes, particularly many German scientists who were employed to work on weaponry and industry in the USA, USSR and UK after World War II (Jacobsen, 2014).

While few would dispute that the Nazis collectively and individually committed 'crimes against humanity', the laws under which some of them were tried were not international law (for example, 'crimes against humanity') at the time the events took place. It was only subsequent to the trials that the 1949 Geneva Conventions were drawn up. The trials did lead to the adoption on 9 December 1948, by the UN General

Assembly, of the Convention on the Prevention and Punishment of the Crime of Genocide. This relates to attempts to exterminate a religious or ethnic group (but not a political group) in peacetime as well as during war.

The Fourth Geneva Convention

The Fourth Geneva Convention (1949), which is actually made up of four conventions, was one result of what happened in World War II and highlighted the limitations of international law up until that point (ICRC, nd b). Agreed subsequent to the Nuremberg and Tokyo trials, they updated and modified the law of war. The Conventions covered:

1. Wounded and sick armed forces on land.
2. Wounded, sick, shipwrecked armed forces at sea.
3. Treatment of prisoners of war.
4. Protection of civilian persons in time of war.

The Fourth Convention was new because for the first time there was now a Convention specific to civilians and how they should be treated in wartime or under occupation. The new elements reflected changes in warfare which occurred during World War II, as well as the concentration camps and the impact on civilian populations of aerial bombardment and reprisal massacres. For the UN, therefore, there was a humanitarian imperative to show that it was doing something to regulate war and protect civilians. IHL thus prohibits: deliberate attacks on civilians, civilian buildings and infrastructure, or the conduct of hostilities in an indiscriminate manner; starvation of the civilian population and the destruction of objects indispensable to its survival; collective punishments of civilian populations, including the destruction of dwellings; and unlawful deportation or transfer of civilians or expropriation of occupied land/property. There are also the rules requiring parties to a conflict to allow relief consignments to reach civilian populations in need. An infringement of any of these rules constitutes a war crime. War crimes include:

- Deliberately killing a 'protected person' (for example, a wounded or sick combatant, prisoner of war or civilian).
- The torture or inhuman treatment of a 'protected person'.
- Wilfully causing great suffering to, or serious injury to the body or health of, a 'protected person'.

- Using prohibited weapons or methods of warfare.
- Making improper use of the distinctive red cross or red crescent emblem or other protective signs.
- Pillage of public or private property.

The Geneva Convention 1949 also gives the International Committee of the Red Cross and Red Crescent (ICRC), an NGO based in Switzerland and set up in 1863, a specific and protected role in wars:

- To organise care for those injured on the battlefield.
- To supervise the treatment of POWs.
- To protect civilians.
- To act as a neutral intermediary.
- To monitor compliance of each side with IHL.

All warring factions are supposed to recognise and respect the ICRC's role and its neutrality during wartime and not abuse the use of its symbols/transport/personnel for military gain.

The four Geneva Conventions have been ratified by all UN member states (193), the two observer states (the Vatican and Palestine) and the Cook Islands. However, one of the major difficulties with the Geneva Conventions has been (and remains) that they were created by nation-states which were members of the UN after World War II to suit the type of mainly conventional wars fought by nation-states, with standing armies and infrastructures. Yet in 1945 when the UN was first set up, only 51 member states existed. Today, there are 193. Most of the new states were colonies of UN founder members. In the post-war period many of them gained their independence through armed struggle against imperial powers. The UN and IHL had little to say about their rights during those struggles, to protection as non-state actors. Indeed, in most cases they were branded 'terrorists' or 'criminals' by the existing power – for example, the Mau Mau (Kenya), the ANC (South Africa) and the PLO (Palestine/Israel). The result was that their struggles were often not recognised as wars or their combatants as soldiers entitled to 'prisoner of war' status. When they obtained power in their respective jurisdictions they set about trying to retrospectively legitimate their actions. For example, on 10 December 1965, the UN General Assembly adopted resolution 2105 (XX) which: 'recognizes the legitimacy of the struggle waged by peoples under colonial domination to exercise their right to self-determination and independence'.

In terms of IHL, Article 3 – common to all four Geneva Conventions (1949) – states that: 'In the case of armed conflict not of an international character occurring in the territory of one of the High Contracting Parties (i.e. states), each party to the conflict shall be bound to apply, as a minimum, the following provisions' (ICRC, nd b). It then goes on to demand that the wounded and captured must not be subjected to violence, torture, ill treatment, sentence/execution without due process and that the parties to a conflict should attempt to form special agreements to bring into force all or part of the other provisions of the Geneva Conventions. It further states that the 'application of the preceding provisions shall not affect the legal status of the Parties to the conflict' (ICRC, nd b). In reality, what that means is that regardless of whether a non-state force abides by the Geneva Conventions, the state they are fighting can refuse to accept that a war exists. The power to enforce IHL rests with the state or with the UN Security Council.

In cases where a 'war' is not recognised as existing and IHL does not apply, IHRL is supposed to apply and the rights of non-state actors and civilians protected by that. Of course in such cases states will usually derogate from some of the protections afforded by IHRL (such as the right to a fair trial) by declaring an 'emergency'. Indeed, most rights under IHRL can be suspended on the grounds of an 'emergency', except the right not to be tortured. In practice, of course, the latter right has proven elusive in many conflict situations. The USA, for example, infamously water-boarded suspected al-Qaeda combatants during the wars in Afghanistan and Iraq with the connivance of the UK and a host of other EU[2] and Arab states. Amnesty International (2014) reported that in the previous five years torture had been used in at least three-quarters of the world's states, 141 countries, despite the fact that 155 states had ratified the UN Convention Against Torture. By 2019, 166 states had ratified it (OHCHR, 2019). One other example of the absence of international human rights protection during conflicts involving non-state actors relates to prisoners held in Guantanamo Bay camp by the US. These prisoners had neither protections under IHL or IHRL (Amnesty, 2017).

How to deal with armed conflicts involving non-state actors became particularly relevant in the post-World War II period given that the vast majority of armed conflicts now involve non-state actors (Chinkin and Kaldor, 2017; Pettersson and Wallensteen, 2015; Pettersson et al, 2019). In an attempt to try to ensure that modern armed conflicts were adequately covered by IHL, two additional protocols were added to the Geneva Conventions (1949) in 1977 (ICRC, nd b). Protocol 1 relates to wars of national liberation or against racism, and classifies them as the same as wars between states – international conflicts – for the first time, thus providing that captured non-state combatants be treated as POWs. However, the question arises, who decides whether such a 'war' exists? It is ultimately up to the state on whose territory the conflict is taking place, or the UNSC, to make that decision. In practice, not many states are going to admit that they are racist or are denying 'national liberation'. The UNSC is only going to intervene if the five permanent members (USA, Russia, China, UK and France) with a veto all agree and that has proven to be rare due to geo-political differences and national self-interests.

Protocol 2 relates to other internal conflicts within a state but only where the insurgent group has control over part of the national territory. Thus, the Protocol tends to favour more powerful groups. Such forces, however, are not provided with the protection of POW status if captured and the state could put them on trial. In this regard, Article 6 paragraph 5 is of interest: 'At the end of hostilities, the authorities in power shall endeavour to grant the broadest possible amnesty to persons who have participated in the armed conflict, or those deprived of their liberty for reasons related to the armed conflict, whether they are interned or detained' (ICRC, nd b). One big advantage of the Protocols, however, is that they give some recognition to the idea that non-state combatants may exist and that they and states have responsibilities to protect non-combatants from harm. Attacks on civilians are clearly prohibited.

One specific area where the operation of IHL has been problematic has been in relation to the Israel/Palestine conflict. The UNSC and the UN Assembly have repeatedly called on Israel to withdraw from Palestinian and Syrian territory it occupied after the 1967 Six Day War and has controlled ever since – the Golan Heights, East Jerusalem, the West Bank and Gaza. Israel, with the active support of the USA and the compliance of most of the EU, has continued to *de facto* annex much of that territory to build Jewish-only settlements on the land in contravention of international law. In Israel's view the territory is 'disputed territory' and like the colonial powers of old it wishes to keep the territory for itself. It refuses to accept that IHL applies in relation to its obligations to care for the Palestinians living under occupation, to refrain from annexing and settling occupied land, or to treat Palestinian combatants it captures as POWs. IHL also calls for the right of return of displaced persons to their homes following the cessation of hostilities. Israel has consistently refused to allow 'the right of return' of some 5.5 million Palestinian refugees displaced by the conflict and registered with the UN via the UNRWA agency. This is despite UN Assembly Resolution 194 which had re-affirmed the 'right of return' every year since 1949.

The Israel/Palestine situation shows one of the major difficulties which exist for realisation of rights bestowed under IHL-enforcement. Oversight and enforcement operate at a number of levels. The UN Assembly, made up of representatives of all 193 member states, may pass non-binding resolutions criticising actions or non-actions under IHL. The most this can produce, however, is embarrassment for the offending party. The UNSC is the only body which can impose sanctions – economic or military – against violators of IHL. However, UNSC decisions need the support, or acquiescence, of all five permanent members and decisions are usually based on geo-political advantage and national interest rather than human rights considerations. Most of the decisions made by the UNSC illustrate this. For example, the UNSC declared war on North Korea (1950–53) after the USSR had temporarily withdrawn from the UN over the non-recognition of the People's Republic of China as the Chinese representative to the UN. It declared war on Iraq in 1991 over the invasion of member state Kuwait. It stated that the USA and UK had the right to wage war against the Taliban in Afghanistan in 2001 – although it refused to sanction war on Iraq in 2003. In most cases, however, where human rights violations have taken place, the UNSC has either been too divided or too uninterested to act – for example, East Timor, Sri Lanka, Palestine, Bosnia, Ukraine, Syria. The UNSC has set up a number of international tribunals to investigate specific conflicts. The International Criminal Tribunal for the former Yugoslavia in 1993 – which was established by the UNSC for the prosecution of genocide, crimes against humanity and war crimes – was the first international criminal tribunal to prosecute war crimes since the 1949 Geneva Conventions. A number of other tribunals have also been set up relating to other specific conflicts – notably, Rwanda (1994), Sierra Leone (2002), Cambodia (2003), Lebanon (2009).

In 2002 the International Criminal Court (ICC) was established in The Hague under the Rome Statute. However, it has many limitations in terms of the enforcement of IHL. Under the Statute, the ICC Prosecutor can initiate an investigation on the basis of a referral from any state signatory or from the Security Council – or, significantly, based on information from individuals or organisations. However, it can only prosecute war crimes committed after 1 July 2002 and only people who belong to states which have agreed to be bound by the Court's statute or have committed their crimes in such a state. The only other option is if the Security Council calls for a state to be brought before the ICC – and this rarely happens. The Court is designed to complement existing national judicial systems and can only exercise its jurisdiction when national courts are unwilling or unable to investigate or prosecute. State parties are expected to implement national legislation to provide for the investigation and prosecution of crimes that fall under the jurisdiction of the Court (Articles 17 and 20 of the Rome Statute). In line with the Rome Statute the UK passed the International Criminal Court Act 2001 (ICC Act, 2001). Corporal Donald Payne became the first British soldier convicted of war crimes in April 2007, convicted of ill-treatment of a detainee in Iraq who eventually died. He was sentenced to one year's imprisonment by a military court in Britain. The USA passed the War Crimes Act in 1996, which applies if either the victim or the perpetrator is a US national or member of US armed forces. While 122 countries had ratified the Rome Statute of the ICC (as of January 2020) the USA, Russia, China, Israel and several Arab states have not. One hundred states have also concluded an 'impunity agreement' with the USA – which excludes US citizens from prosecution.

The main form of enforcement of IHL is through universal jurisdiction, though the doors to this type of enforcement appear to be closing. States are obliged to search for persons alleged to have committed war crimes, or who ordered them to be committed, and to bring them to trial regardless of their nationality and of the place where the crimes took place. They are also required to arrest suspects that land on their territory, put them on trial, or extradite them. However, who is accused of 'war crimes' and who is pursued is often more related to political concerns than anything else.

Since World War II there has been a steady expansion of legal mechanisms designed to prevent those accused of violating IHL from seeking refuge in other states. Many states now have complementary national legislation which enables prosecutions of their own citizens, or citizens of other states, for war crimes. This has sometimes allowed citizens to demand arrest warrants for people the government does not want arrested. For example, in 1998 a Spanish judge obtained an international arrest warrant for General Pinochet, the former dictator of Chile (1973–90), for crimes against Spanish citizens. In 1998 he was arrested in London where he was receiving medical treatment.[3] Chile objected because he was travelling on a diplomatic passport. He was held for 18 months under house arrest before being released on medical grounds in 2000 and returned to Chile (*The Guardian*, 1998). In 2009, UK Palestinian supporters got an arrest warrant issued for Israeli politician and former Foreign and Justice Minister, Tzipi Livni, who was expected at a conference and was accused of perpetrating war crimes. She cancelled the trip and the British government later changed the law on 'universal jurisdiction' to require prior approval from the Director of Public Prosecutions (DPP) before an arrest warrant in connection with international war crimes could be issued. Previously, citizens could apply directly to a judge for an arrest warrant. In 2014, Livni was granted immunity by the UK government (*The Guardian*, 2014). In February 2014, a Spanish court issued international arrest warrants for former Chinese President Jiang Zemin and four other top officials, as part of an investigation into alleged human rights abuses in Tibet (CNN, 2014). No action followed, however. States have tended to be reluctant to try non-citizens over war crimes committed elsewhere against citizens of other states. It is complicated by political, strategic and other considerations, and difficult due to 'evidence' availability in other jurisdictions (Kissinger, 2001).

Conclusion

The Geneva Conventions of 1949 and the 1977 Additional Protocols (almost 600 articles) are the main instruments of IHL. A range of other conventions and protocols exist – for example, protecting cultural property, restricting or prohibiting the use of certain weapons (landmines, booby traps, cluster bombs, biological, chemical weapons) and limiting the proliferation of others (such as the 1970 Nuclear Proliferation Treaty). Some areas where military activities *are* prohibited by international agreements are: the Moon (Moon Treaty, 1979), Antarctica (Antarctic Treaty, 1959) or on the territory (including the airspace) or territorial waters of neutral states. In addition, nuclear weapons or other weapons of mass destruction cannot be orbited around the Earth (Outer Space Treaty, 1967) or placed on the seabed (Seabed Treaty, 1971). While there are many difficulties with the articulation and enforcement of IHL, with its practical application to modern-day non-state and low-intensity conflicts and with geo-political and national interests often superseding human rights concerns, at the very least IHL promotes thinking and practice around protecting the welfare of people during war. It provides the tools to pursue those guilty of war crimes and prevent impunity. It provides 'universal' rights in that it does not matter who the person is (race, colour, creed) – they are entitled to equal protection. It also ostensibly applies to all types of conflict including those involving non-state combatants. In the case of the latter, however, it depends whether a state (or the UN) is prepared to declare a 'conflict' with non-state forces as a war. Many states view such 'conflicts' as 'internal' disputes, criminal conspiracies or 'terrorism' and are not therefore prepared to call the opposition 'soldiers' with the protections that secures. Ultimately, concepts of human rights at times of war/conflict remain contested sites, often decided by who is the most powerful or influential.

Notes

[1] Accurate statistics for the deaths in World War I and II are difficult to calculate. There has also been some dispute as to whether World War I was the deadliest war up to 1918; the Taiping rebellion in southern China in the nineteenth century has been estimated to have led to 20 million deaths.

[2] In July 2014 the European Court of Human Rights (ECtHR) censured Poland for helping CIA secret renditions and in October 2018 it made rulings in relation to the involvement of Poland, Romania, Lithuania, (North) Macedonia and Italy. Available at: www.echr.coe.int/Documents/FS_Secret_detention_ENG.PDF

[3] A copy of the Arrest Warrant can be found here: http://www.haguejusticeportal. net/Docs/NLP/UK/Pinochet_Arrest_warrant_16-10-1998.pdf

References

Amnesty (2014) *Amnesty International Launches Worldwide Campaign to Expose Global Crisis on Torture*, 12 May 2014. Available from: www. amnestyusa.org/press-releases/amnesty-international-launches-worldwide-campaign-to-expose-global-crisis-on-torture/

Amnesty (2017) *USA: Guantanamo, Impunity and Global Anti-Torture Day*, 25 June 2017. Available from: www.amnesty.org/en/documents/ amr51/6574/2017/en/

Chinkin, C. and Kaldor, M. (2017) *International Law and New Wars*, Cambridge: Cambridge University Press.

CNN (2014) 'Spanish judge issues arrest warrants for China's former President, Prime Minister', 12 February 2014. Available from: http://edition.cnn.com/2014/02/10/world/europe/ spain-chinese-officials-arrest-warrants/

The Guardian (1998) 'Pinochet arrested in London', 19 October 1998. Available from: www.theguardian.com/world/1998/oct/18/ pinochet.chile

The Guardian (2014) 'Israeli minister Tzipi Livni given diplomatic immunity for UK visit', 13 May 2014. Available from: www.theguardian.com/ world/2014/may/13/israel-tzipi-livni-diplomatic-immunity-uk

ICC Act (2001) *International Criminal Court Act*. Available from: www. opsi.gov.uk/acts/acts2001/ukpga_20010017_en_1

ICRC (nd a) *History of the ICRC*. Available from: www.icrc.org/en/ document/history-icrc

ICRC (nd b) *The Geneva Conventions and Their Additional Protocols*. Available from: www.icrc.org/en/war-and-law/treaties-customary-law/geneva-conventions

Jacobsen, A. (2014) *Operation Paperclip: The Secret Intelligence Program to Bring Nazi Scientists to America*, New York: Little, Brown and Company.

Jewell, N.P., Spagat, M. and Jewell, B.L. (2018) 'Accounting for civilian casualties: from the past to the future', *Social Science History*, 42: 379–410. Available from: https://doi.org/10.1017/ssh.2018.9

Kissinger, H.A. (2001) 'The pitfalls of universal jurisdiction', *Foreign Affairs*, 80(4): 86–96. Available from: www.jstor.org/pss/20050228

Labuda, P.I. (2014) 'Lieber Code', *Oxford Public International Law*. Available from: http://opil.ouplaw.com

Pettersson, T., and Wallensteen, P. (2015) 'Armed conflicts, 1946–2014', *Journal of Peace Research*, 52(4): 536–550.

Pettersson, T., Hogbladh, S. and Oberg, M. (2019) 'Organized violence, 1989–2018 and peace agreements', *Journal of Peace Research*, 56(4): 1–15.

OHCHR (2019) UN Office of the High Commissioner on Human Rights, Convention against Torture and Other Cruel, Inhuman or Degrading Treatment or Punishment. Available from: http://indicators.ohchr.org/

PART II

Key issues for universal human rights-based approaches

7

The European Union, human rights and international development policy

Gerard McCann

This chapter considers the influence of the European Union (EU) on international development with respect to social and economic rights. All but a few countries outside the EU are former colonies of member states and with the legacy of colonialism being so invasive there continue to be systemic and paternalistic ties. While ongoing links between the EU states and the various countries of Asia and the African, Caribbean and Pacific Association (ACP) have been crucial for development purposes, recent changes to the structure and form of international cooperation have altered the way in which the EU considers former colonies (Holland and Doidge, 2012: 70–94; Beringer et al, 2019; Carbone and Orbie, 2018). This chapter will survey the implications of key socio-economic policies with respect to the EU's influence on former colonies, arguing that developmental and rights-based approaches have been frustrated by ideologically driven positions characterised most often by self-interest on the part of EU member states. While acknowledging various efforts and commitments that have been made by member states (indeed, half of the world's development aid comes from the EU) this chapter has the intention of opening up the debate to look through the fault-lines that exist between former colonies and former colonial powers. Its aim is to examine the manner in which certain EU policies have contributed to under-development and a diminution of rights in many of the most vulnerable regions around the world. In assessing the potential contribution of the EU to Least Developed Countries (LDCs), this chapter recognises a need to reconsider the legacy of colonialism and examine policy-based reasons for continued under-development and the negation of human rights in former colonies (Gamble, 2013: 15–26).

The policy framework

All member states of the EU are party to the Charter of the United Nations, which, in Articles 55 and 56, places an obligation on these states to: 'promote … universal respect for, and observance of, human rights and fundamental freedoms for all without distinction as to race, sex, language or religion'. In practical terms this means that: 'Member States have an obligation to promote and protect human rights and fundamental freedoms as stated in the Charter of the United Nations and elaborated in the Universal Declaration of Human Rights, the International Covenants on Human Rights and other applicable human rights instruments' (UNHRO, 2009: 7; also see Carbone and Orbie, 2018: 1–11). All of the member states of the EU are party to the 'core' human rights treaties as presented under the aegis of the United Nations (UN). This has provided, in principle, a compliance framework for subsequent EU legislation.[1]

While fundamental rights are built into the *acquis communautaire* (the legislation) of the EU for its citizens, EU partnership arrangements with third countries also include rights obligations and a range of protocols. The 25 June 2012 'Human Rights and Democracy: EU Strategic Framework and EU Action Plan' set out the manner in which the member states could enhance partner human rights policies. Along with the appointment of an office of EU Special Representative for Human Rights, these initiatives aimed 'to make EU policy on human rights in non-EU countries more effective and to bring it to public attention' (EC, 2012). The 'universal and indivisible nature' of human rights is emphasised as key to the EU institutional engagement with third countries and external organisations. Indeed, every agreement on trade or international cooperation must now include a human rights clause. If breached the EU has the mechanism to impose sanctions. Progress is monitored and set out in the *Annual Report on Human Rights and Democracy*, an annual statement of intent backed up by the European Instrument for Democracy and Human Rights (EIDHR) with a not insubstantial €1.3 billion budget (from 2014 to 2020).

The nature of policy-making in the EU has influenced the manner in which it has shaped the rights-based approaches of external partners. This is notable with the adaptation of treaties in particular. The application of the Reform Treaty of the European Union (the Lisbon Treaty), for example, has been problematic in terms of its practical outworking and methods of ensuring that a more effective policy base could be put in place to engage with rapidly changing geo-political situations. Constitutional wrangling within the EU itself, the failed Constitution, Brexit and an increasingly evident 'Fortress Europe', have represented a restructuring of power relations and policies, including international cooperation and the place of fundamental rights in international relations from the EU's perspective (Beringer et al, 2019: 7–10; de Búrea, 2011: 649–693; Dinan, 2010: 523–524). While noticeable internally – with incidents such as the French government's ongoing deportation of the Roma communities or the Polish government's refusal in 2016 to take in Syrian victims of war – frustration can be seen, particularly in the policy field of international development.

Continuity on the ideal of universal rights can be sourced to the formative Article 3 of the original Treaty of Rome, building 'association ... in order to increase trade and to promote joint economic and social development'. While 'rights' in an external context are not overtly mentioned in treaties until Lisbon, coordination, coherence and complementarity ('associationism') in development partnership can be read explicitly in clauses on the sustainable economic and social development of developing countries – and, more succinctly, the most disadvantaged among them. The treaty's progress into policy-making in this regard has been caught up in the turmoil that accompanied the global financial crisis, the Syrian and African wars, and events such as unprecedented vulnerable migrant flows and the rise of xenophobic populism – all of which have destabilised the Union itself. Arguably, the key external policy initiatives within the Lisbon Treaty pre-dated the global recession, and whereas the institutional reconfiguration and ordering of the *acquis communautaire* represented a clarification of the treaty base of the European Union, the effects on policy implementation have proved increasingly dysfunctional (Holland and Doidge, 2012: 123–133).[2]

With this noted, the EU remains the single most powerful global influence on international development. Even with the UK out, it still dominates the Group of Eight leading industrial countries (G8) and has a disproportionate influence on the Group of Twenty leading financial countries (G20). It contributes most to international aid budgets and its member states are active in more developing regions of the world than any other power bloc. On the ground, these countries have an immense influence on the protection of rights and poverty alleviation for the most disadvantaged people on earth. In 2017, EU Official Development Assistance (ODA) represented 57 per cent of the total flow from the most developed to the least developed regions. Its shortcomings are, however, important to register in relation to plans that do not match reality and the means by which developing countries have had to deal with a bureaucracy weighed down by the prejudices of various departments, politicians and policy-makers within the EU itself. In effect, the legacy of colonialism is there to see. After over 60 years of the Community's international development cooperation policy, the vast majority of LDCs, the most impoverished and conflict-ridden regions on Earth, remain caught in the orbit of major EU powers.

The Lisbon Treaty, as a strategy to engage third countries, addresses the practicalities of development intervention and awkwardly approaches the questions of rights and responsibilities, aid, trade and debt relief, through a number of principles and rhetorical statements which mirror the questionable approach taken by the EU to developing vulnerable regions since the Maastricht Treaty of 1992. Article 3.5 introduces the issues with the clause that the EU:

> shall contribute to peace, security, the sustainable development of the Earth, solidarity and mutual respect among peoples, free and fair trade, eradication of poverty and the protection of human rights, in particular the rights of the child, as well as to the strict observance and the development of international law, including respect for the principles of the United Nations Charter. (Lisbon Treaty, Article 3.5)

Article 21.2 of the Lisbon Treaty states that the EU will: 'promote an international system based on stronger multilateral cooperation and good global governance'. These clauses link in with general statements that are attached to the work of the EU in regard to third countries and do not differentiate between regions or the myriad of complications that exist across the globe. The problems are self-explanatory. In effect, the USA is placed in the same policy matrix as Syria or the Democratic Republic of Congo, yet the relationships are substantially different (Howorth, 2013: 65–78). Complicating this is the fact that the EU is facing its most challenging set of crises ever, with the Middle East in turmoil, North Africa in various states of civil war, war in Ukraine and internal disintegration driven by disruptive and emboldened 'exit' movements (Beringer et al, 2019: 2–4).

A further clause in the Treaty that has had an adverse impact on international development and the protection of rights has been the security clause of Article 42.5 which states quite categorically that threats to the vested interests of the member states of the EU 'will lead to a common defence, when the European Council, acting unanimously, so decides'. This is underwritten by the possibility of mutual defence and solidarity actions – that is, going to war to protect EU vested interests. It would thus put actions such as the Afghan war on a firm legal footing and within the *acquis communautaire* of the EU, leaving war against developing states subject to arbitrary political intervention. Article 42.7 enhances this commitment by stating that this obliges member states to intervene militarily in defence of the interests of other member states 'by all the means in their power', the nuclear option included. The Treaty, to an extent, had been introduced with the objective of realigning the EU to adapt to changing global contexts and security considerations *apropos* protecting interests. The human rights implications of this and possible interstate conflict have become evident (Holland and Doidge, 2012: 92–94). Across Iraq, Afghanistan, Libya and Syria – where EU forces continue to be active with thousands of bombings and drone raids – hundreds of thousands of civilian causalities have been affected without recourse to rights, compounded by the creation of millions of refugees. The United Nations High Commissioner for Refugees (UNHCR) estimated that in 2016 alone 362,000 refugees and migrants tried to make it across the Mediterranean to flee war, with thousands dying in the attempt.

Cotonou

The development cooperation strategy of the EU has tenure going back to the Lomé Conventions operating from 1975 until 2000. Its replacement, the Cotonou Agreement, was designated to last until 2020. In this the EU has been seeking to rationalise engagement with the ACP bloc in particular by bringing together bespoke and flexible economic partnership. Its Preamble is a veritable list of human rights conventions. In form, it is an affirmation of globalisation (European Commission, 2010: 14–16). There were also prerequisites that would satisfy the political interests of the EU states in the uncertain environment of an evolving new Cold War. Security, competition and compliance – all aspects that were built into the Reform Treaty – were to become a framework for the Cotonou system. Cotonou would be long term, adaptable, with an extension option. Different economies would be dealt with in different ways; the ACP bloc would be broken up and with annual reviews and more fluid approaches to finance, free trade mechanisms could be established with one region while aid commitments could be agreed with another. The liberalisation of trade, particularly imports under the Generalised System of Preferences (GSP), would drive it towards World Trade Organization (WTO) criteria and compatibility, while the ACP would be given a level of flexibility until preferential produce could be managed out of the network (Holland and Doidge, 2012: 70–94). The private sector would be encouraged throughout the ACP partners to enhance market activity and facilitate EU Transnational Corporations with increased access to natural and human resources (Dinan, 2010: 524–526).

The overarching objective that Cotonou carried was the need for differentiation and competitive engagement, secured through the ongoing and highly problematic Economic Partnership Agreement (EPA). As stated in the Commission's 'Main Objectives and Principles': 'The *central objective* of the Partnership Agreement is to reduce and eventually eradicate poverty while contributing to sustainable development and to the gradual integration of ACP countries into the world economy' (European Commission, 2001: section 2: 1). Article 43, Objective 1 of the Cotonou Agreement is more targeted: 'Economic and trade cooperation shall aim at fostering the smooth and gradual integration of the ACP states into the world economy'. This was mirrored in Article 3.5 of the Lisbon Treaty and continues to have immense policy implications, economic and social. Countries not sufficiently developed to engage in WTO activities could, and would, be penalised. Sub-Saharan Africa was to become a particular target of this punitive structural adjustment strategy. In real terms it forced impoverishment on many regions.

Cotonou stipulated that the EU would negotiate EPAs with the most economically developing states or groups of states, mostly former colonies. Different ACP countries – by way of consultation with the European Commission – were to decide if they could sign and implement these types of agreements. Many countries also attempted to embark on negotiations through EPAs. The LDCs may have the option of a backstop – if the EPA negotiations failed, they could argue for duty-free, quota-free access to the EU through the 'Everything but Arms' (EBA) initiative, that is, as stated, trade in all but armaments. This was named after the EU's Council regulation on the initiative and granted: 'access to imports of all products from the LDCs without any quantitative restrictions except for arms and munitions' (Dinan, 2010: 526; Hadfield, 2007: 39–66). In doing this the EU moved for the first time from giving priority to former colonies – and many of the poorest regions on Earth – to looking at development policy in terms of LDC engagement and geo-political security. Badly managed, it subsequently led to colonial-type dependency for some countries, with regions being locked into specific trade flows without the protection of reciprocity.

One long-term EPA objective was to deepen regional economic integration (between the ACP countries) and not – as in the case of the Lomé Convention – only to intensify the trade between the Community and its partners from the ACP Association. As part of the EPAs, the EU and the ACP states were to cooperate for business climate improvement, regional market development and the promotion of good management in the economy. The negotiations between Brussels and many ACP regions are still ongoing, 19 years after the Cotonou Agreement was signed. Progress in the negotiations in different regions varied extensively with different contentious issues remaining unresolved in different regions, such as a 'Most Favoured Nation' clause, the rules of origin, export taxes, accompanying development support, and so on. Difficulties in recurrent EPA negotiations invariably created tensions between the EU and its ACP partners, and consequently in the poorest regions EPAs emerged as a controversial issue. In the meantime, some states (for example, Ivory Coast, Cameron) signed so-called interim EPAs with the EU to ensure they had access to the EU market and more beneficial rules of origin (PAH, 2011).

Aside from Cotonou, which specifically targeted 77 ACP states for partnership, the EU also negotiated agreements with other LDCs such as India, Bangladesh and Egypt. The EU noticeably targeted the Maghreb and Mashreq groups (Algeria, Libya, Mauritania, Morocco, Tunisia, Egypt, Jordan, Lebanon and Syria). The engagement with these states was an assurance of sorts where favoured regions – mostly on the periphery of the EU itself – were facilitated with support to encourage stability in an increasingly volatile geo-political environment (Gillespie, 2013: 121–134). This became particularly urgent during the US-led 'War on Terror' in which most EU states compliantly participated even though it was being directed on questionable legal and human rights grounds (for example, extraordinary rendition, the use of torture, the killing of civilians, drone use and military activities against states not at war). Intervention in these regions by the EU often included financial support for development projects, support for EU private sector investment, aid and loans. After the Arab Spring of 2011 onwards and the rise of Daesh (McCann and McCloskey, 2015: 233–250), EU arms companies became more flexible and indeed opportunistic. In response, EU political leaders complied with the facilitation of arms deals, for example, to Libya, Syria, Saudi Arabia and Yemen, feeding the growing instability. The social policy and human rights implications have been catastrophic in these regions (Yemen and Syria in particular), with conflict and impoverishment accelerating, migration becoming the only way to escape war, poverty and oppression, and interregional conflict spiralling across the volatile areas affected. By the end of 2018, in Syria alone, the Syrian Observatory for Human Rights listed over half a million dead, including tens of thousands of children. Arms sales from EU states have soared as the wars have escalated.

The changing patterns of EU development policy – demanding a reciprocation of trade and governance compliances, prioritising security issues and protecting member state trade concerns – could be seen through the ongoing quarrels that the ACP has had with the EU representatives. Disputes are not new, dating back to the 2003 Cancun lockout where the 650-strong EU delegation to a WTO summit refused to admit the dozen ACP representatives to discussions on social and economic policies that would adversely affect the development of ACP regions. After this low point in the relationship between the former colonies and EU powers, any platform that had sustained a flawed – albeit operable – communication of interests had effectively come to an end. Many ACP states believed that their societies could not cope with such aggressive neo-colonial interventions and the securitisation of interstate relations. Perhaps the most telling commentary on the EU came from Oxfam:

> The deals currently on the table will strip ACP countries of important policy tools they need in order to develop. EPAs severely constrained effective regulation and threaten universal access to vital services; the deals would only slightly improve market access for the ACP to the EU, but the ACP countries would 'dramatically' open their markets to the EU, giving concern to the increased competition of EU exports. (Oxfam, 2008)

Given that most ACP regions and LDCs depend on revenue generated by tariffs placed on imports for public services (health and education in particular), the reduction or wholesale removal of this revenue has adversely affected the health and social services provided by governments across these least developed regions. The process is, as always, essentially about the distribution of capital, power and wealth. The social policy effects of this diverging two-world strategy (a first and a third), as with the WTO liberalisation strategy, can be seen across the globe. Thomas Piketty, in *Capital in the Twenty-First Century*, highlighted the point:

> The dynamics of the global distribution of capital are at once economic, political, and military. This was already

the case in the colonial era, when the great powers of the day, Britain and France foremost among them, were quick to roll out the cannon to protect the investments. Clearly, the same will be true in the twenty-first century. (Piketty, 2014: 458)

Apart from the obvious implication of having left many regions at a competitive disadvantage in a disintegrating but liberalising economic environment, other complications for development policy (and the rights implications) have been emerging throughout the tenure of Cotonou and Lisbon. Multilateral and bilateral engagements have been formulating under different precedents and at different paces. Multilateral activities would include those that the EU as an organisation would support, whereas bilateral activities would include state-to-state activities. Within the EU itself the differences can be extreme. The Scandinavian countries have been contributing significantly and imaginatively to global development and have taken an avowedly equality-based and rights-based approach, but this stands in stark contrast to the southern and eastern states of the EU. The example of Italian and Spanish border patrols – notably during the migrant crisis of 2015–16 – forcing starving migrants back out into the Mediterranean Sea and possible death, gives one stark picture of EU member state intervention, whereas other regions are willing to facilitate support. The 175 kilometre long, 4 metre high, razor fence erected by the Hungarian government to stop those fleeing the Syrian war entering the country was another desperate measure, and exposed an increasing disregard for human rights. Indeed, across the EU, since 2015, 1,000 kilometres of fence has been erected against migrants. In 2017 alone, 3,915 migrants were killed trying to get into the EU. The lack of compassion shown by many EU member states can be seen as a reconstruction on many fronts of a 'Fortress Europe'. Increasing numbers of governments are condemning the rescue of asylum seekers stranded at sea and whereas some states have shown immense and world-leading intervention, others have ignored basic development and rights commitments (*Independent*, 9 November 2018; Howorth, 2013: 65–67).

Conclusion

Since the introduction of the Lisbon Treaty, the development policies of EU member states have not shown any significant change of direction from those operating since the start of the 2000s. The rights-based aspects, seemingly rhetoric, remain subject to the needs of member states and the populism of EU political leaders. This has meant that securitisation and liberalisation of trading arrangements continue to be the most pronounced priorities that there are for the EU in dealing with developing countries. Other aspects of development policy are also subject to this trajectory. Due to the fact that its design has historically been in the interests of Europe, developing countries will continue to be adversely pressurised by the various EU institutions and states involved. Arguably, in the past, member state interventions have disrupted attempts at genuine humanitarian development (Keukeleire and MacNaughtan, 2008: 200–203; Beringer et al, 2019: 8–10). Aggressive attempts to alter socio-economic relations in LDC regions and for groups that are highly vulnerable (such as migrants and minority ethnic groups) have proved to be catastrophic, with Sub-Saharan Africa and the Middle East – former European colonies – the case in point, where support systems for the most vulnerable have virtually collapsed under dependency, conflict and impoverishment.

The two drivers of EU external policy, trade liberalisation and security, have come to dominate the discourse around the design of development policy and the rights discourse therein. Both aspects have been shaped to enhance the role of the EU as a global actor and this comes into direct conflict with the principles of development partnership and indeed the universality of human rights (Koeb, 2008: 1–16). On the first count, with trade liberalisation, the agricultural basin of developing regions have been provoked into an unbalanced competitive process with the over-protected agricultural sectors of the EU. It has led to issues of food security. On the second count, compliance with transnational agendas towards EU member states' priorities regarding security have frustrated regional balances of power – as can be seen in North Africa. EU power and security intentions and developmental activities (including humanitarian aid) stand together uneasily (Howorth, 2013: 77–78). One fear in this shift is that humanitarian aid and development assistance will eventually be utilised as a method of ensuring strategic military positioning. The pressures are already there, as can be seen from the withholding of aid to Sri Lanka in return for political compliances, French and UK arms deals to Libyan warlords, a proxy war with the Russian Federation in Syria, and the withdrawal of aid from many of the more impoverished regions of Sub-Saharan Africa. Circumstances, again, weighed against the Global South as the world crashed into the Arab Spring and its aftermath of conflict across Africa and the Middle East. Over a half century after the European development policy was first introduced, a productive workable framework has remained elusive – to the poverty of humanitarian aid, genuine development and basic human rights.

Notes

[1] This 'core' under the aegis of the UN includes: the International Covenant on Civil and Political Rights (ICCPR), the International Covenant on Economic, Social and Cultural Rights (ICESCR), the International Convention on the Elimination of All Forms of Racial Discrimination (ICERD), the Convention on the Elimination of All Forms of Discrimination against Women (CEDAW), the Convention against Torture and Other Cruel, Inhuman or Degrading Treatment or Punishment (CAT) and the Convention on the Rights of the Child (CRC). All EU member states have also ratified or signed the Convention on the Rights of Persons with Disabilities (CRPD) (UNHRO, 2009: 7).

[2] All Lisbon Treaty references will refer to the Treaty on European Union (TEU) and the Treaty on the Functioning of the European Union (TFEU) as published by the Council on 30 April 2008; 2010/C83/01, www.eu-lex.europa.eu

References

Beringer, S., Maier, S. and Thiel, M. (eds) (2019) *EU Development Policies*, London: Palgrave Macmillan.

Carbone, M. and Orbie, J. (eds) (2018) *The Europeanisation of Development Policy*, Abingdon: Routledge.

De Búrca, G. (2011) 'The road not taken: the European Union as a global human rights actor', *The American Journal of International Law*, 105(4): 649–693.

Dinan, D. (2010) *Ever Closer Union*, London: Palgrave.

European Commission (2001) *Cotonou Infokit*, Brussels: EC.

European Commission (2010) *The Cotonou Agreement*. Available from: http://www.europarl.europa.eu/intcoop/acp/03_01/pdf/mn3012634_en.pdf

European Commission (2012) 'Human rights and democracy', Brussels: EC. Available from: http://data.consilium.europa.eu/doc/document/ST-11855-2012-INIT/en/pdf

Gamble, A. (2013) 'The EU and the evolving shift of power in global governance', in M. Teló and F. Ponjaert (eds) *The EU's Foreign Policy*, Farnham: Ashgate, pp 15–26.

Gillespie, R. (2013) 'The European neighbourhood policy and the challenge of the Mediterranean southern rim', in M. Teló and F. Ponjaert (eds) *The EU's Foreign Policy*, Farnham: Ashgate, pp 121–134.

Hadfield, A. (2007) 'Janus advances? An analysis of EC development policy and the 2005 amended Cotonou Partnership Agreement', *European Foreign Affairs Review*, 12(1): 39–66.

Holland, M. and Doidge, M. (2012) *Development Policy of the European Union*, London: Palgrave.

Howorth, J. (2013) 'The Lisbon Treaty, CSDP and the EU as a security actor', in M. Teló and F. Ponjaert (eds) *The EU's Foreign Policy*, Farnham: Ashgate, pp 65–78.

Keukeleire, S. and MacNaughtan, J. (2008) *The Foreign Policy of the European Union*, Basingstoke: Palgrave Macmillan.

Koeb, E. (2008) 'A more political EU external action: implications of the Treaty of Lisbon for the EU's relations with developing countries', European Centre for Development Policy Management, *InBrief 21*, Maastricht.

McCann, G. and McCloskey, S. (eds) (2015) *From the Local to the Global: Key Issues in Development Studies*, London: Pluto Press.

OXFAM (2008) *Partnership or Power Play: How Europe should Bring Development into its Trade Deals with Africa, Caribbean and Pacific Countries*, Oxford: Oxfam International.

PAH (2011) *The European Union's Development Cooperation Policy in the Context of the Polish Presidency in the EU Council in 2011*, Warsaw: PAH.

Piketty, T. (2014) *Capital in the Twenty-First Century*, Cambridge, MA: Belknap Press.

UNHRO (2009) *The European Union and International Human Rights Law*, New York: UN High Commissioner for Human Rights. Available from: https://europe.ohchr.org/Documents/Publications/EU_and_International_Law.pdf

8

Socio-economic rights

Giovanni Farese

This chapter provides a critical analysis of some of the difficulties experienced in attempting to promote the development of universal social and economic rights. Drawing on the historical development of concepts of socio-economic rights in nation-states and then in international human rights mechanisms, it discusses the importance of ideology, human agency and power. It also discusses contemporary attempts by non-governmental organisations (NGOs) and other campaigning organisations to promote the recognition and realisation of universal socio-economic rights.

Socio-economic rights are human rights that generally refer to social and economic conditions accepted as necessary for individuals and groups to live sustainably in dignity and freedom within society. These rights have a *dual* function. They are *means* for livelihood and they are *ends* – pillars of human dignity. As happens with most freedoms, these rights have reinforcing connections too (Sen, 1999: 54–86). They include the right to an adequate standard of living, the right to work and related rights, and the right to social security. These rights are recognised and protected through a network of legal instruments, which create an obligation to respect, protect, facilitate and fulfil them, and to take progressive measures to secure their recognition and observance. An essential aspect of these rights comes from the duty of international cooperation as recognised in Article 55 of the Charter of the United Nations (Eide et al, 1995).

> With a view to the creation of conditions of stability and well-being which are necessary for peaceful and friendly relations among nations based on respect for the principle of equal rights and self-determination of peoples, the United Nations shall promote:
>
> a. higher standards of living, full employment, and conditions of economic and social progress and development;

    b. solutions of international economic, social, health, and related problems; and international cultural and educational co-operation; and

    c. universal respect for, and observance of, human rights and fundamental freedoms for all without distinction as to race, sex, language, or religion. (UN Charter, Article 55)

This has been embedded to varying degrees in international and regional legal systems since the signing of the Charter on 26 June 1945 in San Francisco. The *universal sources* of social and economic rights include: the Universal Declaration of Human Rights (1948); the Convention on the Elimination of All Forms of Racial Discrimination (1963); the International Covenant on Economic, Social and Cultural Rights (1966); the Convention on the Elimination of all Forms of Discrimination against Women (1979); the Convention on the Rights of the Child (1989); and the Convention on the Rights of Migrant Workers and Their Families (1990). *Regional sources* include: the American Declaration of the Rights and Duties of Man (1948) adopted in Bogotá, Colombia, by the Organization of American States; the American Convention on Human Rights (1969), adopted by the same organisation in San José, Costa Rica; the Additional Protocol to the American Convention on Human Rights in the area of Economic, Social and Cultural Rights (1988), adopted in San Salvador, El Salvador; the African Charter on Human and People's Rights (1981), adopted by the Organization of African Unity (since replaced by the African Union) in Nairobi, Kenya; the European Social Charter (1961, revised in 1996) adopted by the Council of Europe to support the European Convention on Human Rights (1950) and also by the Council; and the Charter of Fundamental Rights of the European Union (2000). Collectively this body of legislation, agreements and conventions represent the basis of an international framework for socio-economic rights.

There are also specific bodies that promote economic and social rights, either at the international or regional level. For example: the UN Committee on Economic, Social, and Cultural Rights; the Inter-American Commission on Human Rights; the African Commission on Human and People's Rights; the European Committee of Social Rights of the Council of Europe; and the European Economic and Social Committee of the European Union. There are few Asia-wide conventions or bodies, although an Association of South-East Asian Nations (ASEAN) Human Rights Declaration (2012) was adopted by the ASEAN in Phnom Penh, Cambodia. Oceania-wide initiatives are also rare, though most countries there have human rights cultures. This is notably the case with the Pacific Plan adopted by the Pacific Islands Forum in 2005, which includes a commitment to a plan for the defence and promotion of human rights in the region. Further to this, there are oversight mechanisms in relation to social and economic rights, such as the UN Committee on Economic, Social and Cultural Rights (UNCESCR) which monitors compliance by member states of the International Convention on Economic, Social and Cultural Rights (ICESCR) and has been in force since January 1976. With these structures in mind, the development of a socio-economic framework for rights needs to highlight the precedents in the international commitment to rights (that is, promoted by international institutions and covenants) by looking at their history, their meaning and, finally, their outlook in today's challenging political environment.

The history

The history of economic and social rights is a recent one. This story can be divided into three periods. First, from the mid-nineteenth century until World War I; second, the inter-war years; and third, the 1940s and the post-war years, an era that give shape to rights as we know them today. Through the first period social and economic rights emerged as a consequence of industrialisation and capital–labour conflicts. Here, Robert Owen in England and Daniel Legrand in France (among others) stand out as pioneers. In 1848, Karl Marx and Friedrich Engels famously wrote in *The Communist Manifesto*, 'Workers of all countries unite!', yet, ironically, it was a German conservative, Otto von Bismarck, who between 1883 and 1885 introduced a set of laws that provided a recognisably modern welfare and social insurance system. In 1890, a conference convened in Berlin by the German government (under Bismarck) considered an international agreement on labour conditions. It sparked the discourse on labour rights that shaped the emerging trade union movement in industrialised countries. Other powerful forces of the day stepped in to enhance a growing international consensus on welfare. In 1891, the encyclical letter *Rerum Novarum* by Pope Leo XIII discussed work, labour conditions and wages. From this moralistic perspective, and drawing on calls from the emerging trade union movement, it was stated that wages should be sufficient for workers to comfortably support their families.

In the decades up to World War I, a small group of states promoted economic and social rights by regulating labour conditions and working time, including child labour and women's labour, as in the United States under Theodore Roosevelt (1901–09), or by introducing schemes for social insurance, as was the case with David Lloyd George's People Budget (1909) and the National Insurance Act (1911) in Great Britain. It is interesting to note that in those years William Beveridge's *Unemployment: A Problem of Industry* (1909) sowed seeds that bore fruit later. Welfare policies were not just a policy trend but were organisational. As early as 1900, the International Association for the Legal Protection of Workers was established in Basle, Switzerland, leading to two ground-breaking conferences in 1905 and 1906, and the adoption of the first international labour conventions.

The developments of the second period gravitate around the consequences of World War I and of the Great Depression in the 1930s. At the end of the war and in the orbit of the League of Nations there came the establishment of the International Labour Organization (ILO, Article 387–427 of the Treaty of Versailles), whose first Secretary-General was Albert Thomas, a French civil servant and politician. The preamble of the ILO's constitution reads:

> Universal and lasting peace can be established only if it is based upon social justice ... conditions of labour exist involving such injustice, hardship and privation to large numbers of people as to produce unrest so great that the peace and harmony of the world is imperilled ... an improvement of those conditions is urgently required; as, for example, by the regulation of the hours of work, including the establishment of a maximum working day and week, the regulation of labour supply, the prevention of unemployment, the provision of an adequate living wage, the protection of the worker against sickness, disease and injury arising out of his employment, the protection of children, young persons and women, provision for old age and injury, protection of the interest of workers when employed in countries other than their own, recognition of equal remuneration for work of equal value, recognition of the principle of freedom of association, the organization of vocational and technical education and other measures.
> (ILO Constitution, Preamble)

This was the result, on one hand, of growing concerns among factory owners and political establishments about labour conditions abroad (since trade and investment already crossed borders frequently) and, on the other hand, of growing ties of solidarity between labour movements. It also signalled the emergence of a new conscience on the supranational interdependence of the world economy. In the inter-war years, the ILO adopted conventions and recommendations on labour standards, supervising their progressive implementation.

Then came the economic crash of 1929, with global mass unemployment. In 1935, the first report on 'Nutrition and Public Health' by the Health Division of the League of Nations showed widespread food shortages. It was the first account of the extent of hunger and malnutrition in the world, and contributed to the emergence of a sense of urgency. It was not a problem felt by poor countries only and became a point of action that has had a global legacy. In the US, the New Deal marked a shift with, in 1935, the Social Security Act being introduced. In his second inaugural address, Roosevelt said: 'I see one-third of a nation ill-housed, ill-clad, ill-nourished' (Roosevelt, 1961a: 105). He went on to point to the right to an adequate standard of living (housing, care, food) that would form the substance of economic and social rights.

During World War II, the principles of the New Deal found larger application. On 6 January 1941, the 'Four Freedoms Speech' of Roosevelt introduced the idea of 'freedom from want' (Roosevelt, 1961b: 278). As for the other three (freedom of speech, of worship, freedom from fear), Roosevelt called for measures to ensure the application of these rights everywhere in the world. In the Atlantic Declaration of August 1941, the American President and the British Prime Minister, Winston Churchill, pledged: 'to bring about the fullest collaboration between all nations in the economic field with the object of securing, for all, improved labour standards, economic advancement and social security'. Shortly after, in May–June 1943, a conference on food and agriculture was convened in Hot Springs, Virginia, on the initiative of Roosevelt. On the other side of the Atlantic, William Beveridge was drafting the report on *Social Insurance and Allied Services* (1942), advocating a standard of living below which no one should be allowed to fall. The Report would be the pillar of the modern welfare state. Beveridge would further develop his ideas (influenced by the welfarism of John Maynard Keynes) in *Full Employment in a Free Society* (1944), which carried the motto 'misery generates hate' (Beveridge, 1944). It became the founding document of the British welfare state. In the US, an interim commission was entrusted with formulating a plan for a permanent organisation to ensure food security, the Food and Agriculture Organization (FAO).

On 10 May 1944, the Declaration of Philadelphia was signed. Drafted by the acting director of the ILO, the Irishman Edward J. Phelan and the British lawyer C. Wilfred Jens, it offered a series of key principles on human development: that labour was not a commodity; that freedom of expression and freedom of association were essential to sustained progress; that poverty anywhere constitutes a danger to prosperity everywhere (a fundamental idea of the Roosevelt doctrine); that war against want requires unrelenting vigour for the promotion of the common welfare; that all human beings, irrespective of race, creed or sex, have the right to pursue both their material well-being and their spiritual development in conditions of freedom and dignity, of economic security, and equal opportunity. A dual culture of world government and world development had emerged (Farese, 2015). By then, the idea of an International Bill of Human Rights or a Universal Declaration of Human Rights, was well under way. When the UN was established in 1946, Eleanor Roosevelt, widow of the President, became the driving force behind its universal declaration and its adoption, along with a drafting committee involving Alexandre Bogomolov (USSR), René Cassin (France), Charles Dukes (UK), William Hodgson (Australia), John P. Humphrey (Canada), Charles Malik (Lebanon), Peng-chung Chan (China) and Hernan Santa Cruz (Chile). The Declaration was adopted on 10 December 1948. In the same year the World Health Organization (WHO) was established, contributing to a web of institutions intent on future socio-economic progress (Staples, 2006).

From 1948 onwards, the UN and the Universal Declaration became standards for other supranational organisations and conventions on the protection of rights across the globe. Supported by the emergence of a global conscience, the age of social and economic rights went together with decolonisation and the rise of a culture of development. This evolving architecture of rights coincided with the emergence of the development sector, non-governmental organisations that were dedicated to campaigning, funding and advocating socio-economic change for the most vulnerable in the most challenging environments. This has been mirrored through the work of the trade union movement globally, which coordinated numerous campaigns for workers' rights and acted as an authoritative oversight to abuses of these rights (www.ictur.org).

Socio-economic rights

The evolving system of rights led to a formative understanding of economic rights as well as definitive universal human rights: the right to an adequate standard of living, the right to work and protection therein, and the right to social security. These collectively provide the framework for work-related rights as they apply across liberal democracies to this day. Even under sustained pressures from neoliberalism and populism they remain the fabric of socio-economic advancement.

The right to an adequate standard of living – food, housing, and health/social care – is fundamental. At the core of social rights is the right to an adequate standard of living. This is recognised in Article 25 of the Universal Declaration of Human Rights: 'everyone has the right to a standard of living adequate for health and well-being of himself and of his family'. In Article 11 of the International Covenant of Economic, Social and Cultural Rights, it states that: 'the State Parties to the present Covenant recognize the right of everyone to an adequate standard of living for himself and his family'. This means that everyone should enjoy necessary subsistence rights. Adequate food has multiple meanings. It means access to food, with a community management of natural resources that has an impact on food supply; adequacy of food supply, that is, culturally acceptable food; food covering nutritional needs in terms of quantity and quality; safe food (free of contaminants or toxic factors); and long-term stability of the supply in terms of economic and social sustainability. In other words, food procurement should not shadow other basic human needs.

Adequate housing has many dimensions. It implies: legal security of tenure which guarantees legal protection (for example, against forced eviction); availability of facilities and services; affordability, meaning that the associated financial cost should not compromise or threaten other basic needs; habitability (protection from cold, heat, rain, wind, and so on); accessibility for disadvantaged groups; location (access to healthcare services, schools, and so on); and cultural adequacy. Adequate care in general is equally important and covers multiple aspects. It is particularly relevant for vulnerable groups in a society, including children and the elderly. It implies the conditions to assure medical services in the event of sickness; the improvement of environmental and industrial hygiene; the prevention, treatment and control of epidemics and other diseases; and the reduction of infant mortality.

As stated, on the part of states there is an obligation to respect these rights, an obligation to protect (for example, against encroachment of the land of indigenous people) and an obligation to facilitate and to fulfil where there is a need for some entitlements to be directly provided by the state. There is also the right to work and related rights. This right is, as noted, a source of both income and livelihood (means) and a source of human dignity and human flourishing (ends). Article 23 of the Universal Declaration of Human Rights refers to the right to work, equal pay for equal work, just and favourable remuneration, while Article 24 provides for the right for everyone to rest and leisure, including reasonable limitation of working hours and periodic holidays with pay. This clause goes across the conventions. Article 15 of the African Charter on Human and People's Rights provides that every individual shall have the right to work under equitable and satisfactory conditions and shall receive equal pay for equal work. In Part II, Article 1 of the European Social Charter, it states that parties: 'accept as one of their primary aims and responsibilities the achievement and maintenance of as high and stable level of employment as possible, with a view to the attainment of full employment' (the legacy of Keynes and Beveridge is evident here). This right is sometimes considered, both from critics and supporters, as a *guarantee of work*, that is, the right to have a job with adequate remuneration. However, no such right exists. Still, states have to take steps to define work as a right, as noted in Article 6 of the International Covenant on Economic, Social and Cultural Rights: 'to achieve the full realization of the right to work and shall include technical and vocational programmes, policies and techniques to achieve steady economic, social and cultural development and full and productive employment under conditions safeguarding fundamental political and economic freedoms to the individual'. Unfortunately, today monetary stability is often seen as a policy goal that has to be prioritised vis-à-vis full employment. The principle of the right to work implies work-related rights, including freedom of association, freedom from forced labour (where occupations should be freely entered upon), the right to healthy and just conditions of work (annual paid holiday, working hours, and so on), and the right to strike, to note a few. Again there is an obligation to respect individuals with basic rights such as freedom from slavery and freedom from forced labour; an obligation to protect people from discrimination in access to work; and an obligation to facilitate and to fulfil, with a view to full employment policy.

With social security, Article 25 of the Universal Declaration of Human Rights refers to the right to social security for everyone as a member of society. In particular, Article 25 (1) mentions this right in relation to disability, old age, sickness, unemployment, widowhood or circumstances beyond one's control. The ILO Social Security (Minimum Standards) Convention of 1952 comprises nine areas of social security: (1) medical care; (2) sickness benefit; (3) unemployment benefit; (4) old-age benefit; (5) employment injury benefit; (6) family benefit; (7) maternity benefit; (8) invalidity benefit; and (9) survivors' benefit. Options can be different, from assistance only to the needy to social insurance based on contributions made in working relationships, to social security in a comprehensive and universalistic approach. There is reference to the right to social security in Article 12 of the European Social Charter, but there is only reference to the aged and the disabled in the African Charter on Human and People's Rights. While there is not an obligation to respect with regard to social security, the obligations to protect, to facilitate and to fulfil are applicable.

Today's challenges

In recent years, the landscape of economic and social rights has been largely shaped by the Millennium Development Goals (MDGs) established at the Millennium Summit of the United Nations held in September 2000, when member states committed to achieving set targets by 2015. These goals aimed to: (1) eradicate extreme poverty and hunger; (2) achieve universal primary education; (3) promote gender equality and empower women; (4) reduce child mortality; (5) improve maternal health; (6) combat HIV/AIDS, malaria and other diseases; (7) ensure environmental sustainability; and (8) develop a global partnership for development. Advances were made in a number of areas and a recognisable appreciation of universal intervention to advance human development was definable. However, the terrorist attacks of 11 September 2001 and the subsequent war of terror marked a shift both politically and culturally. As the economist Jeffrey Sachs noted: 'a single minded pursuit of a war on terror was doomed to fail, undermining global cooperation, addressing symptoms rather than causes, and draining attention and resources away from the fundamental challenges of the new world economy' (Sachs, 2009: 14). The impact on socio-economic rights has been disastrous.

The impact of a changing and challenging geo-political context has had a significant effect on the attempts to realise the original MDGs and subsequently with the Sustainable Development Goals (SDGs) which will run until 2030. Results have been mixed. The global child mortality rate has reduced by more than half over the past 25 years – falling from 90 to 43 deaths per 1,000 live births – but it has failed to meet the target of a drop of two-thirds. Some 2.6 billion people have gained access to improved drinking water since 1990. Indeed, the target of halving the proportion of people without access to improved sources of water was achieved as early as 2010. However, 663 million people across the world still do not have access to improved drinking water.

The number of people living on less than $1.25 a day has been reduced from 1.9 billion in 1990 to 836 million in 2015, but the target of halving the proportion of people suffering from hunger has been missed (*The Guardian*, 2015). One may ask if the threshold of $1.25 grasps reality or not. Today, the new formula seems to be shared prosperity, that is, caring about the poorest and the vulnerable 40 per cent in a country, however rich it may be (*The Economist*, 2016).

The SDGs comprise 17 global goals. The socio-economic banners are worth noting and give a sense of the intentions of the authors. Number one reads, 'End poverty in all forms everywhere'; number three reads, 'Ensure healthy lives and promote well-being for all at all ages'; and number eight reads, 'Promote sustained, inclusive and sustainable economic growth, full and productive employment and decent work for all'. Each goal is connected to a number of specific targets, totalling 169. Crossing all of them is a growing concern for the effects of climate change, especially for vulnerable groups in less developed areas, causing migration and displacement, and adding to the effects of war (Ansuategi et al, 2015). Since 2016 the global migrant crisis added a new critical dimension to the protection of socio-economic rights. The extreme poverty of vulnerable individuals, such as migrants and refugees, combined with often racist reaction on the part of states, has led to inhuman and degrading conditions (Ktistakis, 2013). The problem is indeed global, but it has become critical for Europe, a continent hit by the financial crisis and by new forms of poverty. In the round, it is still in the Global South that these socio-economic rights are more imperilled and need more action and protection.

In 2017, the Ordinary Session of the African Commission on Human and People's Rights included the following among current challenges: human rights violations stemming from the conflict in South Sudan; the rise in violent extremism and terrorism as well as the proliferation of terrorist attacks; increasing youth unemployment; climate change and related unpredictable weather patterns; and increased strains on scarce resources such as arable land and potable water (African Commission, 2017). Individually and collectively they have led to persistent under-development, systemic impoverishment and widespread destabilisation. It could be viewed in this context as a reversal of the processes that have been put in place since the UN Charter, to bring the poorest communities on earth to an enhanced and equal social and economic context. Indeed, the injustices and inequalities of today's situation has been captured by remarks from an unusual source, Pope Francis, on the rights related to land property, housing and work (the 3 'Ts': *Tierra, Techo, Trabajo*):

Land and water grabbing, deforestation, unsuitable pesticides are some of the evils which uproot people from their native land ... The other dimension of this already global process is hunger ... Second, Housing. I said it and I repeat it: a home for every family ... Third, Work. There is no worse material poverty – I really must stress this – there is no worse material poverty than the poverty which does not allow people to earn their bread, which deprives them of the dignity of work. (Francis, 2014)

Given the adverse effects of a decade of contradictions where we have seen the principles of socio-economic rights juxtaposed with increasing dehumanisation on a global scale, and over 70 years after the Universal Declaration of 1948, it seems that time has, for many of the most vulnerable people, passed in vain. With this noted, the framework and commitment by many remains: covenants and courts, institutions and fundamental ideals have been built along the way. Furthermore, we must take into account the contemporary attempts by NGOs and other campaigning organisations to promote the recognition and realisation of universal socio-economic rights, using the SDGs and the UN monitoring committees. There is still a significant amount of work that needs to be done to build more humane societies everywhere in the world, regardless of those ever-present destructive forces, both old and new, that can affect good governance, and in particular challenge us with exclusion, capture, and clientelism (World Bank, 2018).

References

African Commission (2017) *Final Communiqué of the 61st Ordinary Session of the African Commission on Human and People's Rights*, Banjul: African Commission on Human and Peoples' Rights.

Ansuategi, A. et al (2015) *The Impact of Climate Change on the Achievement of the post-2015 Sustainable Development Goals*, Cape Town: Climate and Development Knowledge Network.

Beveridge, W. (1944) *Full Employment in a Free Society*, London: Allen and Unwin.

The Economist (2016) 'How the other tenth lives', 8 October.

Eide, A., Krause, K. and Rosas, A. (eds) (1995) *Economic, Social and Cultural Rights*, Dordrecht: Martinus Nijhoff Publishers.

Farese, G. (2015) 'The rise of the dual culture of world government and world development, 1930–1950', *International Affairs*, Virtual Issue, 1–17.

Francis (2014) *Address of Pope Francis to the Participants in the World Meeting of Popular Movement*, 28 October.

The Guardian (2015) 'What have the Millennium Goals achieved', 6 July.

Ktistakis, Y. (2013) *Protecting Migrants under the European Convention on Human Rights and the European Social Charter*, Strasbourg: Council of Europe.

Roosevelt, F.D. (1961a) 'Second inaugural address, January 20, 1937', in B.D. Zevin (ed) *Nothing to Fear: The Selected Addresses of Franklin Delano Roosevelt, 1932–1945*, New York: Popular Library, 102–106.

Roosevelt, F.D. (1961b) 'The four freedoms speech, January 6, 1941', in B.D. Zevin (ed) *Nothing to Fear: The Selected Addresses of Franklin Delano Roosevelt, 1932–1945*, New York: Popular Library, pp 270–278.

Sachs, J. (2009) *Common Wealth: Economics for a Crowded Planet*, New York: Penguin.

Staples, A.L.S. (2006) *The Birth of Development: How the World Bank, Food and Agriculture Organization, and World Health Organization Changed the World*, Kent: Ohio State University Press.

Sen, A. (1999) *Development as Freedom*, Oxford: Oxford University Press.

World Bank (2018) *World Development Report 2018*, Washington, DC: World Bank Group. Available from: http://www.worldbank.org/en/publication/wdr2018

9

Cultural rights

Adam Nowakowski

It cannot be overstated how essential culture is in our lives. It penetrates most of our daily actions, it binds us together with our community, it helps to constitute our identity and is especially important when we represent a cultural minority. A visit to venues such as the cinema, theatre, museums, festivals, monuments and heritage sites quite obviously qualifies as participation in cultural life. However, we also take part in culture by communicating a shared language and engaging in various intercultural activities. Since it is clear why culture is so important, it should not be difficult to understand why the right to take part in cultural life needs special protection in the present world of complex borders, ethnically and culturally diverse societies, and rising xenophobia (Belder and Porsdam, 2017; Mende, 2016; Porsdam, 2019).

Defining culture as rights

Cultural rights are considered an integral part of human rights and are as important as civil, political, economic and social rights. The promotion of and respect for cultural rights is fundamental for the maintenance of human dignity and positive interaction between individuals and communities in such a diverse world. The first international legal document to underline their importance was the Universal Declaration of Human Rights (UDHR), adopted by the United Nations General Assembly in 1948. Article 22 of the UDHR proclaims:

> Everyone, as a member of society, has the right to social security and is entitled to realization, through national effort and international cooperation and in accordance with the organization and resources of each State, of the economic, social and cultural rights indispensable for his dignity and the free development of his personality.

Adoption of the UDHR was a milestone and the first step in the process of formulating the International Bill of Human Rights, which consists of two other elements: the International Covenant on Civil and Political Rights (ICCPR) and the International Covenant on Economic, Social and Cultural Rights (ICESCR). Both were adopted in 1966 but entered into force in 1976 after a sufficient number of countries had ratified them.

Whereas the ICESCR still remains the central treaty in the area of cultural rights, both are referenced in numerous UN treaties that deal with discrimination – for example, in the Convention on the Protection and Promotion of the Diversity of Cultural Expressions, adopted in 2005, and in protocols such as the 2007 Fribourg Declaration. The first United Nations International Conference on Human Rights, which took place in Teheran in 1968, should also be mentioned. Proclamation No 5 of the Final Act of the Conference states:

> The primary aim of the United Nations in the sphere of human rights is the achievement by each individual of the maximum freedom and dignity. For the realization of this objective, the laws of every country should grant each individual, irrespective of race, language, religion or political belief, freedom of expression, of information, of conscience and of religion, as well as the right to participate in the political, economic, cultural and social life of his country.

Proclamation No 13 of the same document adds: 'Since human rights and fundamental freedoms are indivisible, the full realization of civil and political rights without the enjoyment of economic, social and cultural rights is impossible'.

Formulating rights is just the first step. Arguably, an even bigger challenge is defining their content and obligations attached to them. In this process institutions play an essential role. This is why an international-level task force of expert bodies was established in the field of cultural rights by the United Nations in 1987, the Committee on Economic, Social and Cultural Rights. This Committee consists of 18 experts from 162 states. Its role is to evaluate the extent to which the states comply with their obligations. Experts do this by examining government reports, information provided by civil society and other sources, and questioning official delegations on this account. The other major activity of the Committee is formulating general comments – authoritative interpretations such as the implication of a cultural right or other obligations flowing from the ICESCR.

Listing cultural rights

Cultural rights are so closely related to other human rights that occasionally it is difficult to clearly distinguish them from each other. However, several of them are widely recognised as specific rights relating to cultural interaction. As mentioned before, the primary cultural right is the right 'freely to participate in the cultural life of the community', as asserted in the UDHR (Article 27, paragraph 1) and repeated in the ICESCR (Article 15). The Committee on Economic, Social and Cultural Rights General Comment No 21 is much more precise in providing the scope and content of cultural rights. Paragraph 3 of the document reads:

> Other international instruments refer to the right to equal participation in cultural activities; the right to participate in all aspects of social and cultural life; the right to participate fully in cultural and artistic life; the right of access to and participation in cultural life; and the right to take part on an equal basis with others in cultural life. Instruments on civil and political rights, on the rights of persons belonging to minorities to enjoy their own culture, to profess and practice their own religion, and to use their own language, in private and in public, and to participate effectively in cultural life, on the rights of indigenous peoples to their cultural institutions, ancestral lands, natural resources and traditional knowledge, and on the right to development also contain important provisions on this subject. (Committee on Economic, Social and Cultural Rights, 2009)

Paragraph 7 of the same document adds to this list another important right, the right not to participate in cultural activities. That is: 'The decision by a person whether or not to exercise the right to take part in cultural life individually, or in association with others, is a cultural choice and, as such, should be recognized, respected and protected on the basis of equality'.

A particularly notable cultural right is the right to 'enjoy the arts and to share in scientific advancement and its benefits', as stated in the UDHR (Article 27, paragraph 1) and repeated in the ICESCR (Article 15). This right was, however, under-developed for a long time. This situation changed only in 2009 with the Experts' Meeting on the Right to Enjoy the Benefits of Scientific Progress and Its Applications. Organised by UNESCO, it was an important step in pushing this issue forward. Closely connected is the right 'to the protection of the moral and material interests resulting from any scientific, literary or artistic production of which he is the author', proclaimed in the UDHR (Article 27, paragraph 2) and in the ICESCR (Article 15). In 2006 the Committee on Economic, Social and Cultural Rights issued a similar clause, General Comment No 17, solemnly dedicated to discussing this particular right and its scope. We should mention as well that the ICCPR (Article 19, paragraph 2) guarantees the right 'to freedom of expression'.

The right to education is also considered a cultural right, as underlined in World Declaration on Education for All. Education is a fundamental dimension of any cultural design. It ensures cultural progress, strengthens cultural identity (if conducted in the native tongue), and enables participation in cultural life. This right is regulated, among others, by the ICESCR (Articles 13 and 14) and the Convention on the Rights of the Child (Articles 28 and 29). Also numerous international legal documents discussing the rights of minorities include references to cultural rights. These documents discuss issues such as respect for one's cultural identity, the use of one's own language, the practice of religion, the cultivation of traditions, participation in cultural life, access to education (also in one's own language and culture) and cultural heritage – all refer to cultural rights. For instance, the ICCPR (Article 27): 'In those States in which ethnic, religious or linguistic minorities exist, persons belonging to such minorities shall not be denied the right, in community with the other members of their group, to enjoy their own culture, to profess and practice their own religion, or to use their own language'. We should also mention the Indigenous and Tribal Peoples Convention (1989), the International Convention on the Protection of the Rights of All Migrant Workers and Members of Their Families (1990), and the Declaration on the Rights of Persons Belonging to National or Ethnic, Religious and Linguistic Minorities (DRPBNERLM) (1993).

The principle of non-discrimination referred to in numerous human rights documents is also important to our discussion. It played a fundamental role in ensuring the judicial basis necessary for the protection and development of cultural rights. These documents provided the definition of discrimination understood as any exclusion, restriction or preference based on race, colour, sex, language, religion, political or other opinion, national or social origin, property, birth or other status which has the purpose or effect of nullifying or impairing the recognition, enjoyment or exercise, on an equal footing, of human rights and fundamental freedoms in the political, economic, social, cultural or any other field of public life. Although this topic has not been sufficiently academically explored as yet, there is also the right to 'rest and leisure' guaranteed by the UDHR (Article 24) and very closely connected to cultural rights. Most adults in a modern society participate in cultural life outside of work and this requires a place within which to experience cultural life. Rest and leisure give this experience space within which to cultivate activities.

Individual or group character

An important issue when examining cultural rights is whether they are individual or group rights. This is a still unresolved dilemma among scholars. According to the individual rights-based view, cultural rights are derived from human dignity and based on shared meanings among individuals in a community (for a detailed discussion see Jakubowski, 2016). As a result, they are held by individuals. The group rights-based approach, on the other hand, sees cultural rights as a product of human interaction, which can only arise out of dialogical relationships among individuals. Since no single individual can constitute a culture, cultural rights are held by the group rather than by its members separately. The international human rights instruments unfortunately do not provide definitional clarity, leaving the issue open for discussion. For example, the already referenced Article 27 of the UDHR recognises the right of every individual to enjoy the cultural life of the community, and share the benefits of scientific advancement. However, because of the definitional vagueness, the UDHR fails to recognise that someone, especially a member of a cultural minority, might not want to participate in the majority group's cultural life. As a result, the UDHR avoids the controversy involved in reconciling cultural rights with individual rights.

The DRPBNERLM (Article 3, paragraph 1) provides more clarity on this dilemma. It states: 'Persons belonging to minorities may exercise their rights, including those set forth in the present Declaration, individually as well as in community with other members of their group, without any discrimination'. Similar statements can also be found in the Indigenous and Tribal Peoples Convention (Article 5). Generally, the individual approach to defining cultural rights is preferable. The notion of group rights seems to be in conflict with the very core of human rights, which derives from the dignity inherent in all individuals simply because they are human beings. Meanwhile culture can be thought of as a set of shared views, meanings, norms and practices that unite a group and contribute to the identity of its individual members. Individuals have the right: to participate in cultural life of one or more groups; free development of various aspects of one's identity; access to one's own cultural heritage and the cultural heritage of others.

Cultural rights have a strong and long-lasting presence in international legal documents, all of the major treaties and in many national constitutions. They are widely recognised and protected. In spite of that, they are not as developed as other human rights. They occupy a secondary role in the work of international human rights organisations, both governmental and non-governmental. Because of this, they are often seen as less important in comparison. It speaks volumes that the Commission on Human Rights adopted its first ever resolution on cultural rights only in 2002, with little progress since. Why did this situation occur? Elsa Stamatopoulou (2008: 7–8) proposes several explanations for the neglect of cultural rights. Firstly, many experts see the discussion of cultural rights as problematic because of the issue of cultural relativism, which seems 'to undermine the delicate and fragile universality concept that has been painstakingly woven over the last five decades' (Stamatopoulou, 2008: 7). It is, indeed, a very complicated issue that originates from the question whether human rights standards can exist in a world of diverse cultures and religions. In theory, international human rights apply universally. After all, the UDHR and other human rights instruments protect the same scheme of rights for all people regardless of their nationality, religion, ethnicity, language, gender, and so on. In practice, countries differ in recognition and enforcement of rights. This is, however, accepted because human rights law generally allows some degree of variation in this aspect. For example, the right to education is not a constitutionally protected right in the USA, with the American constitution only recognising a commitment to free public education.

Such treatment of human rights is more than just unwritten custom. It is grounded in the very human rights instruments. For example, the ICESCR (Article 2, paragraph 1) proclaims that:

> Each State Party to the present Covenant undertakes to take steps, individually and through international assistance and co-operation, especially economic and technical, to the maximum of its available resources, with a view to achieving progressively the full realization of the rights recognized in the present Covenant by all appropriate means, including particularly the adoption of legislative measures.

As we see, this Article leaves a lot of room for differences in the development and capacity of economic, social and cultural rights. States are not required to fulfil them immediately or even in a specified amount of time, but should just take steps towards fulfilling this goal. Of course it is not cultural relativism, but nonetheless the presented example shows that profound differences in rights protection among states are permitted in international human rights law. What is the reason for division between universalists and relativists then?

Supporters of the universality of human rights believe that human rights standards are universal and can apply to any society, in spite of the variety of their national and cultural features. They claim that human rights are not a product of one particular culture, but can be drawn up by the shared efforts of the entire international community. On the other side of this argument stand cultural relativists. Supporters of this conception see the idea of the universality of human rights as an attempt to impose the principles of one culture on the representatives of another. They underline the fact that the conception of human rights originates in Western Europe and naturally reflects Western views. It is tied closely to social, political and economic conditions, and the history, culture and values specific to that part of the world. Therefore, these rights are not applicable everywhere and should not be seen as such. The diverse background of different peoples and cultures results in different understandings and practices in the sphere of human rights (this discourse is addressed by Barth, 2008; and Francioni and Scheinin, 2008).

What adds fuel to the discussion is uncertainty on the definition, scope and content of cultural rights. For example, the DRPBNERLM (Article 2, paragraph 1) states: 'Persons belonging to national or ethnic, religious and linguistic minorities have the right to enjoy their own culture, to profess and practice their own religion, and to use their own language, in private and in public, freely and without interference or any form of discrimination'. However, what happens when a particularly conservative cultural group limits the rights of its female and child members? On one hand, this group after all is allowed to freely practise its own culture without any interference from the state. On the other hand, the very first Article of the UDHR reads: 'All human beings are born free and equal in dignity and rights'. The answer of which human right deserves more protection in this instance is unclear. According to Stamatopoulou (2008: 7), many experts prefer not to talk about cultural rights in order to avoid such discussions.

Cultural relativism becomes even more problematic when certain national or regional values which contradict human rights outweigh human rights norms. A good example is the Bangkok Declaration (1993), which codified the so-called 'Asian values' advocated by Mahathir Mohamad (Prime Minister of Malaysia) and Lee Kuan Yew (Prime Minister of Singapore). These leaders pushed forward a set of values based on Confucianism that preferred communal harmony (loyalty towards the family, corporation, nation and figures of authority) to individual rights and personal freedom. Article 8 of the Declaration controversially provides that: 'while human rights are universal in nature, they must be considered in the context of a dynamic and evolving process of international norm-setting, bearing in mind the significance of national and regional particularities and various historical, cultural and religious backgrounds'. Commentators have noted that these 'Asian values' have, in practice, been used to suppress universal values such as the freedom of speech and human rights, and to justify authoritarian regimes in Asia, including Malaysia and Singapore.

Problems with defining culture

When asking people whether they understand what culture is, a handful will hesitate to answer yes. But when asked to define culture, few will manage to cope with this challenge and provide a definition. One could argue that what speaks vocally about the essentialness of cultural life is the problem of defining it. What is culture? Arguably, culture simply is. However, this explanation cannot be accepted when dealing with legal documents. Cultural rights are obviously tightly connected to the concept 'culture', so in order to promote cultural rights, culture needs to be precisely explained. This task has proven to be a struggle and for this reason Stamatopoulou names problems with defining culture as a reason for the neglect of cultural rights.

Even though both the UDHR and the ICESCR imply the essentialness of cultural rights and strive to protect them, neither of these documents provides any definition of culture. In fact, most UN documents explain culture simply as 'a way of life', which is a definition too vague to base rights and obligations on. The Committee on Economic, Social and Cultural Rights General Comment No 21 (Articles 10–13) is much more precise and successful in the attempt of explaining with words a phenomenon as fluid and ever-changing as culture. According to the Committee, culture is:

> a broad, inclusive concept encompassing all manifestations
> of human existence ... a living process, historical, dynamic

and evolving, with a past, a present and a future ... Culture ... encompasses, inter alia, ways of life, language, oral and written literature, music and song, non-verbal communication, religion or belief systems, rites and ceremonies, sport and games, methods of production or technology, natural and man-made environments, food, clothing and shelter and the arts, customs and traditions through which individuals, groups of individuals and communities express their humanity and the meaning they give to their existence, and build their world view representing their encounter with the external forces affecting their lives. (Committee on Economic, Social and Cultural Rights, 2009)

This leads to the question of the abuse of cultural rights. Human rights abuses did not end when the UDHR was adopted. The international human rights legal architecture helped many in securing freedom from torture, unjustified imprisonment, as well as providing fair access to education and healthcare. In the light of this fight for human lives, a fight which still continues, some people see cultural rights, as Stamatopoulou puts it, as a 'luxury'. Why focus on providing access 'merely' to culture when there are countless people who are deprived of food and water? Is economic development and rights not more important than culture? Stamatopoulou argues that economic development generally goes with cultural development. Culture represents 'the soul' of a community, everything it holds dear and strives for, without which all life loses purpose and meaning. In that sense, cultural development is not a luxury but rather a means for obtaining economic development, a rights-based *demos* – human development in its fullest form.

Another reason for the neglect of cultural rights noted by Stamatopoulou is political in nature. As she explains, cultural rights are often an inconvenient topic to raise in an international diplomatic context. To speak publicly of cultural rights for many means being ready to talk of cultural wrongs as well – that is, violations of internationally proclaimed human rights. Understandably, this is a topic approached cautiously by state actors and reaching any conclusions requires a lot of time. To illustrate this issue, Stamatopoulou references the case of female genital mutilation (FGM). It took UN bodies over two decades (from the 1950s to the late 1970s) to reach agreement that it is not only a health issue but a human rights issue as well. It was only in 1993 that the United Nations General Assembly moved to include female genital mutilation in the Declaration on the Elimination of Violence Against Women.

The final arguments discussed by Stamatopoulou are closely related to politics. Dealing with cultural rights, especially the rights of minority cultures, regardless if understood as individual or group rights, proves to be difficult because some governments see them as a possible threat to national and territorial integrity. Official state support, according to Stamatopoulou (2008: 8), often merely takes the form of promoting 'seemingly innocent folklore' without addressing cultural issues that are the centre of community development for many people. The promotion of minority languages, for example, through education systems and the state media is generally met with silence or even hostility.

Justiciability

There is much discussion as to whether and how courts should enforce cultural rights. Economic, social and cultural rights are sometimes referred to as 'non-binding' or 'non-enforceable' rights, in contrast to civil and political rights (Belder and Porsdam, 2017: 2–4). This is because the former are generally expressed in aspirational language and immediate enforcement is not expected in their case. Limitation of the enforcement of economic, social and cultural rights is often justified by states. With the first two, the reason is often that courts have only limited time and resources to investigate such cases, and there is a concern that judicial enforcement of these rights would challenge the separation of powers. However, in the context of cultural rights, the fear is not that courts would assume too much authority if they enforce these rights, but rather law would get frustrated by definitional vagueness. Moreover, as noted, it is not clear precisely what qualifies as culture in most states. Belder and Porsdam, in *Negotiating Cultural Rights*, highlight the legal complexity of protecting cultural rights:

> the protection of cultural rights is incomplete without the ethical imperative of the protection of cultural diversity. Respect, protection and promotion of cultural diversity being essential for ensuring the full respect of cultural rights means neither, however, that cultural diversity can be invoked to infringe upon or limit the scope of human rights guaranteed by international legal instruments, nor that all cultural practices are automatically condoned by these instruments. (Belder and Porsdam, 2017: 3–4)

Certain elements, such as shared history, language, literature, religion, and so on, are agreed upon, but this is not an exclusive or exhaustive list. Unless this definitional confusion is clarified, cultural rights will remain very difficult to enforce.

Conclusion

Cultural rights are an integral part of human rights. Universal and indivisible, they are an expression of human dignity. Since violations of cultural rights give rise to tensions and conflicts – one of the principal causes of violence, wars and terrorism globally – they require special protection. This is guaranteed by a large number of international human rights instruments and often through regional and domestic law as well. The list of cultural rights has an immensely broad, complicated and diverse base and includes rights such as to participate in cultural life, to education, to enjoy the arts and to share in scientific advancement and its benefits, to freedom of expression, to rest and leisure. Because of this, cultural rights are surrounded by a myriad of complexities and controversies. They derive from such issues as the definitional vagueness of both culture and cultural rights, the risk of cultural relativism, various political reasons that result in the neglect of cultural rights when compared to other human rights and the interface with basic human rights. There is also a justiciability concern with cultural rights, caused by general definitional confusion, which could lead to inconsistent judicial enforcement.

References
Bangkok Declaration, 2 April 1993. Available from: https://www. hurights.or.jp/archives/other_documents/section1/1993/04/ final-declaration-of-the-regional-meeting-for-asia-of-the-world-conference-on-human-rights.html
Barth, W. (2008) *On Cultural Rights: The Equality of Nations and the Minority Legal Tradition*, Boston: Brill Nijhoff.
Belder, L. and Porsdam, H. (eds) (2017) *Negotiating Cultural Rights*, Cheltenham: Edward Elgar.
Committee on Economic, Social and Cultural Rights (2006) *General Comment No 17: The Right of Everyone to Benefit from the Protection of the Moral and Material Interests Resulting from any Scientific, Literary or Artistic Production of which He or She is the Author*, 12 January 2006. Available from: www.refworld.org/docid/441543594.html

Committee on Economic, Social and Cultural Rights (2009) *General Comment No 21: Right of Everyone to Take Part in Cultural Life*, 21 December 2009. Available from: https://www.refworld.org/docid/4ed35bae2.html

Francioni, F. and Scheinin, M. (eds) (2008) *Cultural Human Rights*, Boston: Brill Nijhoff.

Jakubowski, A. (ed) (2016) *Cultural Rights as Collective Rights*, Boston: Brill Nijhoff.

Mende, J. (2016) *The Human Right to Culture and Identity*, London: Rowman and Littlefield.

Porsdam, H. (2019) *The Transforming Power of Cultural Rights*, Cambridge: Cambridge University Press.

Stamatopoulou, E. (2008) *Right to Take Part in Cultural Life*, 9 May 2008. Available from: http://humanrightscolumbia.org/sites/default/files/pdf/stamatopoulou_ecescr.pdf

Cultural Human Rights Instruments

Convention on the Rights of the Child, 2 September 1990.

Declaration on the Elimination of Violence Against Women, 20 December 1993.

Declaration on the Rights of Persons Belonging to National or Ethnic, Religious and Linguistic Minorities, 3 February 1993.

Final Act of the International Conference on Human Rights, 13 May 1968.

Fribourg Declaration, 18 March 2007.

Indigenous and Tribal Peoples Convention, 5 September 1991.

International Convention on the Protection and Promotion of the Diversity of Cultural Expressions, 18 December 1990.

International Convention on the Protection of the Rights of All Migrant Workers and Members of Their Families, 1 July 2003.

International Covenant on Civil and Political Rights, 19 December 1966.

International Covenant on Economic, Social and Cultural Rights, 16 December 1966.

The Right to Enjoy the Benefits of Scientific Progress and its Applications, 17 July 2009.

Universal Declaration of Human Rights, 10 December 1948.

World Declaration on Education for All, 9 March 1990.

10

Migration and refugees: applying human rights to 'everyone'?

Michal Cenker and Daniel Holder

By definition 'human' rights apply to 'everyone'. In practice, despite the post-World War II consensus on the universality of rights, there has been significant variance of state practice from this principle, with increasingly differentiated restrictions on migrants as rights holders. This is itself reflected in the United Nations (UN) Migrant Worker Convention, sitting alone among the core UN human rights treaties in having a low rate of ratification, and having been largely shunned by migrant-receiving states. Original provisions of other core UN treaties, including the International Convention on the Elimination of All Forms of Racial Discrimination (ICERD), permitted differentiations between citizens and non-citizens. While the evolving interpretation of the ICERD has led to this not extending to discrimination, the international human rights system is clearly a long way from affording effective protection to people who are not citizens of a state. Into this context came the global financial crisis, the forced migration of millions of refugees from areas at war (such as Syria and Myanmar), and the rise of 'populist' ethnocentric governments challenging basic human rights protections for migrants and refugees. A major tendency of such movements has been the fuelling of anti-migrant and refugee racism, even in places such as Hungary where there is little migration (Guild, 2018: 661–663). The impact of such practices is manifest not so much in amending migrant flows dependent on other factors, but in a further squeeze on the rights of migrants and refugees, and the dismantling of existing standards. In 2016 the UN General Assembly adopted the New York Declaration for Refugees and Migrants, from which, in 2018, flowed separate Global Compacts on Migration which reiterated undertakings on the human rights of migrants. All in all there has been little practical strengthening of effective rights protections. This chapter will outline these developments and seek to highlight the distance yet to travel for human rights to effectively apply to 'everyone' who is human.

Migration: regional changes, global connections

The movement of people is a global issue, yet given the hyperbole that can often surround the subject it is worth noting that the vast majority of the world's population goes nowhere. Only a few per cent of the global population are international migrants. Of the 7 billion-plus global population there were an estimated 258 million international migrants in 2017 (of which 146 million were in the Global North and 97 million in the Global South).[1] In the Global North migrants constitute 11.6 per cent of the total population, whereas in the Global South it is only 1.6 per cent (UNDESA, 2017). However, migrants from the Global South tend to stay in the Global South more than they migrate to the Global North and, more recently, in contrast to past trends, it is the Global South where migration rates are increasing. The most significant increases in the last two decades have been on the Asia–Asia and Africa–Africa axes. Higher levels of migration are found in the hundreds of millions of people migrating within their own countries of origin. Put together, it is estimated that there are approximately a billion migrants, which accounts for almost one in every seven people globally (UNDESA, 2015).

Migration takes place due to numerous push and pull factors, which can range from social (family reunification), employment and education reasons to persons seeking to escape conflict or persecution. Recent migration trends have been further influenced by the increased globalisation of markets, global inequalities, uneven development, economic and environmental crises, climate change, and the instability and wars of the twenty-first century. While detailed examination is beyond the scope of this chapter, there are a range of significant benefits from migration flows with tremendous potential to improve the livelihoods of migrants and the societies that surround them. In addition to stemming demographic time-bombs in places such as Europe where there are shrinking populations, there are also significant economic benefits in redressing skills and labour shortages (KNOMAD, 2018). Migrant remittances are also a major source of income in countries of origin.[2]

A failure to ensure respect of human rights can lead to significant misery. Migrants and refugees can be victims of arbitrary detention, family separation, trafficking and racial discrimination. They are vulnerable to a denial of social protection and other core civil rights, as well as labour exploitation and modern slavery (with broader implications for working conditions for which migrants themselves can be scapegoated). The next section will explore how international human rights law has related to the rights of international migrants.

Migrant rights as human rights

The principles of the post–World War II human rights framework were embodied in the Universal Declaration of Human Rights (UDHR) proclaimed by the UN General Assembly on 10 December 1948. Article 1 of the UDHR provides that: 'All human beings are born free and equal in dignity and rights'. Article 2 opens with: 'Everyone is entitled to all the rights and freedoms set forth in this Declaration, without distinction of any kind', before a range of substantive rights are listed as applying to 'everyone'. Rights to political participation are a rare exception, being limited to persons in their 'own country'.

The UDHR was followed by legally binding treaties to take forward its provisions, this includes the two UN Covenants – on civil and political rights (ICCPR) and economic, social and cultural rights (ICESCR) respectively – that were adopted in 1966 and entered into force in 1976. Alongside this, adopted in 1965, and entering into force in 1969, was the UN International Convention on the Elimination of All Forms of Racial Discrimination (ICERD). While ICERD has obvious relevance for the rights of migrants, its opening article – setting out its scope – provides that it does not apply to differentials between citizens and non-citizens. The first subsection of Article 1 ICERD defines racial discrimination as encompassing 'any distinction, exclusion, restriction or preference based on race, colour, descent, or national or ethnic origin' that impacts on equality of exercise of human rights. This is then qualified as follows: '[ICERD] shall not apply to distinctions, exclusions, restrictions or preferences made by a State Party to this Convention between citizens and non-citizens' (Article 1(2)). A further qualification sets out that the ICERD does not apply to a state's citizenship law provided that such law does not discriminate against any particular nationality.[3] Many of the human rights provided for in ICERD are also to be found in other core instruments, including the two UN Covenants, without such an explicit restriction.[4]

The scope of rights in UN instruments are subject to evolving interpretations from the expert treaty bodies appointed to monitor their compliance, that, among other mechanisms, issue general comments or recommendations clarifying their scope. In 2005 the ICERD Committee adopted such a general recommendation clarifying the scope of ICERD in relation to non-citizens. This states that Article 1(2): 'must be construed so as to avoid undermining the basic prohibition of discrimination' and not be 'interpreted to detract in any way from the rights and freedoms recognized and enunciated in particular in the' UDHR, ICESCR and ICCPR. It also holds that under ICERD:

> differential treatment based on citizenship or immigration status will constitute discrimination if the criteria for such differentiation, judged in the light of the objectives and purposes of [ICERD], are not applied pursuant to a legitimate aim, and are not proportional to the achievement of this aim.[5]

In summary, under ICERD, while some differential treatment may be allowed between citizens and non-citizens, 'discrimination' (distinctions which are unfair, unjustifiable or arbitrary) is not, nor is their limitation on human rights that are enshrined in other instruments.

One of the most significant Conventions from the UDHR era is the UN 1951 Convention Relating to the Status of Refugees, which defines a refugee as a person who:

> owing to well-founded fear of being persecuted for reasons of race, religion, nationality, membership of a particular social group or political opinion, is outside the country of his nationality and is unable or, owing to such fear, is unwilling to avail himself of the protection of that country; or who, not having a nationality and being outside the country of his former habitual residence as a result of such events, is unable or, owing to such fear, is unwilling to return to it. (UNHCR, 2010)

The 1951 Convention was largely limited to European refugees in the aftermath of World War II. Its scope was expanded by a 1967 Protocol that removed geographical and time limits. The core principle of this Convention is 'non-refoulement', that a refugee should not be returned to a country where they will not be safe. This principle has become a rule of customary international law. The Refugee Convention does not cover other migrants who may not meet the definition of refugee but are 'in vulnerable situations'. In 2018, the Global Migration Group (GMG), together with the Office of the United Nations High Commissioner for Human Rights prepared the document *Principles and Guidelines* which defines the 'migrant in vulnerable situations' in broad terms as someone who is 'unable effectively to enjoy his or her human rights and who accordingly is entitled to call on a duty-bearer's heightened duty of care' (GMG, 2018: 5). Causes which generate vulnerability may happen in the country of origin before departure, in the country of destination after arrival, during migration in transit, and may also be associated with migrants themselves, for example, with their ethnicity, religion, sexual orientation, and so on.

Other instruments from the same era as the UDHR include the International Labour Organization Migration for Employment Convention of 1949. Revised from a 1939 predecessor, this Convention includes provisions to prevent less favourable treatment and discrimination against migrants in a range of matters, including wages and working conditions, social security, taxation and trade union membership. However, this is restricted to 'immigrants lawfully within [a state party's] territory'.[6] It was 1990 before a core UN human rights treaty specifically dealt with the rights of migrant workers. This treaty – the International Convention on the Protection of the Rights of All Migrant Workers and Members of Their Families was to become the seventh core UN Human Rights instrument. The Convention contains rights which apply to all migrant workers, including those in an irregular situation, and differentiates further rights for migrants in a regular situation. However, the Migrant Worker Convention has, uniquely among such instruments, not received widespread global ratification, with only 54 contracting states (as of May 2019). All other core UN human rights treaties have over 150 state parties – notably, no 'Western' migrant-receiving country has ratified the Migrant Worker Convention.

The divergence of state practice, even from the present human rights standards, has become increasingly apparent in relation to recent migration flows. This includes the practice in Western countries in relation to migration flows that are a direct consequence of conflicts in the Middle East and North Africa, despite Western countries' roles as protagonists in these conflicts. Such practices are further outlined in the next section.

Migrant ill-treatment at state level

2015 bore witness to the horrific mass drownings in the Mediterranean of thousands of people. Within the context of the Arab Spring, the disintegration of Iraq and Libya, wars in Syria, Congo and Sudan, and other crises, there were 66 million forcibly displaced persons worldwide with a significant rise due to the war in Syria. Eighty-four per cent of the world's refugees live in developing countries (Panizzon and van Riemsdijk, 2019). While the majority of migration flows are entirely different to such patterns and consist of regular labour migration, such flows have led to changes in policy – much of it detrimental.

Hungary, a country with little inward migration, decided to limit to a minimum the entry of migrants in 2018, mostly Syrians seeking international refuge, by allowing only one single person per day to apply for asylum in transit zones between Serbia and Hungary. Given that there are two such transit zones, in Röszke and Tompa, by July Hungary was only accepting two asylum applications per day from migrants traversing the Balkans to Hungary by land (UNHCR, 2018). Before this decision, most migrants had already waited in the camps at the borders for up to 12 months to claim asylum. With the new regulation in place, it became practically impossible for thousands of people on the Serbian–Hungarian border to claim asylum, even though non-governmental organisations (NGOs) warned that it would increase human trafficking and criminal activities in the region. Earlier, the Hungarian government had adopted a law on the so called '8-kilometre rule', which allowed Hungarian police to apprehend migrants within an 8-kilometre zone along the borders with Croatia and Serbia to 'push them back' to the external side of the Hungarian border fence without allowing migrants to submit asylum claims. This law was passed despite being contrary to international law and violating the rights of migrants as recognised in international treaties (The Hungarian Helsinki Committee, 2016). The Hungarian authorities went as far as using starvation as a 'deterrent', refusing food to some asylum seekers in their border detention camps and prompting intervention from the European Court of Human Rights (Reuters, 2018).

Evidence of horrendous experiences for migrants came to light, for example, in Libya in 2017, with women facing a particularly hazardous route with the dual threat of violence and sexual exploitation. According to a report of the Panel of Experts on Libya, presented to the Security Council of the United Nations, the Libyan Department to Counter Illegal Migration, as well as the coastguard, were directly involved in 'grave human rights violations' (UN, 2017: 21). While the response of states such as Hungary and Slovakia, which have 'decoupled' from EU relocation quotas,[7] may sit outside the EU framework, the response of the EU itself in agreements with non-EU states violates the core principle of non-refoulement by returning refugees to war zones and countries of persecution. According to Webber, the EU's response to refugee flows has involved:

> entering into dubious agreements with countries outside the EU. Using bribery (aid, promises of investment, even the prospect of membership of the EU) and blackmail (threats of withdrawal of support for educational and health programmes), the EU has inveigled and browbeaten countries around the Mediterranean and as far afield as sub-Saharan Africa, to undertake immigration controls on its behalf. This has involved the EU in agreements with repressive regimes such as Turkey, Sudan and Eritrea, designed to block the movements of millions of people in the Middle East and Africa necessitated by war, climate change and religious conflict. (Weber, 2017: 36)

The rise of hard right and populist movements and administrations, which nurture and exploit anti-migrant racism, and the co-opting of migration control agendas by many mainstream parties, has formed the background music to such policy developments. In addition to Hungary, there has been the issue of building 'border walls' by Presidents Trump and Bolsonaro in the Americas; the racist treatment of new migrants and refugees in Israel (Beaumont, 2018; Lior, 2018); the 2016 pan-European 'Exit' mobilisation; and the 'hostile environment' policies of the UK government. All represent just some examples of this policy swing. The UK 'hostile environment' (a series of policies involving denial of essential services including healthcare, freezing monies in bank accounts and bestowing immigration control functions on a range of private and public sector actors) was intentionally designed to make lives so difficult for migrants with a perceived irregular status as to compel people to voluntarily leave the country. Such practices form part of a pattern of social policy changes designed to directly restrict the rights of migrants. A systematic analysis by Ludz (covering 1990–2014) of the direct and indirect effect of 'radical right anti-immigration parties' on migration policy reforms in 17 Western European states, comments that: 'anti-immigrant mobilisation is more likely to influence immigrants' rights than their actual numbers' (Lutz, 2019: 517–544). This is by virtue of the radical right in government office enacting more restrictions on integration policies. The changes have even affected more liberal regions. A study by Hernes of integration policies in Scandinavian countries after the 'refugee crisis' of 2015 found all three states taking more restrictive steps in areas such as permanent residence, citizenship, family reunification and access to social benefits, and explicitly adapted policies relative to the other countries (Hernes, 2018: 1305–1329).

The 2016 UN Declaration and 2018 compacts

This final section will examine key developments at UN standard-setting level in response to the above events and is centred around the September 2016 UN High-level Meeting on Addressing Large Movements of Refugees and Migrants. It was considered 'the most high-profile plenary meeting to take place on human movements at the United Nations' (IOM, 2018: 125), a 'historic opportunity … a watershed moment' (UN, 2018). As well as institutional changes, including the formal entry of the IOM into the UN system, the main output of the summit was the New York Declaration for Refugees and Migrants. The Declaration provides a framework for furthering international cooperation in the area, and it called for and eventually led to the adoption of two global compacts by the end of 2018, one on migration and the other on refugees.

There was initial resistance from some European states to this UN summit, not wishing for it to focus only on the Mediterranean and EU measures (Thouez, 2019: 1242–1257). A critique by Elspeth Guild (2018) of the Migration Compact notes 30 references to human rights in the New York Declaration and 45 in the Migration Compact, with its preamble referencing the UDHR, ICCPR, ICESCR and other core human rights treaties as well as other international obligations, including the UN Sustainable Development Goals (SDGs). However, Guild contends that despite this reaffirmation of commitments, many of the key ICCPR rights relied upon by migrants (rights to liberty, private and family life, regarding expulsion) are not specifically referred to in the Migration Compact, which only contains 'vague references'. Guild also highlights a change in language from the UN SDG 10.7 of the 2030 agenda on facilitating 'orderly, safe, regular and responsible migration' with the Compact dropping the commitment of state 'responsibility', noting that: 'States only act responsibly where they act in a manner consistent with human rights law. This includes non-discrimination between citizens and migrants'. Guild concludes that: 'The Migration Compact provides a new undertaking by States to uphold the human rights of migrants. However, this needs to be strengthened by an enhanced commitment to eliminating discrimination between citizens and migrants, and between different categories of migrants' (Guild, 2018: 663).

Conclusion

The whole concept of human rights rests on humanity and not citizenship. The early development of post-World War II human rights standards distinguished 'everyone' as rights holders with qualifications on the rights of non-citizens. In particular, differentials and discrimination on the basis of citizenship and immigration status had been narrowed. At the same time, the UN Migrant Worker Convention remained the only core UN human rights instrument not to receive widespread ratification in light of wealthier migrant-receiving countries declining to become state parties. In many instances state practice has significantly diverged from such standards and in recent years there have been further flagrant examples of refugee and migrant policy approaches that directly violate even the most embedded of human rights principles. In response to the migrant crisis of 2016 a fresh UN declaration and global compacts on both migrants and refugees have been produced reiterating rights-based standards. However, in the absence of any enhanced commitments to eliminating discrimination based on citizenship or immigration status, we remain a long way off such rights applying to 'everyone'.

Notes

[1] 'International migrant' is defined as a person that is foreign-born or is a foreign citizen – depending on a country's residence laws. International migrant stock – the total international migrant population referred to in this chapter – is the sum of all people that were either considered legally as foreign citizens or were born outside of the country in which they were residing.

[2] According to World Bank estimates, in 2017, US$466 billion in remittances were sent to low- and middle-income countries (KNOMAD, 2018), which is more than three times the amount of official development assistance as measured by the Development Assistance Committee of the OECD (OECD, 2017). Sending costs are, however, very high – on average 7.1 per cent of remittances in the first quarter of 2018 (WB BRIEF, based on transfer $200), rising to 9.4 per cent for Sub-Saharan Africa, despite a UN Sustainable Development Goal target to reduce costs to less than 3 per cent by 2030 (UN, 2015: target 10c).

[3] Article 1(3) ICERD.

[4] Article 2(3) ICESCR, however, does allow developing countries only to restrict the economic rights recognised in ICESCR to non-nationals.

[5] CERD General Recommendation XXX on discrimination against non-citizens, paragraphs 2 and 4.

[6] C097 – Migration for Employment Convention (Revised), 1949 (No 97), Article 6.

⁷ *Slovak Republic and Hungary v Council of the European Union*, C-643/15 and C-647/ 15 (Panizzon and van Riemsdijk, 2019: 8).

References

Beaumont, Peter (2018) 'Netanyahu asks if African "infiltrators" can be forcibly removed from Israel', *The Guardian*, 3 January. Available from: www.theguardian.com/world/2018/jan/03/benjamin-netanyahu-asks-if-african-migrants-can-be-forcibly-removed-from-israel

GMG (2018) 'Principles and guidelines, supported by practical guidance, on the human rights protection of migrants in vulnerable situations'. Available from: www.ohchr.org/EN/Issues/Migration/Pages/VulnerableSituations.aspx

Guild, E. (2018) 'The UN global compact for safe, orderly and regular migration: what place for human rights?', *International Journal of Refugee Law*, 30(4): 661–663. Available from: https://doi.org/10.1093/ijrl/eey049

Hernes, V. (2018) 'Cross-national convergence in times of crisis? Integration policies before, during and after the refugee crisis', *West European Politics*, 41(6): 1305–1329.

IOM (2018) *World Migration Report 2018*, Geneva: IOM.

KNOMAD (2018) 'Migration and remittances: recent developments and outlook', *Migration and Development Brief*, 29 April. Available from: www.knomad.org/sites/default/files/2018-04/Migration%20and%20Development%20Brief%2029.pdf

Lior, I. (2018) 'Asylum seekers struggle to make ends meet after Israel enforces cash deposit', *Haaretz*, 1 December. Available from: www.haaretz.com/israel-news/.premium-asylum-seekers-struggle-to-make-ends-meet-after-israel-enforces-cash-deposit-1.5627452

Lutz, P. (2019) 'Variation in policy success: radical right populism and migration policy', *West European Politics*, 42(3): 517–544.

OECD (2017) 'Development co-operation report 2017', Paris: OECD Publishing. Available from: www.oecd.org/dac/development-co-operation-report-20747721.htm

Panizzon, M. and Van Riemsdijk, M. (2019) 'Introduction to special issue: migration governance in an era of large movements: a multi-level approach', *Journal of Ethnic and Migration Studies*, 45. Available from: https://doi.org/10.1080/1369183X.2018.1441600

Reuters (2018) 'European rights court says Hungary must feed asylum seekers on border', 23 August.

The Hungarian Helsinki Committee (2016) 'Hungary: access denied'. Available from: www.helsinki.hu/en/hungary-access-denied/

Thouez, C. (2019) 'Strengthening migration governance', *Journal of Ethnic and Migration Studies*, 45(8): 1242–1257.

UN (2015) 'Resolution adopted by the General Assembly on 25 September. 7/1. Transforming our world: the 2030 Agenda for Sustainable Development', A/RES/70/1. Available from: http://www.un.org/ga/search/view_doc.asp?symbol=A/RES/70/1andLang=E.

UN (2017) 'Final report of the Panel of Experts on Libya established pursuant to Resolution 1973 (2011)', S/2017/466, 1 June. Available from: www.un.org/sc/suborg/en/sanctions/1970/panel-experts/reports

UN (2018) 'UN summit for refugees and migrants 2016'. Available from: https://refugeesmigrants.un.org/summit

UNDESA (2015) 'Trends in international migrant stock: the 2015 revision. United Nations database', POP/DB/MIG/Stock/Rev.2015. Available from: www.un.org/en/development/desa/population/migration/data/estimates2/docs/MigrationStockDocumentation_2015.pdf

UNDESA (2017) 'International migration report 2017'. Available from: www.un.org/development/desa/publications/international-migration-report-2017.html

UNHCR (2010) 'Convention and protocol relating to the status of refugees'. Available from: www.unhcr.org/3b66c2aa10.pdf

UNHCR (2018) 'Hungary: UNHCR dismayed over further border restrictions and draft law targeting NGOs working with asylum-seekers and refugees', Press Release, 16 February. Available from: www.unhcr.org/news/press/2018/2/5a86dcff4/hungary-unhcr-dismayed-further-border-restrictions-draft-law-targeting.html

Webber, F. (2017) 'Europe's unknown war', *Race and Class*, 59(1): 36–53. Available from: https://doi.org/10.1177/0306396817701657

11

Conflict, 'terrorism' and non-state actors

Féilim Ó hAdhmaill and Mike Ritchie

One obstacle in the realisation of universal human rights in the world today is the continuing existence of armed conflict. It directly impinges on the most fundamental of rights – the right to life – as well as a host of others: for example, the right to family life, employment, housing, education, health, security, privacy, travel, and so on. While international human rights law (IHRL) is supposed to operate at all times, the reality is that during armed conflict it is often suspended/derogated from, or is simply inoperable in practice.

International humanitarian law (IHL), embodied in the main in the 1949 Geneva Conventions, is supposed to provide protections to civilians and captured or wounded combatants during wartime and, indeed, regulate war to make it more 'humane'. However, enforcement may be limited by ambiguity or lack of knowledge about IHL, ambiguity about the distinction between non-combatants and combatants, troop indiscipline, emotions (the politics of the last atrocity) and, especially where non-state forces are involved, the lack of infrastructure for holding captured enemy combatants. Violation of human rights may also be viewed as a necessary means to winning a conflict – bombing populations into submission or torturing captives for information (Amnesty, 2014, 2017; Cobain, 2012, 2016). This is all compounded by the fact that no state and few non-state groups want to admit that they, or their allies' combatants, violate human rights. This has had profound implications for the enforcement of IHRL/IHL.

The human rights mechanisms created since the end of World War II have also faced challenges from changing forms of armed conflict in the world. Most armed conflicts up until then had been between states. Since World War II the vast majority of conflicts have not been *directly* between states but have usually involved states and non-state actors (sometimes sponsored by or acting as surrogates for other states). Most wars have also been fought in the Global South: in Africa, Asia and Latin America, former colonies of Western European powers. Most conflicts have been influenced by colonialism, or the ongoing neo-colonial control of the resources and destinies of the vast majority of the population of the world by rich and powerful states, or by the geo-political interests of competing world powers. The vast majority of casualties (75–90 per cent) have been civilian, which is a change from earlier wars. Most casualties have occurred in developing countries and most war refugees have found themselves in other developing countries rather than in the rich countries of Western Europe or the United States. The major powers, nevertheless, remain deeply involved in conflicts in the world, either directly, or through the provision of funding, weaponry, political support, or through setting the conditions which lead to armed conflicts (Harbom and Wallensteen, 2009; Kaldor, 2013; Chinkin and Kaldor, 2017; Pettersson et al, 2019).

There have been conflicts in Europe of course. In Eastern Europe, the collapse of the Eastern bloc and the more independent Yugoslavia led to a series of different conflicts among the new emerging states. In Western Europe there have been a small number of low-intensity conflicts involving separatist nationalists (for example, the Basque conflict, 1959–2011; the Irish 'Troubles', 1956–62, 1968–98), or revolutionary Marxists (for example, Red Army Faction, West Germany, 1969–to 1980s; Red Brigades, Italy, 1970 to 1980s). There have also been sporadic isolated attacks by Islamist, neo-Nazi and other groups which have affected both the Global North and South.

One of the main challenges posed for human rights by such conflicts involving non-state actors is that, on the one hand, most are not recognised at the time as 'wars' but referred to as 'emergencies' or 'terrorism' and consequently IHL does not apply, while on the other, IHRL is often derogated from due to the 'emergency'. The Geneva Conventions (1949) were designed by and for states and ratified by them, not non-state forces. Common Article 3 of the Conventions requires all armed forces (state and non-state) to abide by the Conventions regarding protecting non-combatants. However, it does not bestow rights to be treated as 'soldiers' – and prisoners of war (POWs) if captured – on non-state forces. In an attempt to address some of these difficulties two additional optional protocols to the Conventions were introduced in 1977 allowing non-state forces to be recognised as engaging in a 'war' under certain conditions. The Protocols emerged after demands from new states that their struggles for independence (branded 'terrorist' at the time) be recognised as legitimate by the UN. In 1965 the UN Assembly had already adopted resolution 2105 (XX), which in paragraph 10: 'recognizes the legitimacy of the struggle waged by peoples under colonial domination to exercise their right to self-determination and independence' (UNGA RES, (XX) para 10, 2015).

Optional Protocol 1 provides for the recognition of 'wars of national liberation', or against 'racism', as 'wars' (or 'international conflicts') and allows for captured non-state combatants to be treated as POWs. Optional Protocol 2 recognises 'wars' where non-state forces have control over some national territory, although captured combatants are not guaranteed POW status and can be placed on trial (ICRC, nd). In theory, this might seem to include the conflict in Colombia where the FARC held 'liberated' territory, the establishment of 'Islamic State' (IS or Daesh) or the 'liberated' areas of Syria or Libya. However, it is up to the state on whose territory the conflict is taking place, or the United Nations Security Council (UNSC), to make the decision about whether the conflict should be given the status of 'war' and thus whether the protocols should come into force. In practice, few states will accept that they are racist or are denying 'national liberation' or that the armed group occupying part of their territory is anything other than 'terrorist' or 'criminal'. The UNSC will only intervene if the five permanent members (USA, Russia, China, UK and France) with a veto all agree – and that is highly dependent on geo-political concerns. In the Syrian conflict from 2011 on, for example, the only unanimity on the UNSC was that IS was a 'terrorist' organisation with no rights under IHL. Russia continually vetoed UN intervention against the Assad government, militarily supporting it against what it claimed was 'terrorism', while the Western powers armed, trained and financed a number of what they viewed as 'legitimate' liberation forces fighting against Assad.

Geo-political divisions in the UNSC have also been reflected in the Israel/Palestine conflict. The vast majority of UN states agree that IHL should apply in relation to the territories occupied by Israel since 1967, including a responsibility on the occupying power to provide for the welfare of the people and not to build settlements. Likewise, Palestinian resistance to the Occupation is not regarded as 'terrorism' as long as civilians are not deliberately being targeted; something which both Palestinian and Israeli forces have done throughout this conflict (Bt'selem, nd a; nd b). However, Israel, supported by the US, regards Palestinian resistance as 'terrorism' and rejects the notion that IHL should apply. Furthermore, the US has continually vetoed UNSC resolutions aimed at challenging alleged Israeli violations of IHL in relation to the stateless Palestinians.

One other problem with the 1977 protocols is that they tend to favour larger, more powerful non-state forces that can occupy land, have the security and funds to provide uniforms for their soldiers, and provide for POWs. The protocols, like the Geneva Conventions, require armed forces to distinguish themselves from the civilian populations by wearing uniforms during combat. Such protocols would have, for example, ruled out recognition of the French Resistance during World War II as being engaged in a 'war of liberation', and indeed many anti-colonial struggles, from Ireland to Algeria or Palestine. One important question is: when a conflict is not recognised as a 'war' where does that leave human rights mechanisms? What happens if IHL is not recognised as operating and IHRL is suspended due to 'the Emergency'? This is the dilemma facing human rights in a world where most conflicts involve non-state forces who are usually labelled 'terrorist' by their state opponents.

Colonialism and the Cold War

When the United Nations (UN) was established in 1945, only 51 nation-states were members; today there are 193 member states. Almost a third of the world's population (750 million people in 1945) lived in territories that were not self-governing, dependent on and subjugated by colonial powers. Since the creation of the UN more than 80 former colonies have gained independence (UN, nd). Most countries in the world have been invaded and occupied at some stage in their history. Fisher (2015) produced a map for Vox Media suggesting that only five currently recognised UN states managed to avoid European control/ invasion during their history – Liberia, Ethiopia, Japan, Korea and Thailand (though the last two were colonised by Japan and there is dispute about both Liberia and Ethiopia (Office of the Historian, nd)). Laycock (2012) details how Britain had invaded or fought conflicts in the territory of 171 out of the 193 current UN member states. Only 22 were not invaded.

During colonial periods, colonial powers exploited natural and human resources and promoted trade inequalities to enrich themselves (Tharoor, 2017). Power was often established and maintained by the divide and rule of native peoples, encouraging pre-existing or promoting new inter-group conflict, favouring one set of people over another, or supporting local elites. In much of Africa, the Middle East, India, Pakistan and indeed Ireland, ethnic/religious inter-group animosity/conflict was reinforced and reproduced, to be played out into the future in the form of racism or sectarianism, and ultimately armed inter-group conflict. A doctrine of racial/ethnic social Darwinism, bringing 'civilisation' or religion to the natives, justified colonial rule by promoting notions of the superiority of the colonists and the inferiority of the natives. Not only did this set colonist against native but laid the seeds for continuing animosities amongst their descendants. It created a psychological and cultural context as future generations absorbed notions of superiority and inferiority, lowering the expectations of native peoples, promoting dependency and subservience, while promoting expectations of entitlements to privilege among others. It also created a discourse of 'the West versus the Rest' and thus negatively impacted on personal and national development, and ultimately global peace (Fanon, 1967; Memmi, 1974; Said, 1978). As the Indian independence leader Mahatma Ghandi once said when asked by a journalist what he thought about Western civilisation: 'I think it would be a good idea!'

Colonialism also led to the drawing of borders, partition and the systematic separation of peoples, reflecting competing imperialist interests not local ethnic and religious divisions. In 1884–85, the Berlin Conference of imperial powers agreed spheres of influence in Africa. As a result, the borders of African states today were drawn by European colonial powers – paying no attention to ethnic, linguistic or religious groups, or existing political organisation during colonisation (Shah, 2010). Since 1970 more than 30 wars have been fought across Africa, the vast majority of them intra-state in origin and resulting in millions of deaths, refugees and continuing instability in many areas. In 2016 Africa continued to have the highest number of conflicts in the world with 19 active conflicts (SIPRI, 2017).

A similar carve-up of much of the Middle East took place with the fall of the Ottoman Empire after World War I. The roots of much of the conflict in Iraq, Syria, Yemen, Lebanon and Israel/Palestine stem from such actions – providing some understanding of the ongoing antipathy felt by many in that region towards the West. Such antipathy was of course further promoted by continuing interference in the region by Western powers since World War II. After 1945, it became more difficult for Western powers to control colonies; colonial imposition appeared to contradict the UN Declaration of Human Rights (1948) for example. However, there was reluctance to give up lucrative colonies and the control of resources or trade, leading to numerous 'wars of liberation' which were invariably termed 'terrorism' by the West before self-determination was achieved in many states. The resolution of such conflicts also often led to further 'internal' conflicts. One reason was the legacy of colonialism; another was the advent of neo-colonialism. Former colonial powers often ensured their economic/political interests, and/or the control of natural resources and trade were maintained by installing and supporting 'friendly' dictators, or cooperative ruling elites. This in turn promoted a legacy of poverty, inequality, grievance, division, dependency, corruption and instability in the new states. Colonialism mutated into neo-colonialism – continuing exploitation through the manipulation of trade, political threats and armed aggression by colonial powers when deemed necessary.

With the onset of the Cold War the geo-political needs of the US, USSR and their allies also became more important. Both sides supported rival groups in conflict zones rather than engaging in direct combat against each other – which in a nuclear age could have been globally fatal. Since the Western powers had had a head start in global control, the Eastern bloc tended to support the non-state opponents of leaders supportive of the West. Peoples in these generally grossly undemocratic states in Africa, Asia, or Latin America, tended to see the 'enemy' as Western interfering powers and looked around for an ideology of liberation. Many found it (as well as Eastern bloc funding, training, arming and political support) in Marxism. Up until the mid-1980s, for example, the vast majority of 'liberation struggles' in Africa, Asia, Latin America and the Middle East were influenced by 'leftist' ideology (for example, the African National Congress (ANC), the Palestinian Liberation Organization (PLO) and the National Liberation Front (NLF) in Vietnam).

The fall of the Eastern bloc meant that many had to look around for a new ideology of liberation. In Islamic countries some returned to the traditional beliefs of Islam and a redrafted version of Islamic Jihad promoted by al-Qaeda, IS, and so on. It was a world view that was not secular or capable of being inclusive and which promoted attacks on 'infidel' civilians rather than global capitalism. The rise of right-wing ethnic populism in the USA and Europe in the aftermath of the recession in 2008–10 (similar to the 1930s) may well be another example of people searching for their own ideology of liberation through Trump (US), Orbán (Hungary), Salvini (Italy) or Le Pen (France).

Throughout the twentieth and twenty-first centuries, the big powers also engaged in direct military intervention in other countries to further their own interests, promote regime change or prevent it when it suited them. For example, historian William Blum listed more than 40 countries bombed by the US (Blum, 2006) and 55 where the US attempted to overthrow foreign governments – succeeding in 34 of them – since the end of World War II (Blum, 2013). US foreign policy interventions included the support of right-wing dictatorships in Latin America and the CIA-orchestrated coup against the democratically elected socialist President Allende by General Pinochet, leading to the torture and execution of thousands of civilians in Chile in 1973. In 1953, a UK/

US-organised coup overthrew the nationalist secular government of Iran and installed the Shah as dictator. After 26 years of dictatorship, supported by Western powers, the Shah was overthrown in the revolution of 1979 and an Islamic republic proclaimed which, probably not surprisingly, continues to be suspicious of and hostile to the West. Blumenthal (2018) listed more than 20 different countries where the US engaged in wars, bombings, detentions and troop deployments since 9/11 in 2001 including Iraq, Afghanistan and Syria. Indeed, Global Research (2015) published evidence showing that the US had been at war 93 per cent of the time since independence in 1776 – 222 out of 239 years.

The role of the big powers is particularly evident in the global arms trade which provides weaponry to fuel conflict involving both state and non-state forces. Between 2003 and 2007, approximately 79 per cent of the exports of major conventional weapons was provided by suppliers from five countries: the US, Russia, Germany, France and the UK. From 2012 to 2016 the US (33 per cent) and Russia (23 per cent) exported approximately half of the world's weapons. In 2014–18, arms transfers were 7.8 per cent higher than in 2009–13, with the USA increasing its dominance, with more than 52 per cent of its exports going to the Middle East. The five largest exporters in 2014–18 were the United States, Russia, France, Germany and China (the latter replacing the UK), accounting for 75 per cent of global arms exports. Thus, the five permanent members of the UN Security Council are the among the world's top six exporters of arms (SIPRI, 2019). Saudi Arabia is the biggest customer of US and UK weapons. In recent years it has been involved in a conflict in Yemen against non-state forces using that weaponry. The UN estimated the death toll in this conflict to be 102,000, with a combined death toll from conflict, disease and starvation of 233,000 up to the end of 2019 (Moyer et al, 2019).

Civilian casualties

Above all else, the vast majority of casualties in conflicts today are civilians. While there may be some academic argument about specific percentages, most analysts accept that between 70 and 90 per cent of deaths are civilians, compared with about 15 per cent during World War I. Indeed, some argue that more children are killed than soldiers in wars/conflicts today (AOAV, 2019a; Petterson and Wallensteen, 2015; UNICEF, nd; Jewell et al, 2018). Action on Armed Violence (AOAV) has been monitoring the harm caused by explosive weapons (which are responsible for most deaths in conflict today) since 2010. Its evidence suggests that in the years 2011–18, 75 per cent of all deaths caused by explosions were civilian, rising to 91 per cent in populated areas. A total of 133,732 people (82,437 civilians) were killed globally and 175,312 (149,472 civilians) injured. Improvised explosive devices (IEDs) (mainly non-state forces), which include so-called 'suicide' bombings, were responsible for over half (53 per cent) of all civilian casualties. Airstrikes (mainly state forces) were responsible for 23 per cent of all civilian deaths and missiles for 20 per cent. While a majority (119 out of 193) of states in the world had been affected by at least one death or injury, more than half of all civilian deaths took place in just two states – Syria and Iraq – and 96 per cent took place across 20 states – all of which were in Asia or Africa with the exceptions of Colombia and Russia (AOAV, 2019a). During the first six months of 2019, a further 12,902 deaths and injuries were by explosive weapons – 63 per cent civilians, rising to 92 per cent in populated areas (AOAV, 2019b).

There are a number of reasons for this. The nature of war has changed. In the past war usually took place at close quarters – soldiers could see their enemy. By the time armies were moved to the battlefield civilians often had a chance to escape. Now missiles, including the new weapon of choice – drones – can be launched in one country and hit another in minutes with more deadly effect. Aerial bombardment and the use of missile firing drones are now normal 'armaments' for large states. Soldiers/combatants are also much better trained, protected and prepared than civilians, enabling them to better avoid death or injury.

In November 2014, the human rights group Reprieve produced a report claiming that the USA attempts to kill 41 men with drones resulted in the deaths of an estimated 1,147 people up to that time. In the course of pursuing 24 men (of whom only six were killed) an estimated 142 children were killed by drone strikes. No one has ever been charged for war crimes in this regard (*The Guardian*, 2014). Military (and political) strategy often prioritises the lives of soldiers or the killing of a target or the taking of a city over the lives of civilians in the enemy's camp. Bombing towns and cities containing civilians may be viewed as a way of terrifying opponents into submission. Non-state forces, such as al-Qaeda and Islamic State, of course, also kill and often deliberately target civilians using IEDs as a modus operandi, killing 'unbelieving' civilians being central to their Jihad, a religious obligation.

'Terrorism'

While the term 'terrorism' has a long history, stretching back at least to the French revolution, it has really been in the period since World

War II and in particular since the 2001 9/11 al-Qaeda attacks in the USA, that it has come to dominate discourse on armed conflict (Townsend, 2002). But what is 'terrorism'? One of the problems for social science and indeed for international human rights is that there is no universally agreed definition. American historian Walter Laqueur (1988) counted over 100 definitions. What we have is a range of legal definitions which differ according to country and circumstance. In essence, in most states 'terrorism' relates to the 'illegal' use of armed conflict, usually by non-state forces to achieve certain ends. The ends and indeed the means associated with 'terrorism', may be defined differently in different states. For example, the UK Terrorism Act 2000 definition of 'terrorism' includes:

> (1) ... the use or threat of action ... designed to influence the government or to intimidate the public or a section of the public and ... made for the purpose of advancing a political, religious or ideological cause ... (a) involves serious violence against a person, (b) involves serious damage to property, (c) endangers a person's life, other than that of the person committing the action, (d) creates a serious risk to the health or safety of the public or a section of the public or (e) is designed seriously to interfere with or seriously to disrupt an electronic system.

Of course most of these actions relate to what any enemy would be attempting to do in a 'war'. It invokes the question again: when is a 'conflict' a 'war' and when is it a 'terrorist campaign'? And, of course, what is illegal at one point in time may become legal in another and vice versa. Thus, an insurgent group's struggle may be initially classified as 'terrorist' but if it eventually wins and forms the government it may be retrospectively regarded as national liberation. For example, most of those who fought against British rule from World War I onwards were regarded as 'terrorists' (by Britain) until they became governments themselves – in Ireland, Israel, Kenya, Cyprus, Aden (Yemen), and so on. Nelson Mandela, winner of the Nobel Peace Prize in 1993, was dubbed a 'terrorist' by Margaret Thatcher's UK government in the 1980s. Indeed, successive US governments kept him on a 'terrorist' watch-list until 2008, barring him from entering the United States (except the UN) without a special waiver from the US government because of his South African apartheid regime-era designation as 'terrorist'.

Different states may also have different views on whether a particular group is 'terrorist' or not. Thus, the USA regards Hezbollah (Lebanon) and Hamas (Gaza) as 'terrorist' even though they have won elections, are in government and are respected as 'freedom fighters' in their own and many other developing world states. The USA views the Kurds as 'freedom fighters' in Syria though not in Turkey, while they are viewed as 'terrorist' by Syria and Turkey. The USA of course has a long history of arming and training non-state forces to fight its enemies, from the Contras in Nicaragua to the Taliban and al-Qaeda.

> Bin Laden was, though, a product of a monumental miscalculation by western security agencies. Throughout the 80s he was armed by the CIA and funded by the Saudis to wage jihad against the Russian occupation of Afghanistan. (Robin Cook, Former British Minister for Foreign Affairs, in *The Guardian*, 2005)

'Terrorism' has come to mean what our enemies do and not what we or our allies do. It is thus a highly subjective term. Yet the notion of 'terrorism' still remains part of 'common sense' parlance in much of academia, despite challenges to this notion from some, such as Chomsky (2015) and Galtung (1987). Indeed, for Gearty (2002) the contemporary language on 'terrorism' has become:

> the rhetorical servant of the established order, whatever and however heinous its own activities are. Because the administration has cast terrorism and terrorists as always the evilest of evils, what the terrorist does is always wrong [and] what the counter-terrorist has to do to defeat them is therefore invariably, necessarily right. The nature of the [established] regime, the kind of action that is possible against it, the moral situation in which violence occurs – none of these complicating elements matters a jot against the contemporary power of the terrorist label. (Gearty, 2002: 36)

Thus the acceptance of 'common sense' notions of 'terrorism' potentially places academia firmly on the side of the status quo, the power elites in society.

In international human rights the highly subjective nature of the concept of 'terrorism' is highly problematic because it does not define particular forms of conduct which all should oppose as 'terrorist'.

Instead, it most often concentrates on defining who is carrying out the act. It might be argued from an IHRL/IHL perspective that a simple definition of 'terrorism', such as the deliberate targeting of civilians by *any* group, would be much more meaningful for the universal protection of human rights through the discouragement of such actions. It might make wars or conflicts more humane (if that in itself is not an oxymoron). Indeed, the illegality of such actions is already included in IHL though it does not appear to stop them, as can be seen from the high percentage of deaths of civilians in modern conflicts. Warring factions may argue that they do not *deliberately* target civilians – but what can be expected when bombs are dropped from planes or missiles fired into highly populated areas? It is also clear that military strategies based on 'shock and awe', as witnessed with the USA's bombing of Iraq in 1991, clearly include terrifying and demoralising the enemy's civilian population. Most warring states, however, are not prepared to accept such a simple definition of 'terrorism'. First, it may open the door to states themselves being accused of 'terrorism'; and second, it might legitimate the actions of an enemy which does not target civilians but property or political/military targets.

One further problem with 'terrorism' for international human rights is not only does IHL not apply, as states will not accept that the 'terrorists' are engaging in 'war', but IHRL is also often suspended to cope with the emergency. This in turn may lead to emergency measures which curtail not just the rights of the 'terrorist' but those of the rest of society – since all may be suspect. Routine mass surveillance of whole populations, both *covert*, such as that revealed by Edward Snowdon and Wikileaks in 2013 in relation to Google searches, Facebook content; and *overt*, such as mass CCTV coverage, face recognition software at airports, or car registration recognition software on motorways, challenge the right to privacy. The 'profiling' of potential 'suspects', the use of artificial intelligence (AI) technology, stop and search, house raids and the encouragement of citizen informers via such programmes as the relatively recent UK Prevent measures, have their own inherent dangers of creating suspect and, indeed, alienated communities, as well as inadvertently promoting racism (Grierson and Dodd, 2019). Special measures, such as arrest and interrogation powers, extraordinary rendition, imprisonment without trial, special courts, special evidence rules, and execution, judicial or extrajudicial; curbs on the right to travel, on freedom of speech, on the media, on freedom of association and the banning of protests, all have the potential to fuel a conflict rather than reduce it, as legal forms of behaviour become illegal and innocents become suspects (CAJ, 2008).

The realisation of universal human rights in today's world is challenged by armed conflict, particularly armed conflict involving non-state forces. The ability to ignore or circumvent IHL and derogate from IHRL makes safeguarding rights difficult. However, at the very least the existence of IHL and IHRL can provide tools and benchmarks for NGOs and individuals to pursue the upholding of a minimum standard of rights, and to campaign and lobby for change into the future. As in so many other areas relating to universal human rights, rights during armed conflicts remain a site of struggle.

References

Amnesty (2014) *Amnesty International Launches Worldwide Campaign to Expose Global Crisis on Torture*, 12 May. Available from: www.amnestyusa.org/press-releases/amnesty-international-launches-worldwide-campaign-to-expose-global-crisis-on-torture/

Amnesty (2017) *USA: Guantanamo, Impunity and Global Anti-Torture Day*, 25 June. Available from: www.amnesty.org/en/documents/amr51/6574/2017/en/

AOAV (Action on Armed Violence) (2019a) *Eight Years of Global Explosive Violence Reviewed: 2011–2018*, Action on Armed Violence. Available from: https://aoav.org.uk/2019/8-year-overview/

AOAV (Action on Armed Violence) (2019b) *Six Months of Explosive Violence in 2019 Examined*, 5 July. Available from: https://aoav.org.uk/2019/6-month-update/

Blum, W. (2006) *Rogue State: A Guide to the World's Only Superpower*, London: Zed Books.

Blum, W. (2013) *America's Deadliest Export: Democracy. The Truth about US Foreign Policy and Everything Else*, London: Zed Books.

Blumenthal, P. (2018) 'Barbara Lee warned AUMF would create "open-ended war" and that's what happened', *Huffington Post*, 14 September. Available from: www.huffpost.com/entry/2001-aumf_n_5b9bc513e4b013b0977a1f83

BT'SELEM (nd a) The Israeli Information Center for Human Rights in the Occupied Territories Statistics. Available from: www.btselem.org/statistics

BT'SELEM (nd b) Attacks on Israeli Civilians by Palestinians. Available from: www.btselem.org/topic/israeli_civilians

CAJ (Committee on the Administration of Justice) (2008) *War on Terror: Lessons from NI*, Belfast: CAJ. Available from: https://caj.org.uk/2008/01/01/war-terror-lessons-northern-ireland/.

Chinkin, C. and Kaldor, M. (2017) *International Law and New Wars*, Cambridge: Cambridge University Press.

Chomsky, N. (2015) *The Culture of Terrorism*, London: Pluto Press.

Cobain, I. (2012) *Cruel Britannia: A Secret History of Torture*, London: Portobello Books.

Cobain, I. (2016) *The History Thieves: Secrets, Lies and the Shaping of a Modern Nation*, London: Portobello Books.

Fanon, F. (1967) *The Wretched of the Earth*, Harmondsworth: Penguin Books.

Fisher, M. (2015) *Map: European Colonialism Conquered Every Country in the World but these Five*, 24 February. Available from: www.vox. com/2014/6/24/5835320/map-in-the-whole-world-only-these-five-countries-escaped-european

Galtung, J. (1987) 'On the causes of terrorism and their removal', Essay. Available from: www.transcend.org/galtung/papers/On%20the%20 Causes%20of%20Terrorism%20and%20Their%20Removal.pdf

Gearty, C. (2002) 'Terrorism and morality', *RUSI Journal*, October: 34–39.

Global Research (2015) Washington's Blog, 20th February 2015, 'America Has Been at War 93% of the Time – 222 out of 239 Years – Since 1776', Montreal: The Centre for Research on Globalisation. Available from: https://www.globalresearch.ca/america-has-been-at-war-93-of-the-time-222-out-of-239-years-since-1776/5565946

Grierson J. and Dodd, V. (2019) 'Prevent strategy on radicalisation faces independent review', *The Guardian*, 22 January. Available from: www.theguardian.com/uk-news/2019/jan/22/prevent-strategy-on-radicalisation-faces-independent-review

The Guardian (2005) 'The struggle against terrorism cannot be won by military means', 8 July. Available from: www.guardian.co.uk/uk/2005/jul/08/july7.development

The Guardian (2014) '41 men targeted but 1,147 people killed: US drone strikes – the facts on the ground', 24 November. Available from: www.theguardian.com/us-news/2014/nov/24/-sp-us-drone-strikes-kill-1147

Harbom, L. and Wallensteen, P. (2009) 'Armed conflicts, 1946–2008', *Journal of Peace Research*, 461(4): 577–589.

ICRC (nd) *The Geneva Conventions and Their Additional Protocols*. Available from: www.icrc.org/en/war-and-law/treaties-customary-law/geneva-conventions

Jewell, N.P., Spagat, M. and Jewell, B.L. (2018) 'Accounting for civilian casualties: from the past to the future', *Social Science History*, 42: 379–410. Available from: https://doi.org/10.1017/ssh.2018.9

Kaldor, M. (2013) 'In defence of new wars', *Stability*, 2(1): 1–16. Available from: http://dx.doi.org/10.5334/sta.at

Laycock, S. (2012) *All the Countries We've Ever Invaded: And the Few We Never Got Round To*, Stroud: History Press.

Laqueur, W. (1988) *The Age of Terrorism*, Boston, MA: Little Brown.

Memmi, A. (1974) *The Colonizer and the Colonized*, London: Souvenir.

Moyer, J.D., Bohl, D., Hanna, T., Mapes, B.R., and Rafa, M. (2019) *Assessing the Impact of War on Development in Yemen*, Yemen: UN Development Programme. Available from: www.arabstates. undp.org/content/rbas/en/home/library/crisis-response0/ assessing-the-impact-of-war-on-development-in-yemen-.html

Office of the Historian (nd) *Founding of Liberia, 1847*. Available from: https://history.state.gov/milestones/1830-1860/liberia

Pettersson, T. and Wallensteen, P. (2015) 'Armed conflicts, 1946–2014', *Journal of Peace Research*, 52(4): 536–550.

Pettersson, T., Hogbladh, S. and Oberg, M. (2019) 'Organized violence, 1989–2018 and peace agreements', *Journal of Peace Research*, 56(4): 1–15.

Said, E. (1978) *Orientalism*, London: Pantheon Books.

Shah, A. (2010) *Conflict in Africa: Introduction, Global Issues*. Available from: http://www.globalissues.org/article/84/conflicts-in-africa-introduction

SIPRI (2017) *Stockholm International Peace Research Institute (SIPRI) Yearbook 2017*. Available from: www.sipri.org/sites/default/files/ 2017-09/yb17-summary-eng.pdf

SIPRI (2019) 'Global Arms Trade: USA increases dominance; arms flows to the Middle East surge, says SIPRI', SIPRI: Stockholm, 11 March. Available from: www.sipri.org/research/conflict-peace-and-security/trends-armed-conflicts

Tharoor, S. (2017) *Inglorious Empire: What the British Did to India*, London: Hurst Publishers.

Townsend, C. (2002) *Terrorism: A Very Short Introduction*, Oxford: Oxford University Press.

UN (nd) *The United Nations and Decolonisation*, New York: UN. Available from: https://www.un.org/en/sections/issues-depth/ decolonization/index.html

UN General Assembly (UNGA) (1965) *Implementation of the Declaration of the Granting of Independence to Colonial Countries and Peoples*. Available from: https://research.un.org/en/docs/ga/quick/regular/20

UNICEF (nd) Available from: www.unicef.org/graca/patterns.htm

12

Gender and human rights

Birgit Schippers

'Woman has the right to mount the scaffold; she must equally have the right to mount the rostrum'. With these words, the French revolutionary Olympe de Gouges (1748–93) threw down the gauntlet for women's rights in the eighteenth century, an era of revolutionary transformation. Her *Declaration of the Rights of Woman and the Female Citizen* (1791) was a witty and sharp rewriting of the *Declaration of the Rights of Man and Citizen*, which had been issued two years earlier, in 1789, by the newly established French National Assembly. De Gouges' *Declaration* demonstrated that struggles for freedom and justice demand the active participation of women, that their voices are heard and their rights addressed. Tragically, her intervention into the politics of revolutionary France ended on the scaffold: she was guillotined in 1793. In the years to come women's rights activists campaigned as trade unionists, abolitionists and suffragettes, and fought for a commitment to the principles and for the effective implementation of equal rights. This struggle is by no means over and its goals have not been fully achieved. Both globally and locally, women continue to be subjected to violations of their rights and dignity, ranging from physical violence to economic and social deprivation, and restrictions on their engagements as equal citizens (Schippers, 2016). If Olympe de Gouges embodied the struggle for women's rights in the late eighteenth century, a young Pakistani woman, Malala Yousafzai, has come to embody this struggle in the early twenty-first century. Shot and wounded by the Taliban in 2012 as a punishment for her campaign in support of the right of girls to be educated, Malala symbolises the dangers and the necessity to continue the struggle for women's and girls' human rights.

Two insights propel this on-going activism. First, the assertion that human rights are interdependent and indivisible, that is, that 'no person's rights are secure unless all people's rights are secure' and that 'no right is secure unless all rights are secure' (Ackerly, 2016: 38). Second, it is the recognition that the figure of the 'human', which underpins the concept of human rights, is in fact gendered. Put differently, although human rights propagate the notion of a universal humanity, we appear to each other, and experience our intimate, social and political relationships with others, as gendered beings. This chapter argues for the importance of the concept of gender to our understanding of human rights. It also highlights the significance of studying human rights through a gendered lens and demonstrates how human rights are framed with respect to the gendered diversity of being human. This commences discussion with a reflection on the role of the human in human rights discourse. Then different perspectives on the concept of gender and its impact on our understanding of human rights are outlined. Subsequently, selected aspects of the institutional implementation of gendered conceptions of human rights are illustrated and some policy issues are mapped. The chapter concludes with a brief reflection on future challenges to gendered understandings of human rights.

Who is the human in human rights? Gender and the challenge of difference(s)

The notion of human rights gives expression to the idea that all humans, as Article 1 of the 1948 Universal Declaration of Human Rights (UDHR) asserts, are 'born free and equal in dignity and rights'. By rejecting practices that discriminate on the grounds of race and ethnicity, religion, and indeed gender, human rights portend the notion of a universal humanity that transcends human difference, or particularity. In other words, human rights foreground what we as human beings share, rather than what makes us different. This commitment to universality is expressed in an often-cited reference by Jack Donnelly (1989: 1), who declares that human rights are the rights we have because we are human. What, though, does it mean to be human? And, who is this 'human' who sustains the notion of human rights?

Different ethical, religious and cultural traditions provide different responses to this question (see for example Ishay, 2008), but there is a broad commitment to define humans based on our capacity for reason and speech (*logos*), our possession of historical memory, and our ability to pursue a purpose in life (*telos*). These qualities, according to Alan Sussman (2014), are intimately connected with the idea and practice of human rights. As he declares, 'we need human rights ... to permit ourselves the possibility of being human'. However, this linkage between human rights and being human presupposes the existence of a universal humanity that rubs against the plurality and diversity of human life. The importance, and indeed difficulty, of thinking about human rights through the lens of difference has been highlighted by Anne Phillips, who contends that: 'human rights discourse relies on an abstracted human who is too often male and white. The challenge is to develop a human rights politics that is inclusive without obliterating differences' (Phillips, 2014). This tension, between the universalist vocabulary of human rights and the exclusion of those who do not conform to the ideal of the universal, acquires the quality of a paradox. Struggles for human rights demand inclusion in the language of universal humanity, but they are articulated in the language of the particular (Scott, 1996). Universal human rights must acknowledge gender-differentiated experiences that reflect the lives of women. Further, gender-sensitive conceptions of human rights must account for the structural division of human life into a public and private sphere. Given women's association with the private realm and with family life, the gendering of human rights must also recognise the public *and* private wrongs that women and girls experience, including violence in the home (see for example Ackerly, 2016; Nash, 2015).

Feminist activists and scholars have been at the forefront of these struggles. By campaigning for women's human rights, they reject a deficit model that excludes women from the language of human rights and seek instead to recognise gender differences, and with them women's specific experiences, in a gender-sensitive rights framework. This deficit model that historically excluded women from the language of universal humanity and thus from the philosophy and practice of human rights, persists to this day, as we continue to grapple with the meaning of gender and its ramifications of what gendered human rights should mean. In fact, the commitment to gendering human rights must acknowledge intersecting particularities. These were brilliantly articulated by Sojourner Truth (1850), a former slave, whose question 'Ain't I a Woman?' challenged those who campaigned for women's rights and equality, yet sought to introduce new exclusions, based on race, from the language of universal womanhood. Thus, masculinist and androcentric interpretations of human rights that have excluded all women are also, as suggested by Patricia Williams (1993), inflected with racialised and colonial imbrications that marginalise and exclude women of colour (see also Ackerly, 2016; Schippers, 2019). The next section will take a closer look at the concept of gender. It will ask, first, what we actually mean when we talk about gender and, second, what kind of conceptual and political work the category 'gender' performs.

The trouble with gender

The category of gender occupies a central position in the feminist critique of power and it has entered mainstream scholarly and public discourses that seek to understand and explain the differential and unequal distribution of resources between men and women, whether in the family, at local and national level, or globally (Nash, 2015). One's gender can have a decisive impact on educational and employment opportunities, on earnings, on health, on access to positions of power, and on the experiences of intimate life, including relationships within the family. Gender also shapes access to human rights entitlements and frames the concrete manifestations of human rights violations. Given the significance of gender to the way we experience and make sense of the social and political world, including human rights, it is judicious to unpack this concept further.

Broadly speaking, 'gender' articulates the claim that social and political inequalities between women and men are the result of political struggles and decisions. By studying social and political life through the lens of gender, we acknowledge that these inequalities are not the product of alleged natural, or biological, differences or capabilities. The biological differences that are said to exist between women and men are captured by the term 'sex'. According to this sex–gender distinction (sociologists also speak of a sex–gender system), the concept of gender refers to the cultural, social and historical meanings that are attached to biological, or natural, bodies. To develop this further, 'gender' challenges the idea that inequalities between women and men are the logical outcome of our biology. In this respect, gender can also be defined as a relational category. It articulates the relationship between historically and culturally modulated conceptions of masculinity and femininity, which are mapped upon biological sexual differences, whether real or perceived, of male and female.

Of course, the sex–gender distinction, as depicted in the previous paragraph, presumes that 'sex', or 'the body', is a stable and fixed biological, or natural, foundation upon which we develop our gender identity. This assertion has been challenged by the historian Thomas Laqueur (1992), who traces the shift in historical understandings of sex and gender, from what he terms a 'one-sex model' to a 'two-sex model'. Whereas the one-sex model presumes that male and female bodies are broadly similar, and that gender differences between men and women are the product of social convention, the two-sex model portends an essential biological difference between males and females, claiming that gender differences derive from these biological distinctions. According to the two-sex model, bodies constitute biological facts or truths that tie gender, and gender inequality, to nature. Therefore, whatever social differences exist between men and women they are said to be anchored in nature. What is peculiar about this shift in thinking about sex and gender is its historical context. Laqueur locates the move towards the two-sex model in the period around 1800, a time we associate with the re-ordering of political power in the wake of the revolutionary transformations in parts of Europe and North America, and with the language of equality, liberty and solidarity. In other words, just as the language of politics began to embrace ideas such as rights and equality, opening up the prospect of women's recognition as being equal to men, a new discourse emerged that sought to anchor gender inequality in nature, in scientific knowledge and thus in the 'hard facts' of sexed bodies.

The two-sex model continues to inform discussions about gender to this day, but it has also come under increasing scrutiny. Challenges to the two-sex model give expression to the claim that the languages of sex and gender – and with them the languages of science and of scientific classification – are part of a set of wider political and moral struggles that seek to order, or overthrow, unequal power relationships. Feminists have refuted the idea that 'anatomy is destiny' – in other words, that biological sex determines our gender identity, and that one's body determines one's social or political status. An emerging new gender politics aims to give recognition to a wider range of experiences of sexed bodies and genders, beyond the two-sex–two-gender model. For example, transgender activists, while also refusing to anchor gender identity in biology, specifically in the body presented to us as birth, challenge the idea that cis-identity – the term used to describe the continuum between the (biological) body presented at birth and one's gender identity – is the only possible form of living in one's body and one's gendered sense of self. Intersex activists criticise the binary language of sex and gender because it limits the vocabulary of bodily and gendered experiences to male/female biological distinctions and masculine/feminine gender identities. They argue instead for the recognition of multiple sexes and genders, beyond male and female (see for example Fausto-Sterling, 2000). Queer scholars and activists contend that gender, and sex, are positioned in a complex relationship with our sexual orientation. As they argue, connecting sexed male and female bodies to socially dominant gender norms of what it means to be masculine and feminine via heterosexual practices produces and stabilises a hetero-normative gender identity, whereas queer identities scramble the relationship between sexed bodies, gender identities and sexuality (Keating and Burack, 2016; see also Butler, 1990).

So far, the discussion has sought to illustrate that gender is a complex and indeed troublesome concept. Its meaning is inherently unstable, shifting historically and culturally with and against dominant ideas about politics, culture and science, and formed by intersecting identity categories, such as race and ethnicity, class and religion, that generate socially and politically produced inequalities which are presented as natural. As Judith Butler (1990) contends, we should conceive of gender instead as a normative ideal. According to Butler, gendered realities are mere approximations of dominant – and fictitious – gender norms. How we experience and live our gendered identities is shaped primarily by social conventions and social prohibitions. As discussed in the next section, the culturally and historically shifting conceptions of these normative ideals are frequently used to legitimise human rights violations, but they also provide the occasion for human rights struggles that enhance the possibilities for accessing human rights entitlements.

Towards gendered human rights: ideas, issues and institutions

Olympe de Gouges' *Declaration of the Rights of Woman and the Female Citizen* (1791), together with Mary Wollstonecraft's *A Vindication of the Rights of Woman* (1792) and John Stuart Mill and Harriet Taylor's *The Subjection of Women* (1869), are important milestones on the path towards women's human rights. However, notwithstanding the important contributions of these, essentially classical liberal, formulations to include women in the discourse of rights, they also mirror the shortcomings of the wider human rights history and its exclusions of subjugated populations on the basis of categories such as class, race and sexual orientation. Thus, as suggested above, the struggles for women's rights have often replicated the exclusionary practices of masculinist models of human rights, for example, by excluding women of colour, but also by failing or refusing to consider what it means to articulate gendered conceptions of human rights.

As intimated earlier, the commitment to universal human rights found its fullest expression in the aftermath of World War II and the Holocaust, leading to the Universal Declaration of Human Rights. Article 2 of the UDHR enshrines an equal entitlement to human rights, regardless of sex or other forms of social distinction. This commitment to equal entitlement to human rights was further strengthened with the International Covenant on Civil and Political Rights and the International Covenant on Economic, Social and Cultural Rights, two instruments in the human rights repertoire that were introduced in 1966. However, neither of these instruments, which together with the UDHR form the International Bill of Rights, sufficiently addresses specific human rights issues that pertain to women, or indeed wider gender-specific forms of human rights entitlements and violations. This situation started to change in the 1970s. In recognition of the need for a specific human rights convention that addresses women's human rights, but also in response to the feminist activism of the late 1960s and the 1970s, the United Nations (UN) embarked on a process that led to the adoption of the 1979 UN Convention on the Elimination of all Forms of Discrimination against Women (CEDAW) (Arat, 2008).

To this day, CEDAW remains an important instrument that recognises women's shared vulnerabilities to violence, to practices of discrimination and to a systematic and systemic denial of opportunities. The institutional apparatus built around CEDAW monitors and seeks to redress these violations. But there has also been recognition that CEDAW should be developed further. The 1995 Beijing Platform for Action was a key staging post in CEDAW's development and it identified priority issues, such as the use of violence against women; women and the environment; and the rights of the girl-child, as areas for further attention. Also discussed in Beijing was the role of women in armed conflict, a topic that has since received significant attention and led to the UN Security Council Resolution (UNSCR) 1325. UNSCR 1325 recognises the importance of women's experiences of conflict and seeks to advance women's rights in conflict resolution and post-conflict settlement, as well as women's participation in peace negotiations and the increase of women's representation in decision-making processes at all levels.

CEDAW's focus on the life experiences of heterosexual and cis women, that is, women assigned a female gender at birth, has also been the subject of criticism. Dominant cultural conventions of what it means to be a woman continue to marginalise lesbian, bisexual and transgender (LBT) women and their specific needs and requirements. These cultural conventions are also at odds with the broader human rights obligations that documents such as CEDAW articulate, and that many states have signed up to. This omission does not make CEDAW obsolete, but it requires a re-reading of CEDAW through the lens of sexual orientation and gender identity (SOGI) rights and an engagement with the needs and entitlements of sexual and gender minorities.

In this context, it is important to stress that neither the experiences nor the needs of lesbian and bisexual women on the one hand and transgender women on the other are identical. However, LBT women are frequently subjected to similar human rights abuses. These include: experiences of violence and the threat of violence, including violence in the home; discrimination, harassment and bullying in public life and in workplaces; restrictions on participation in public life; attempts to regulate sexuality, reproduction and the right to a family life, including restrictions on access to fertility treatment; restrictions on marriage rights, rights to inheritance and adoption rights; unequal access to healthcare and insensitive engagement with health concerns and needs; as well as the absence of a social recognition of already established legal rights. Efforts to include SOGI rights in the human rights canon have become part of a movement that aims to expand the existing human rights framework beyond the narrow confines of heterosexuality and cis-gender (Keating and Burack, 2016). The Yogyakarta Principles (2006), formulated by a group of distinguished human rights scholars (and named after the Indonesian city where they met), constitute a landmark document in this process. The Yogyakarta Principles seek to redress blind-spots in existing human rights provisions and to shed light on the human rights of LGBT populations. Crucially, Yogyakarta also re-affirms the obligation of states to protect all populations, an obligation that stems from the international human rights framework already in place.

Conceptions of gender that are informed by ideas about respectability and sexual propriety, and that marginalise and discriminate against gender and sexual minorities, also circulate in discourses that seek to prioritise cultural traditions, whether long-established or recently invented, over the human rights of women and gender and sexual minorities. Often couched in the language of religious values, cultural tradition arguments are used to justify practices such as the male guardianship system in Saudi Arabia; practices of female genital mutilation (FGM); honour killings; and the criminalisation of gay and trans people, to give just a few examples. Furthermore, invoking cultural traditions or cultural defence arguments to justify human rights violations is by no means exclusive to states and communities in the Global South or to states with majority Muslim populations. It is important to remember that cultural tradition arguments are also deployed in the Global North. For example, calls for a ban on Muslim women wearing the hijab or other religious garments in the public realm constitute an infringement of these women's freedom of religion; it also illustrates how disputes over culture serve to regulate and to police women's appearance. To give another example, for many decades, girls and women in the Republic of Ireland were confined in institutions under the authority of religious organisations, typically for what were regarded as acts of sexual transgression, such as pre-marital sexual relationships and pregnancies outside marriage; yet to this day, as highlighted by the UN Committee against Torture, the Irish state has failed to fully investigate claims of ill-treatment of women and children in these institutions and to punish and prosecute the perpetrators.

These examples illustrate the complex relationship between culture and gendered conceptions of human rights. As the anthropologist Sally Engle Merry (2006) has pointed out, the universalist and often abstract language of human rights must be translated into the languages and practices of local communities if it wants to become and remain meaningful (see also Nash, 2015). Notwithstanding the continued significance of the interdependent and indivisible quality of human rights, it is important to remember that cultural contexts and attachments matter to people's lives and that they require a human rights vernacular that individuals and communities can relate to.

Conclusion: gender and human rights in dark times?

The central tenet of the discussion in this chapter was the claim that gender is integral to our conception of human rights. The idea that we should regard human rights as gender-neutral was rejected, and it was suggested instead that gendered conceptions of human rights presume that the figure of the human, which underpins and sustains the concept of human rights, is diverse, plural and contested. To think about human rights through the lens of gender is but one such effort to do justice to this plurality.

What, though, is the future for gendered conceptions of human rights? The matter of human rights, as demonstrated here, is not a settled issue, and requires constant attention and responses that will galvanise new generations of human rights activists and lead to the creation of new political alliances. Recent months and years have witnessed the growth of human rights activism at local and global levels, committed to tackling old and new human rights abuses. For example, the #MeToo movement responded to on-going practices of sexual assault and harassment. Activists also challenge threats of violence in online communities and on social media that seek to police the participation of women and gender and sexual minorities in public discourse. In the Republic of Ireland, a long-running campaign succeeded in overturning a constitutional ban on girls' and women's access to pregnancy terminations, while a referendum in 2015 paved the way for the introduction of marriage equality for same-sex couples. The success of these struggles depended on the commitment to advancing the rights of women and sexual minorities, and on the persistent work to tackle those dominant norms that produce, regulate and police gender identities.

However, while we witness a renewed energy for the protection and expansion of human rights by activists, we are also confronted with a retreat from human rights commitments on the part of many governments. Despite a growing number of states expressing their support for the protection of gendered and sexual minorities, for example, by legislating for marriage equality, introducing anti-discrimination legislation and expanding the rights of transgender people, we also observe a retreat from human rights protection or a continued refusal to introduce and effectively implement already established rights. For example, while reproductive rights for women in the Republic of Ireland are being expanded, these rights are under threat in Central America and increasingly in the United States. In fact, it is not just women's human rights or SOGI rights, but the very notion of gender that is increasingly coming under attack. A campaign driven by conservative religious forces to root out the so-called 'gender ideology' is garnering support in the Americas and in parts of Europe. 'Anti-gender' campaigners challenge the notion that gender, and gendered power relations, are socially produced and instead seek a return to a 'biology is destiny' ideology that denies the very existence of diverse gender identities, and that associates women primarily with their reproductive capacities. For example, 'anti-gender' campaigners in Brazil, motivated by the electoral success of Jair Bolsonaro, seek to delete reference to gender from educational guidelines. The Trump administration in the US has launched a campaign against the rights of transgender people and seeks to enshrine in law that the gender ascribed at birth cannot be changed. In Hungary and elsewhere, we see an assault on gender studies programmes at universities and colleges, while the Spanish far-right Vox party deploys a discourse of 'feminist supremacism' and 'gender totalitarianism' to discredit serious engagement with and critical analysis of gender politics and gendered inequalities. To persist with the struggle for gendered conceptions of human rights is a key challenge for our contemporary era and for the future.

References

Ackerly, B. (2016) 'Feminist and activist approaches to human rights', in M. Goodhart (ed) *Human Rights: Politics and Practice*, Oxford: Oxford University Press, pp 28–43.

Arat, Z.F.K. (2008) 'Women's rights as human rights', *UN Chronicle*, XLV(2 and 3): 9–13.

Butler, J. (1990) *Gender Trouble: Feminism and the Subversion of Identity*, New York: Routledge.

CEDAW (1979) *Convention on the Elimination of all Forms of Discrimination against Women*. Available from: https://www.ohchr.org/documents/professionalinterest/cedaw.pdf

De Gouges, O. (1791) *Declaration of the Rights of Woman and the Female Citizen*. Available from: http://chnm.gmu.edu/revolution/d/293

Donnelly, J. (1989) *Universal Human Rights in Theory and Practice*, Ithaca, NY: Cornell University Press.

Fausto-Sterling, A. (2000) *Sexing the Body: Gender Politics and the Construction of Sexuality*, New York: Basic Books.

Ishay, M. (2008) *The History of Human Rights: From Ancient Times to the Globalization Era*, Berkeley: University of California Press.

Keating, C. and Burack, C. (2016) 'Sexual orientation, gender identity, and human rights', in M. Goodhart (ed) *Human Rights: Politics and Practice*, Oxford: Oxford University Press, pp 182–197.

Laqueur, T. (1992) *Making Sex: Body and Gender from the Greeks to Freud*, Cambridge, MA: Harvard University Press.

Merry, S.E. (2006) *Human Rights and Gender Violence: Translating International Law into Local Justice*, Chicago: Chicago University Press.

Mill, J.S. and Taylor, H. (1869/2006) 'The subjection of women', in J.S. Mill, *On Liberty and the Subjection of Women*, London: Penguin.

Nash, K. (2015) *The Political Sociology of Human Rights*, Cambridge: Cambridge University Press.

Phillips, A. (2014) 'Who is the human in human rights?' Available from: www.opendemocracy.net/anne-phillips/who-is-human-in-human-rights

Schippers, B. (2016) 'Women's human rights and diversity politics', *agendaNI*, February–March: 106–107.

Schippers, B. (2019). 'Introduction', in B. Schippers (ed) *Critical Perspectives on Human Rights*, London: Rowman and Littlefield International, pp ix–xxi.

Scott, J.W. (1996) *Only Paradoxes to Offer: French Feminists and the Rights of Man*, Cambridge, MA: Harvard University Press.

Sussman, A. (2014) 'Why human rights are called human rights', *Ethics and International Affairs*, 28(2). Available from: www.ethicsandinternationalaffairs.org/2014/why-human-rights-are-called-human-rights/

Truth, S. (1850) *The Narrative of Sojourner Truth*, Philadelphia, University of Pennsylvania. Available from: https://digital.library.upenn.edu/women/truth/1850/1850.html

Williams, P. (1993) *The Alchemy of Race and Rights*, Cambridge, MA: Harvard University Press.

Wollstonecraft, M. (1792/1992) *A Vindication of the Rights of Woman, with Strictures on Political and Moral Subjects*, London: Everyman.

Yogyakarta Principles (2006) *The Yogyakarta Principles*. Available from: http://yogyakartaprinciples.org/principles-en/yp10/

PART III

Human rights approaches to social policy development

13

Human rights-based approaches to social policy development

Margaret Buckley and Fiona Dukelow

The development of a range of global, regional and national human rights frameworks since the end of World War II has led, particularly since the 1990s, to a growth in their use by a range of non-governmental organisations (NGOs) and other campaigning bodies as tools to promote national and global recognition of human rights in policy and in practice. However, the formulation of specific rights often involves struggle and campaigning, and is thus a contested site. The presentation of a right does not ensure that it can be realised. Often attention must be given to wider social and economic policy developments as well as the promotion and facilitation of community empowerment, development, advocacy and campaigning to ensure rights are realisable and extended in line with changing contexts and circumstances. This chapter analyses some of these issues alongside a discussion of contemporary attempts by NGOs and other campaigning organisations to promote the recognition of universal human rights, in areas such as the right to social protection, housing, health and education; and the rights of particular groups, such as women, children, older people, disabled people and the lesbian, gay, bisexual, and transgender (LGBT) community.

Setting the context: from a high tide to a hostile climate?

There was an enormous growth in human rights NGOs in the latter decades of the twentieth century (Posner, 1997; Hegarty, 1999). The field encompasses well-established international non-governmental organisations (INGOs) such as Amnesty International, Human Rights Watch, Care International and the Centre for Economic and Social Rights, and it extends to a myriad of regional, national and local NGOs. While domestic NGOs focus on human rights issues within a particular country, their activity often involves strategic linkages with INGOs. Related to this has been the enormous growth of NGOs in the Global South. There has also been a proliferation of interest groups that have a sectoral focus and specialise in pursuing the human rights of particular groups, such as children and women. The work of human rights NGOs spans a range of activities, including information gathering and fact finding which is used for monitoring and reporting work, but also for lobbying governments and inter-governmental organisations (IGOs), and for human rights education/consciousness-raising activities. These NGO activities serve both to diffuse human rights discourses and norms, and to mobilise shame in the context of a state's lack of human rights or poor implementation record (Kim, 2013). Besides such rights-focused NGOs, a wide range of other voluntary and community sector organisations have also begun to develop human rights-based approaches to advance policy and practice in their own particular fields.

The growth and evolving nature of human rights NGOs is linked to the proliferation of international and regional human rights treaties since the end of World War II, and particularly since the end of the Cold War in the 1980s. Yet, despite this, universal rights continue to be challenged throughout the world, such as LGBT rights in countries like Russia and Nigeria; the continued lack of gender equality and religious persecution in Islamic countries; issues such as Islamophobia, migration, 'terror' and the rise of political authoritarianism in Eastern Europe and Latin America; and financial crises taking priority over the traditional championing of human rights by Europe and the US. Arguably, this context has created a hostile climate for human rights NGOs. Indeed, since 2012 more than 60 countries have adopted legislation and/or practices to restrict the human rights-based work of NGOs, including in Azerbaijan, Russia, Turkey and several European countries including Hungary, Bulgaria and Slovakia (Muižnieks, 2017).

These problems build on long-standing issues concerning the nature and promotion of universal human rights, and contestation in these areas is entangled with contestation about the authority and practices of human rights NGOs. One of the longest standing arguments about universal human rights relates to the extent to which they are actually universal and whether, indeed, it is possible to create universal rights. This is reflected, on the one hand, by conceptual debates about universalism and cultural relativism and, on the other hand, by the politics of international human rights institutions (Le, 2016; Reichert, 2006; O'Sullivan, 1998). Specifically in relation to politics, this concerns the extent to which these institutions reflect power imbalances and tensions between the Global North and the Global South, or between the G8 and the G77 coalition of 134 developing countries, to the effect that the institution of international human rights is ultimately about establishing a global order built upon Western liberal democratic values, governance systems and the liberal model of society. More negatively, it could be that social and economic rights on issues such as labour standards, for example, simply reflect the concerns of 'self-interested and hypocritical northern governments' (Deacon, 2007: 12). These are well-worn debates (Le, 2016). As for the role of NGOs, issues are raised about their representativeness and the degree to which they are complicit with established power relations (Dryzek, 2012). Regarding the latter issue, Heins suggests that civil society is 'composed of self-appointed representatives, coming mostly from wealthy countries, and so helping to constitute a global elite, not a counterweight to established power' (2005, in Dryzek, 2012: 106). While Dryzek suggests that this criticism may be 'overdrawn', in practice NGOs are necessarily selective in the issues they choose to pursue at any particular time, not least for the pragmatic reason that their funding is drawn from donors whose propensity to give is influenced by the issues that motivate and outrage from a Western perspective, but may not be the most pressing from a local perspective in Asian or African contexts (Posner, 2014). Interestingly, an alternative view proposed by Kim (2013), writing from a South-East Asian perspective, is that INGOs can more readily mobilise shame against human rights violations as opposed to domestic NGOs that may be more sensitive to local populist discourses. As for complicity, there are questions about the degree to which NGOs prioritise cooperation with states and IGOs over opposition and resistance in order to have influence and, in the process, simply contribute to maintaining the status quo. There is also a politics to NGOs on these points, with NGOs from the Global South asking serious questions about the elitism and imperialism of NGOs centred in the Global North. A key example is the instigation of the 'Nothing About Us Without Us' campaign in reaction to 'Make Poverty History', which was led by Northern NGOs with minimal input from African NGOs and their perspectives on poverty and debt (Hodkinson, 2005).

There are other issues which also need to be brought to bear when it comes to the extent to which socio-economic rights in particular can be realised and implemented. While civil and political rights do involve investment in legal and regulatory resources in order to be realised, Nolan and colleagues (2009) point out that in many cases public representatives and officials see a large difference between political and civil rights, and social, economic and cultural rights, in terms of costs. This hampers political will to implement the latter sets of rights which are perceived to be particularly resource dependent and costly. This is the rationale articulated most frequently by governments to explain why human rights-based policies are not implemented (Nolan et al, 2009). Realising social and economic rights in the Global South involves further layers of resource complexity. In this case, social and economic rights, if they are to have any practical effect, require redistribution (Deacon, 2007), the architecture of which, at the global level, is far from reality. The practices of INGOs in particular are again entangled in these issues. Over time NGOs, like many other actors in the areas of social policy governance and service provision, have become increasingly managerialised and are incentivised to become more instrumentalist in their work, acting as if they are '"for profits" in a non-profit environment' (Bieckhart, 1999: 74, in Deacon, 2007: 95). In this context Deacon (2007) refers to the paradox of NGOs which, on the one hand, have a campaigning face that advocates for universal human rights, including the provision of social rights based on universal/public provision, and simultaneously act as agents that are required to compete for contracts to deliver aid and services. As such, they end up substituting for state-provided welfare and become invested in the continued provision of non-state/voluntary services, undermining universal and comprehensive social policy.

To conclude this section, while the discussion might read like a 'recital of failings', the point is rather to set a general context for our review of human rights mechanisms at various levels in the subsequent sections. In essence, it is important to recognise that complex issues are at play in how rights are potentially realised and the respective role of states, IGOs and NGOs in that process.

The United Nations

One of the main ways in which NGOs promote human rights in practice is through the reporting committee mechanisms of the various UN covenants and conventions. There are two main covenants – the International Covenant on Civil and Political Rights (ICCPR) and the International Covenant on Economic, Social and Cultural Rights (ICESCR) – as well as a number of specific conventions each with their own reporting or monitoring committee which review each ratifying state's rights record every few years. There is also a Universal Periodic Review (UPR) of all of the rights each state has ratified. Each of these reporting exercises can include lobbying and input from NGOs. Indeed, NGO advocacy has been pivotal to the negotiation of some of these conventions themselves.

The thrust of the Convention on the Rights of Persons with Disabilities (CRPD) is heavily influenced by the international disability rights movement, to the effect that it presses states to move from their continued adherence to a medicalised model of disability services to a rights-based model (Degener, 2017). In the case of the Convention on the Rights of the Child (CRC), which advances children's rights in four domains – survival, development, protection and participation – an NGO alliance was central to negotiations and content (Kamminga, 2005), and this alliance, Child Rights Connect, continues to have a central role in treaty monitoring work. Yet the evolution of the CRC exemplifies the paradoxes and politics of securing international human rights. Of all the conventions, it has the most signatories. Since Somalia ratified it in 2015, the US is the only country not to do so. On the one hand, the CRC is judged to be enormously impactful, it has established the norm of children as individual right holders, with specific entitlements as distinct from adults. It has prompted domestic law and policy reform (such as Thailand abolishing the death penalty for those aged under 18 in 2003), and further standard setting at regional and country level (such as the Brazilian Children's Code passed in 1990). However, these achievements sit side by side with the fact that globally child poverty is hugely problematic; children remain highly vulnerable to violence, migrating children are especially vulnerable to a range of risks, and children's rights to education and healthcare fall far short in many regions. Surveying such issues, Liefard and Sloth-Nielsen suggest that: 'it is not the CRC's success but its failure to promote and protect the rights of children which is the dominant motif, a failure all the more pronounced seeing as the treaty is almost universally endorsed' (2017: 3).

NGOs engage with the specific monitoring committee of independent experts associated with each treaty and the UPR (covering all treaties ratified) along with the Special Rapporteur process by which the UN Human Rights Council can instigate individual country reports on their general or specific human rights record. However, UN regulatory architecture is only as powerful as its member countries are collectively comfortable with. It is constrained not only by this but also by the continued tensions between different member countries and regions, in particular, between the Global North and South (Posner, 2014).

These issues are also reflected in the gap between the rhetorical hailing of NGOs as the 'guardians of reform' (Annan, 2005) and the actual role and opportunities NGOs and activists have in monitoring and implementation mechanisms. NGOs may submit shadow reports and these can be used by monitoring bodies to pose questions and raise issues regarding state reporting. NGO recommendations may also be included in concluding observations and in their preparation of recommendations (Edwards, 2009). NGOs may participate in international complaint mechanisms, associated with some but not all of the treaties, and so may file on behalf of themselves or on behalf of individual or group victims. NGOs may also submit information to Special Rapporteurs. However, an examination of, for example, UPR processes and outcomes reveals some of the problems with monitoring procedures and gaps therein. Research by the NGO Universal Rights Group on the first two cycles of the UPR (2006–16) found that while 48 per cent of recommendations accepted by states during the first cycle were implemented by the second cycle, in reality the majority of states do not consult with NGOs in preparing their reports and limited time during UPR meetings means that alternative reports are not considered (Gujadhur and Limon, 2016). For NGOs and other activists the ability to draw on a discourse of human rights to hold states to account and to mobilise shame in the face of state failure to meet their treaty obligations still appear to be the most effective tools they have at their disposal (Roth, 2004).

The European Convention on Human Rights (ECHR) and the EU Charter of Fundamental Rights (CFR)

The European Court of Human Rights (ECtHR), which rules on complaints made in relation to the ECHR, is one of the most influential mechanisms NGOs have been able to use in the implementation of human rights at state level. The decisions of the ECtHR create legally binding responsibilities for states. Some of the decisions have led to significant changes in national law (Donnelly and Whelan, 2018). For example, in the case of *Oliari and Others v Italy* (2015), the decision held that Italy had violated Article 8 of the ECHR (the right to respect for family and private life) due to the lack of legal recognition for same-sex relationships. The judgement resulted in the introduction of a civil union law in Italy open to same-sex couples (Marinai, 2016). Likewise, the *Norris v Ireland* (1983) case led to the decriminalisation of homosexual activity in Ireland. One big advantage of ECtHR decisions is that they create case law applicable to all ECHR states. However, not all ECtHR cases are successful. In 2011, France's new law prohibiting the covering of the face in public was challenged by a Muslim woman in the ECtHR, claiming it violated her rights under Articles 3, 8, 9, 10, 11 and 14 of the ECHR (*S.A.S. v France*).

Although targeting all types of face covering, it was perceived as aimed primarily at Muslim women who wear a niqab (Erlings, 2015). The ECtHR ruled to uphold the French law in order to 'protect the rights and freedoms of others' through the concept of *vivre ensemble*[1] (Erlings, 2015: 7). The national law and the decision of the ECtHR have resulted in protests, assaults on police and popular debate on whether or not upholding the rights of one group has removed rights from another. Since the ruling of the ECtHR, many countries, municipalities and cities in Europe have now followed suit and banned full-face coverings. Therefore, it must be valid to question whether or not the ECtHR has, in this case, allowed for exclusionary laws to come into effect (Edmunds, 2012).

The incorporation of the ECHR into national law in many European states, as well as the European Union, has made it easier and less costly for NGOs and others to take cases under the ECHR. The ECHR and ECtHR require the implementation and protection of human rights in domestic law and, as a result, individual state courts can now hear test cases. Individuals and groups can also bring cases before the ECtHR, although this is usually a last resort, having exhausted the national system (Cozzi et al, 2016). Judgements of the ECtHR are not automatically executed and, as a result, the execution of judgements is overseen by the Committee of Ministers that supervises and monitors action plans submitted by states (Paris, 2015). Apart from judicial systems, enforcing the ECHR relies on 'peer pressure and political persuasion' (Harris et al, 2018: 183). Thus, the role of NGOs, national human rights institutions (NHRIs) and campaigners is essential to highlighting deficiencies and creating an embarrassing situation for governments that are perceived to be reluctant to carry out their responsibilities.

Separate from the ECHR, the EU's Charter of Fundamental Rights guarantees certain political, social and economic rights to EU citizens and residents under EU law (Lenaerts, 2012). Within the EU, the rights and freedoms of citizens have historically been established at different times and under different circumstances depending on the individual state. The CFR has attempted to provide a set of EU-wide rights with EU oversight. The CFR is consistent with the ECHR and is updated in relation to changes in society (such as data protection). Although drafted in 2000, it was not until 2009 – after all member states had ratified the Lisbon Treaty – that the CFR became legally binding. Primarily, the CFR applies to EU bodies and institutions, and only to national courts when they are implementing EU law. One of the important mechanisms in implementing the CFR is EU directives. EU directives require member states to achieve particular outcomes but, taking into account individual member states' different legal systems, they do not specify the means by which an outcome should be achieved (Donnelly and Whelan, 2018).

As the CFR applies mainly to European bodies and institutions, including the European Court of Justice (ECJ), an important aspect of implementing the CFR is the ability of individuals, groups and NGOs to take legal action to ensure rights and freedoms are secured in EU states. Initially, a number of countries had opposed the CFR (for example, the UK and Poland) and argued that new legal responsibilities would undermine national sovereignty (Barnard, 2019). As a result, both the UK and Poland negotiated 'opt-out' caveats which limit the extent to which EU courts can rule on issues relating to the CFR, if brought to national courts. In addition, unless the UK and Poland have provided for them in their national laws, the social and economic rights contained in the CFR are not justiciable rights (Barnard, 2019). After the UK withdrawal from the EU (Brexit), the CFR will no longer apply explicitly in the UK, giving rise to concerns around reduced power to protect rights, possible gaps in basic human rights and legal uncertainty (Barnard, 2019).

The national context

National human rights institutions are independent bodies whose function is to promote and protect human rights at national level by providing assessments of government compliance with human rights covenants (Universal Rights Group, 2018). There are over 100 such institutions globally. Through research, publications and consultations, NHRIs form one mechanism of implementing human rights at a national level. NHRIs often work closely with NGOs to advance their goals. In the UK, research undertaken by NHRIs and NGOs in the form of surveys and critiques of human rights in the country forms the majority of reporting to parliament on the issue of human rights. NHRIs will often produce domestic 'shadow reports' on policy implementation, which can then be compared to the government claims on human rights (Universal Rights Group, 2018). This results in a degree of embarrassment for the government concerned (if the shadow report does not correspond to the governmental report). As with the ECHR, and as previously seen with UN Conventions, embarrassment and peer pressure can be used to exert pressure on a government to amend policies.

Incorporating international law and mechanisms of implementation into national law can be complicated. An example, of the complexity involved in altering legislation, the role of NGOs, campaigners and activists, and the influence of international law on domestic provision, is the 2018 Irish Referendum on the 36th Amendment of the Constitution of Ireland (commonly known as the 8th Amendment referendum). Since the 1980s in Ireland, there have been a number of debates, campaigns and controversies surrounding the illegality of abortion. In 1983 the 8th Amendment to the Constitution recognised the equal right to life of the mother and the unborn child. In 1992 the Supreme Court interpreted this as meaning that an abortion was admissible if a mother's life was in danger (the 'X' case). In 2005, three women brought a case before the ECtHR which became known as *A, B and C v Ireland*. All three of the women involved had been obliged to travel to the UK to have abortions due to the illegality of the procedure in Ireland. While the majority of complaints were dismissed, the ECtHR held that Ireland had violated Article 8 with regard to complainant C because though Irish law ostensibly allowed a pregnancy termination where the mother's life was in danger, in practice this was not provided for in this case. The result placed pressure on the Irish government to clarify the circumstances under which an abortion may be performed to save the life of a pregnant woman. In response, an expert group was convened to outline the options available to the government. The recommendations, for legislative reform, were submitted the night before the death of Savita Halappanavar. Savita Halappanavar's death in 2012 led to calls for more extensive reform. The Abortion Rights Campaign (ARC) was founded and Repealthe8th hashtag was started on Twitter. The result of the 2018 referendum removed the 8th Amendment from Bunreacht na hÉireann[2] and was followed by the introduction of the Health (Regulation of Termination of Pregnancy) Act 2018.

The involvement of individuals, groups, NGOs and campaigners in the promotion of human rights has resulted in substantial change at national level in many countries. The use of the ECtHR to exert pressure on governments, combined with publicising issues on a global stage and thereby highlighting a potentially embarrassing situation, has helped to bring about significant change.

Notes

[1] Live together.
[2] Constitution of Ireland.

References

Annan, K. (2005) 'Without vital role of NGOs, world could hardly respond to myriad crises, UN Secretary-General Annan tells DPI/NGO conference', *Secretary General Statements and Messages*, 9 September. Available from: www.un.org/press/en/2005/sgsm10085.doc.htm

Barnard, C. (2019) 'So long, farewell, auf wiedersehen, adieu: Brexit and the Charter of Fundamental Rights', *The Modern Law Review*, 82(2): 350–366.

Cozzi, A., Sykiotou, A., Rajska, D., Krstic, I., Filatova, M., Katic, N., Bard, P. and Bourgeois, S. (2016) *Comparative Study on the Implementation of the ECHR at the National Level*, Belgrade: Council of Europe.

Deacon, B. (2007) *Global Social Policy and Governance*, London: Sage.

Degener, T. (2017) 'A human rights model of disability', in P. Blanck and E. Flynn (eds) *Routledge Handbook of Disability Law and Human Rights*, London: Routledge, pp 31–49.

Donnelly, J. and Whelan, D. (2018) *International Human Rights*, 5th edition, New York: Routledge.

Dryzek, J. (2012) 'Global civil society: the progress of post-Westphalian politics', *Annual Review of Political Science*, 15: 101–19.

Edmunds, J. (2012) 'The "new" barbarians: governmentality, securitization and Islam in Western Europe', *Contemporary Islam*, 6(1): 67–84

Edwards, G. (2009) 'Assessing the effectiveness of human rights non-governmental organisations (NGOs) from the birth of the United Nations to the 21st century: ten attributes of highly successful human rights NGOs', *Michigan State Journal of International Law*, 18(2): 165–228.

Erlings, E. (2015) ' "The government did not refer to it", *SAS v France* and *Ordre Public* at the European Court of Human Rights', *Melbourne Journal of International Law*, 16: 1–22.

Gujadhur, S. and Limon, M. (2016) *Towards the Third Cycle of the UPR: Stick or Twist?*, Geneva: Universal Rights Group.

Harris, D.J., O'Boyle, M., Bates, E.P. and Buckley, C.M. (2018) *Law of the European Convention on Human Rights*, Oxford: Oxford University Press.

Hegarty, A. (1999) 'Non-governmental organisations: the key to change', in A. Hegarty and S. Leonard (eds) *Human Rights an Agenda for the 21st Century*, London: Cavendish, pp 267–285.

Hodkinson, S. (2005) 'Make the G8 history', *Red Pepper*, 1 July. Available from: www.redpepper.org.uk/make-the-g8-history/

Kamminga, M. (2005) 'The evolving status of NGOs under international law: a threat to the inter-state system?', in P. Alston (ed) *Non-state Actors and Human Rights*, Oxford: Oxford University Press.

Kim, D. (2013) 'International nongovernmental organizations and the global diffusion of national human rights institutions', *International Organisation*, 67(3): 505–39.

Le, N. (2016) 'Are human rights universal or culturally relative?', *Peace Review*, 28(2): 203–211.

Lenaerts, K. (2012) 'Exploring the limits of the EU Charter of Fundamental Rights', *European Constitutional Law Review*, 8(3): 375–403.

Liefaard, T. and Sloth-Nielsen, J. (2017) '25 years CRC: reflecting on successes, failures and the future', in T. Liefaard and J. Sloth-Nielsen (eds) *The United Nations Convention on the Rights of the Child*, Leiden: Brill Nijhoff, pp 1–13.

Marinai, S. (2016) 'Recognition in Italy of same-sex marriages celebrated abroad: the importance of a bottom-up approach', *European Journal of Legal Studies*, 9(1), 10–37.

Muižnieks, N. (2017) *The Shrinking Space for Human Rights Organisations*. Available from: www.coe.int/en/web/commissioner/-/the-shrinking-space-for-human-rights-organisations?desktop=true

Nolan, A., Porter, B. and Langford, M. (2009) 'The justiciability of social and economic rights: an updated appraisal', *Centre for Human Rights and Social Justice Working Paper*, No 15. Available from: https://papers.ssrn.com/sol3/papers.cfm?abstract_id=1434944

O'Sullivan, D. (1998) 'The history of human rights across the regions: universalism vs cultural relativism', *International Journal of Human Rights*, 2(3): 22–48.

Paris, M. (2015) 'The European Convention on Human Rights Act: implementation mechanisms and compliance', in S. Egan (ed) *International Human Rights: Perspectives from Ireland*, London: Bloomsbury, pp 91–114.

Posner, M. (1997) 'Human rights and non-government organisations: foreword', *Fordham Law Review*, 627: 627–628.

Posner, M. (2014) 'The case against human rights', *The Guardian*, 4 December.

Reichert, E. (2006) 'Human rights: an examination of universalism and cultural relativism', *Journal of Comparative Social Welfare*, 22(1): 23–36.

Roth, K. (2004) 'Defending economic, social and cultural rights: practical issues faced by an international human rights organisation', *Human Rights Quarterly*, 26(1): 63–73.

Universal Rights Group (2018) *The Global Human Rights Implementation Agenda: The Role of National Parliaments*, London: Commonwealth Secretariat.

14

The right to education

Benjamin Mallon

This chapter critically analyses the idea of education as a universal human right. It outlines existing international human rights mechanisms which have relevance to education as a right and discusses contemporary multilateral attempts by non-governmental organisations (NGOs) and other campaigning organisations to promote the recognition and realisation of a universal right to education. It assesses some of the possibilities and difficulties of making the right to education a reality in a world of social, economic, cultural, ideological and political diversity, different levels of 'peace', stability, governmental organisation and conflict, changing contexts and circumstances. While recognising that the right to education includes all people regardless of age, the chapter mainly focuses on education as a right for children and, in particular, how the right to education for children can be affected by violent conflict. It considers some of the problems faced and suggests that for the right to education to be realised the context in which education takes places needs to be considered.

International human rights and the right to education

While the idea of a right to education, especially for children, had been progressively developed in most industrialised nation-states by the nineteenth and twentieth centuries with state provision of schooling, it was not until after World War II and the development of the United Nations (UN) in 1945, that the idea of education as a *universal human right* began to be considered in any substantive way.

The UN's focus on maintaining global peace and cooperation (Page, 2008: 75–83), together with the World Bank and the International Monetary Fund, became 'central pillars of post-war multilateralism' (Mundy, 1998: 452). They would also go on to have a significant impact in the development of a universal right to education. In 1946 two further organisations were established which were also to play an important role, the United Nations Children's Fund (UNICEF) – initially to provide nutrition and healthcare to the many European children facing post-war poverty – and the United Nations Educational, Scientific and Cultural Organization (UNESCO), which, by 1948, had recommended that member states make primary education free, compulsory and universal (Bailliet and Larsen, 2015; UNESCO, 2010). In 1948, the UN Universal Declaration on Human Rights, adopted by all UN member states, declared the right to education as a universal human right (Article 26):

(1) Everyone has the right to education. Education shall be free, at least in the elementary and fundamental stages. Elementary education shall be compulsory. Technical and professional education shall be made generally available and higher education shall be equally accessible to all on the basis of merit.

(2) Education shall be directed to the full development of the human personality and to the strengthening of respect for human rights and fundamental freedoms. It shall promote understanding, tolerance and friendship among all nations, racial or religious groups, and shall further the activities of the United Nations for the maintenance of peace.

(3) Parents have a prior right to choose the kind of education that shall be given to their children.

This was complemented in 1959 by the Declaration of the Rights of the Child (United Nations General Assembly, 1959). It was to take another seven years of negotiations between UN member states before this right to education was incorporated into Articles 13 and 14 of the more legally binding 1966 UN International Covenant on Economic, Social and Cultural Rights (ICESCR). A UN reporting committee on the ICESCR was established in 1985 to oversee each ratifying member state's record in upholding those rights and to provide a five-yearly report in this regard. As with all UN reporting committees, however, the powers were mainly limited to persuasion or encouragement. Nevertheless, the existence of such a mechanism along with a range of other international 'conventions, declarations, recommendations, charters and programmes of action' (Bailliet and Larsen, 2015: 419), has promoted moral expectations on member states, and, when ratified and signed into law, set legal obligations. Besides the ICESCR, a number of other international frameworks have reinforced the concept of education as a universal right, such as the UNESCO Convention against Discrimination in Education (1960) and, at a European level, the European Social Charter (1996), dovetailing with the European Convention on Human Rights (1950), to provide a pan-European commitment to the right to education (Council of Europe, 2006).

Further international instruments have focused on pursuing the right to education for specific groups. These include: women, with the Convention on the Elimination of All Forms of Discrimination against Women (CEFDW) (1979); migrant workers and their families, with the International Convention on the Protection of the Rights of All Migrant Workers (ICPRMW) (1990); people with disabilities, with the Convention on the Rights of People with Disabilities (CRD) (2006); and, of particular importance in relation to the universal right to education for children, the Convention on the Rights of the Child (CRC) (1989). All these UN conventions have overseeing reporting committees which report on each ratifying state's compliance with rights on a regular periodic basis. In addition, the UN Special Rapporteur on the Right to Education, reporting to the UN General Assembly, investigates rights violations (Bailliet and Larsen, 2015: 419). These mechanisms provide a significant opportunity for individuals, organisations and broader coalitions to contribute towards the monitoring of children's rights within signatory states.

Throughout this period UNESCO has also acted as an important intermediary between developing countries in search of funding and those bodies with funds, such as the UN and the World Bank, despite being weakened politically and financially by the withdrawal of the USA (1984–2002, and again in 2019, with Israel) and the UK (1985–97) over geo-political issues. Less impacted by the political and funding constraints experienced by UNESCO, UNICEF's pursued focus on 'basic human needs', including education, garnered political support from social democratic member states as well as emerging international NGOs. Increasingly, children's rights became 'the normative and operational cornerstone of UNICEF' (Jones, 2006: 601). UNICEF, indeed, had been developing a focus on promoting 'basic education' from the 1980s, eventually proposing the 1990 World Conference on Education for All in Jomtien, Thailand, supported by UNESCO and the World Bank (Mundy, 1998). This launched the Education for All (EFA) goals (UNESCO, 2010) which were revisited ten years later in Dakar, Senegal, at the World Education Forum, and which – alongside the Millennium Development Goals (MDGs) – obliged governments to achieve universal primary education by 2015. Despite the impetus created by these targets, by the late 1990s it became apparent that the EFA goals would not be universally achieved and that political, social and economic situations, particularly in conflict-affected countries, were negatively affecting the education rights of many children (Novelli, 2010: 271–285). UNICEF was also actively involved in the drafting of the UN CRC, the 'most widely- and rapidly-accepted human rights treaty in history' (UNICEF, 1989) and which, with its overseeing reporting committee mechanism, was to have a significant impact on the promotion of educational rights for children.

The CRC and education rights

Prior to 1989, children's rights were perceived as 'a slogan in search of a definition' (Rodham, 1973: 487), with little recognition of children's agency or limited consideration of the importance of children's views in tackling widespread barriers to educational access. Despite the difficulties in achieving consensus, the CRC provided the 'fullest legal statement of children's rights to be found anywhere' (Freeman, 2000: 277) and the most far-reaching statement of educational rights ever formulated (Hammarberg, 1990: 97–105). Seeking to address the barriers to well-being faced by groups of children in light of socio-economic status, ethnicity and gender, the CRC is underpinned by a series of cross-cutting General Principles, which include non-discrimination (Article 2), serving the best interests of the child (Article 3), the child's right to development (Article 6) and respect for the views of the child in matters affecting them (Article 12). Through Articles 28 and 29, the CRC provides specific engagement with the right to education. The former demands that, underpinned by international cooperation: every child has the right to education, with primary education free to all children; secondary education available and accessible to all; and that school discipline respects children's dignity. Article 29 focuses on the goals of education and the development of children's 'personality, talents and mental and physical abilities to their fullest potential'. It does have its critics though. Lundy and colleagues criticise the scope of Article 28, describing it as the 'lowest common denominator that falls short of the levels of provision that many states make in relation to education' (2017: 365), in contrast to the broad aspirations of Article 29. Each Article identifies governmental obligations in relation to children's rights which are considered universal (applying to all children, everywhere, without exception), inalienable (belonging to every child and cannot be taken away under any circumstances) and indivisible (part of an inseparable framework). Exemplifying this indivisibility, many of the Articles are directly connected to a child's right to education. Tomaševski also argues that the right to education has a significant impact on other rights:

Education operates as a multiplier, enhancing the enjoyment of all individual rights and freedoms where the right to education is effectively guaranteed, while depriving people of the enjoyment of many rights and freedoms where the right to education is denied or violated. (Tomaševski, 2001: 10)

Where the right to education is denied, by consequence other rights, in the present or future, may also be compromised. While the right to education certainly epitomises the indivisibility and interdependence of all human rights, Lundy and colleagues argue that the right to education does not adequately capture how the interwoven framework has 'evolved and been articulated in international human rights law' (2017: 365). For this reason, they suggest that 'education rights' represent a more inclusive definition of the rights which directly and indirectly influence children's development.

A lack of clarity was judged problematic in early analyses (Hammarberg, 1990), with the vagueness leaving pivotal concepts open to manipulation. Freeman (2000) criticises the drafting of the CRC, highlighting the lack of input from children (within a document which espouses the importance of respecting their views) as well as a failure to engage with issues such as disability, gender and sexuality. Conflicts have also arisen around concepts related to freedom of thought and religion, adoption, the rights of the unborn child and 'traditional practices' (Johnson, 1992; Freeman, 2000). Despite claims of universality, several authors question the CRC's leanings towards Western norms (Nieuwenhuys, 2009). As with human rights, context is very important to the realisation of a right to education. Thus, it may be necessary to address existing social, economic and cultural inequalities, political instability, the need for peace-building and alleviation of conflict, the development of culturally relevant forms for educational provision with relevant progression pathways, the education of empathetic teaching staff, and the promotion of positive attitudes to education amongst families, peers and communities.

Violence within schools is one challenge to the realisation of a right to education (Hammarberg, 1990). Schools may harbour many forms of violence (Harber, 2004). With the presence of bullying, prejudice and corporal punishment, schools may be sites of both direct physical and often hidden symbolic or structural violence both inside and outside conflict-affected states. Schools may reproduce unequal gender relations and may be the sites of gender-based violence. The presence of such violence challenges children's right to be protected from all forms of violence, as entitled within Article 19 of the CRC, and considering the indivisibility of these Articles, presents a barrier to education rights. Thus the realisation of a right to education may also require the realisation of a whole range of other rights working in tandem with one another. Conversely, schools can be an environment in which a culture of peace can be created and promoted.

The impact of armed conflict on children's rights

One context in which a universal right to education faces particular challenges relates to education in conflict-affected parts of the world. A quarter of the world's population lives in countries affected by violent conflict. Globally, the number of armed conflicts appears to be decreasing; however, the indiscriminate nature of conflict has changed (Smith, 2011: 1–7; Shields and Paulson, 2015: 212–230). Contemporary armed conflicts are protracted, usually include non-state combatants, usually take place in developing world/former colonised countries and have an increasingly direct impact on non-combatants (Smith, 2014: 113–125). Indeed, the vast majority of casualties in conflicts in the early twenty-first century have been civilians. Children are disproportionately affected by such conflicts with tens of millions of children growing up in conflict-affected regions (UNESCO, 2011). Comprehensive human rights-based research has revealed the stark physical and psychosocial impact of armed conflict upon young people. Children are physically attacked, trafficked, are victims of sexual violence, are forcibly recruited into armed groups, are displaced from their homes and suffer significant disruption to their lives.

Attacks on education present a significant barrier to children's rights (Martinez, 2013; Novelli, 2010: 271–285). These attacks can be defined as 'threats or deliberate use of force against students, teachers, academics and any other education personnel, as well as attacks on education buildings, resources, materials and facilities, including transport' (GCPEA, 2014: 34). Save the Children, now a global children's charity, estimated that over 3,600 separate attacks on education had taken place in 2012 alone (Martinez, 2013). The Global Consortium to Protect Education from Attack, a coalition of NGOs and UN bodies, highlighted 30 countries where there had been significant attacks on educational institutions, educators and learners in the five years previous, and another 40 countries where isolated incidents had occurred (GCPEA, 2018). Progress on inclusion, educational access, school attendance and school completion are also hindered in countries affected by conflict (Poirier, 2012: 341–351). In

2013, 50 million children remained out of school in conflict-affected countries (Martinez, 2013). Evidence suggests that the impact of conflict may be greater on younger children, but it is also recognised that conflict may affect girls and boys differently (Burde et al, 2017). For example, conflict may place girls at an increased risk of violence within schools (Winthrop and Kirk, 2008: 639–661). Elsewhere, conscription of young males into armed groups presents a barrier to access for boys. Violent conflict also has an unexpected impact on certain educational markers. Studies have shown that in low-intensity conflict, educational enrolment may indeed increase as people seek the opportunity to migrate (de Groot and Göskel, 2011), or due to the pro-education policies of warring factions. Other research questions whether armed conflict is singularly responsible for the denial of education rights. Shields and Paulson (2015) argue that while poor educational outcomes are associated with countries affected by conflict, wider societal factors, described as 'fragility', may underpin both the conflict and low educational outcomes. As such, a focus on state fragility may provide a useful lens to consider education rights.

In a comprehensive critical examination of the relationship between education and conflict, Davies (2004) analysed several educational approaches which have attempted to address violence, while also providing an exploration of educational contributions to violent conflict. In conflict-affected contexts, there is often a recognised imperative to adapt educational practices aimed at discouraging violence and creating peace-building environments (Davies, 2004; Smith, 2014). Often the scope of such transformation is perceived to be vast: 'the existing educational systems, including the overall educational vision, institutional structure within schools, classroom climate and teacher education, need to shift' (Gill and Niens, 2014: 21). As such, creating conditions which make violence less likely might seem more realistic. Exploring the relationship between education and conflict in more depth, Bush and Saltarelli (2000) categorise the positive and negative effects of education on larger scale violent conflict. On the negative side, they argue that the uneven provision of schooling may perpetuate educational and socio-economic inequalities, and in doing so serve to fuel conflict. On the positive side, inclusive peace-centred practices can challenge violent conflict.

Within the Education for All Global Monitoring Report (UNESCO, 2011), consideration is given to the quality of education and the importance of 'ensuring excellence of all so that recognized and measurable outcomes are achieved by all, especially in literacy, numeracy and essential life skills' (Davies, 2013: 83). While the focus on literacy and numeracy is important, Davies argues strongly that any conceptualisation of educational quality should move beyond numeracy and literacy to consider issues such as pupil agency, the understanding of democracy, peace education, human rights and ecology – and even lingualism. The inclusion of human rights education (HRE) within this consideration is significant, as it is increasingly viewed as an integral component of education in post-conflict societies (Osler and Starkey, 2006). Furthermore, HRE provides a means of grounding children's educational experiences within the CRC (Osler and Starkey, 2010). Such a focus also complements the considerable HRE work undertaken by multilateral organisations (Waldron et al, 2011).

Both violence towards and violence within schools has tremendous negative impact on the educational rights, well-being and lives of children throughout the world (eg Davies, 2004; Harber, 2004). Within conflict-affected regions, it may be unclear whether conflict itself remains the sole cause of rights infringements, but it is clear that in many cases, armed conflict – often connected to globalised networks – lessens enrolment, weakens attendance, reduces school completion, destroys educational infrastructure and reduces the chance for many children to lead a life of peace and educational opportunity (Martinez, 2013; Novelli, 2010; O'Malley, 2010).

UNESCO has argued for strengthened human rights protection for children living in conflict-affected countries, increased funding for education systems through humanitarian aid, greater support for peace-building and reconstruction and wider commitment to developing education systems that challenge the causes of violent conflict and foster peace (UNESCO, 2011). Similarly, Save the Children has called for improved monitoring of attacks on education (Martinez, 2013). Indeed, NGOs and non-state actors have held pivotal roles in shaping the work of the UN and the development of educational policies (Hartung, 2017; Jones, 2006). Global collaborations offer important coalitions to challenge the impact of violence on children's rights. For example, the Inter-Agency Network for Education in Emergencies (INEE), formed by educators connected to UN agencies and the International Rescue Committee, holds significant membership and seeks to research, understand and campaign against attacks on education through a commitment to the Safe Schools Declaration (Burde et al, 2017). Child Soldiers International, developed by Amnesty International, Human Rights Watch and Save the Children, led a successful campaign for the Optional Protocol to the Convention on the Rights of the Child (2002), which sought to limit the involvement of children in armed conflict. They continue to advocate against the use of children in armed forces (Coalition to Stop the Use of Child Soldiers, 2008).

Conclusion

Ensuring that the right to education is met for all people, regardless of individual or group identity, remains one of the pressing challenges for social policy across the globe. While the UN human rights conventions, their reporting committees and collaboration between multilateral institutions, states and NGOs, presents opportunities for the universal realisation of education as a human right, there is still no country where all children have their educational rights realised (Lundy et al, 2017). As Novelli noted 'education systems are embedded in complex social systems and local and global political economies' (2010: 272). In the developing world in particular, it is imperative to consider how broader economic frameworks – such as those pursued by the World Bank, International Monetary Fund and Western governments – shape education, children's rights and violence. Klees identifies the challenge of such an approach in this way: 'if education is seen as a human right, then examining the obstacles to fulfilling a child's right to an education becomes even more subversive of the economic order' (Klees, 2002: 470). Criticisms of global economic and human rights alignment with Western perspectives need to be addressed with processes that are inclusive of those voices and perspectives absent in its development. This is particularly pertinent for conflict-affected regions, where a deeper understanding of the context is imperative (Burde et al, 2017), but where humanitarian approaches to education rights may represent new forms of imperialism.

An urgent requirement for those concerned with children's education rights appears to be an honest appraisal of the extent to which formal education contributes towards perpetuating violence and, within regions more directly affected by war, reinforces the foundations of violent conflict (for example, Davies, 2004). In short, 'education can be part of a solution to injustice in the world, but equally it can promote violence and injustice' (Osler and Starkey, 2010: 129). At the very least, education must ensure that it is not reinforcing the wider societal norms which are causes of conflict, before it may consider operating as a force for positive change.

While the focus on literacy and numeracy dominates particular conceptualisations of the right to education, Article 42 of the CRC states that governments have an obligation to make the Convention known to children, signifying the need for children's rights which are grounded within education as 'part of an emergent "common sense" and are articulated with social practices'. Even if the barriers towards the realisation of education rights are created by violent conflicts or state fragility, it remains imperative that children's rights must form a central tenet of any conceptualisation of quality education: 'the right *to* education needs to be complemented by rights *in* education and rights *through* education' (Osler and Starkey, 2010: 129). Furthermore, children's perspectives on and experiences of violence, such as those gathered through the University of Oxford's Young Lives project in Ethiopia, India, Peru and Vietnam (Pells and Morrow, 2018), offer significant insight and should shape the development of approaches to support the educational rights of all.

References

Bailliet, C.M. and Larsen, K.M. (2015) *Promoting Peace through International Law*, Oxford: Oxford University Press.

Burde, D., Kapit, A., Wahl, R.L., Guven, O. and Skarpeteig, M.I. (2017) 'Education in emergencies: a review of theory and research', *Review of Educational Research*, 87(3): 619–658.

Bush, K. and Saltarelli, D. (2000) *The Two Faces of Education in Ethnic Conflict: Towards a Peacebuilding Education for Children*, Florence: UNICEF. Available from: https://doi.org/10.1038/nchem.944

Coalition to Stop the Use of Child Soldiers (2008) *Child Soldiers: Global Report,* Volume 45, Coalition to Stop the Use of Child Soldiers.

Council of Europe (2006) *The Right to Education Under the European Social Charter*. Available from: www.right-to-education.org/sites/right-to-education.org/files/resource-attachments/ESC_The_Right_to_Education_under_the_European_Social_Charter_2006_en.pdf

Davies, L. (2004) *Education and Conflict: Complexity and Chaos*, London: RoutledgeFalmer.

Davis, L. (2013) 'Education, change and peacebuilding', *FriEnt*, 1, 1–7.

De Groot, O.J. and Göksel, I. (2011) 'Conflict and education demand in the Basque region', *Journal of Conflict Resolution*, 55(4): 652–677.

Freeman, M. (2000) 'The future of children's rights', *Children and Society*, 14: 277–293.

Gill, S. and Niens, U. (2014) 'Education as humanisation: a theoretical review on the role of dialogic pedagogy in peacebuilding education', *Compare: A Journal of Comparative and International Education*, 44(1): 10–31.

Global Coalition to Protect Education from Attack (GCPA) (2014) *Education Under Attack*, New York: GCPA. Available from: www.protectingeducation.org/sites/default/files/documents/eua_2014_full_0.pdf

Global Coalition to Protect Education from Attack (GCPA) (2018) *Education Under Attack*, New York: GCPA. Available from: www.protectingeducation.org/sites/default/files/documents/eua_2018_full.pdf

Hammarberg, T. (1990) 'The UN Convention on the Rights of the Child and how to make it work', *Human Rights Quarterly*, 12(1): 97–105.

Harber, C. (2004) *Schooling as Violence: How Schools Harm Pupils and Societies*, London: Routledge.

Hartung, C. (2017) 'Global citizenship incorporated: competing responsibilities in the education of global citizens', *Discourse: Studies in the Cultural Politics of Education*, 38(1): 16–29.

Johnson, D. (1992) 'Cultural and regional pluralism in the drafting of the UN Convention on the Rights of the Child', in M. Freeman and P. Veerman (eds) *The Ideologies of Children's Rights*, Dordrecht: Nijhoff, pp 95–114.

Jones, P.W. (2006) 'Elusive mandate: UNICEF and educational development', *International Journal of Educational Development*, 26(6): 591–604.

Klees, S.J. (2002) 'World Bank education policy: new rhetoric, old ideology', *International Journal of Educational Development*, 22(5): 451–474.

Lundy, L., Orr, K. and Shier, H. (2017) 'Children's education rights: global perspectives', in M. Ruck, M. Peterson-Badali and M. Freeman (eds) *Handbook of Children's Rights: Global and Multidisciplinary Perspectives*, Abingdon: Taylor and Francis, pp 364–380.

Martinez, E. (2013) *Attacks on Education: The Impact of Conflict and Grave Violations on Children's Futures*, London: Save the Children.

Mundy, K. (1998) 'Focus on world order educational multilateralism and world (dis)order', *Comparative Education Review*, 42(4): 448–478.

Nieuwenhuys, O. (2009) 'Editorial: is there an Indian childhood?', *Childhood*, 16(2): 147–153.

Novelli, M. (2010) 'Education, conflict and social (in)justice: insights from Colombia', *Educational Review*, 62(3): 271–285.

O'Malley, B. (2010) *Education Under Attack*, Paris: UNESCO. Available from: http://unesdoc.unesco.org/images/0018/001868/186809e.pdf

Osler, A. and Starkey, H. (2006) 'Education for democratic citizenship: a review of research, policy and practice 1995–2005', *Research Papers in Education*, 21(4): 433–466.

Osler, A. and Starkey, H. (2010) *Teachers and Human Rights Education*, Stoke-on-Trent: Trentham Books.

Page, J. (2008) 'The United Nations and Peace Education', in M. Bajaj (ed) *Encyclopedia of Peace Education*, Charlotte, NC: Information Age Publishing, pp 75–83.

Pells, K. and Morrow, V. (2018) *Children's Experiences of Violence: Evidence from the Young Lives study in Ethiopia, India, Peru and Vietnam*. Available from: www.younglives.org.uk/content/childrens-experiences-violence-evidence-young-lives-study-ethiopia-india-peru-and-vietnam

Poirier, T. (2012) 'The effects of armed conflict on schooling in sub-Saharan Africa', *International Journal of Educational Development*, 32(2): 341–351.

Rodham, H. (1973) 'Children under the law', *Harvard Educational Review*, 43(4): 487–514.

Shields, R. and Paulson, J. (2015) ' "Development in reverse"? A longitudinal analysis of armed conflict, fragility and school enrolment', *Comparative Education*, 51(2): 212–230.

Smith, A. (2011) 'Education and peacebuilding: from "conflict-analysis" to "conflict transformation"?', *FriEnt*, 4: 1–7.

Smith, A. (2014) 'Contemporary challenges for education in conflict affected countries', *Journal of International and Comparative Education*, 3(1): 113–125.

Tomaševski, K. (2001) *Human Rights Obligations: Making Education Available, Accessible, Acceptable and Adaptable*, Gothenburg: Sida.

UNESCO (2010) *UNESCO at a Glance*, Paris. Available from: http://unesdoc.unesco.org/images/0018/001887/188700e.pdf

UNESCO (2011) 'The hidden crisis: armed conflict and education', *EFA Global Monitoring Report*. Available from: https://news.harvard.edu/wp-content/uploads/2016/02/190743e.pdf

UNICEF (1989) *Convention on the Rights of the Child*. Available at: https://www.unicef.org.uk/rights-respecting-schools/wp-content/uploads/sites/4/2017/01/UNCRC-in-full.pdf

United Nations General Assembly (1959) *Declaration of the Rights of the Child*. Available at: https://doi.org/10.1017/S0020860400013243

Waldron, F., Kavanagh, A., Maunsell, C., Oberman, R., O'Reilly, M., Pike, S. and Ruane, B. (2011) *Teachers, Human Rights and Human Rights Education: Knowledge, Perspectives and Practices of Primary School Teachers in Dublin*. Available from: www.dcu.ie/sites/default/files/chrce/pdf/CHRCE-primary-teacher-human-rights-report.pdf

Winthrop, R. and Kirk, J. (2008) 'Learning for a bright future: schooling, armed conflict, and children's well-being', *Comparative Education Review*, 52(4): 639–661.

15

The right to healthcare

Ann Marie Gray

This chapter explores the relationship between human rights and health and social care. It begins by setting out the main international mechanisms and the obligations that these place on governments. It then discusses the impact of international and domestic human rights instruments through an examination of developments in social care policy, and with regard to reproductive healthcare rights in Northern Ireland. It also highlights issues relating to devolution and the implementation of human rights in the UK.

International mechanism relating to the right to health and social care

In 2015, the principles of a human rights–based approach to health were endorsed in the United Nations 2030 Agenda for Sustainable Development (United Nations, 2015), including the target of universal health coverage. However, the right to the highest attainable standard of health has long been internationally recognised as a fundamental human right. In 1946, the constitution of the World Health Organization (WHO) set out the principles which it described as basic to happiness, harmonious relations and the security of all peoples. These included the statement that: 'The enjoyment of the highest attainable standard of health is one of the fundamental rights of every human being without distinction of race, religion, political belief, economic or social condition' (WHO, 1946: 1). The Universal Declaration of Human Rights, adopted by the United Nations in 1948, for example, refers to the:

> right to a standard of living adequate for the health and well-being of himself and of his family, including food, clothing, housing and medical care and necessary social services, and the right to security in the event of unemployment, sickness, disability, widowhood, old age or other lack of livelihood in circumstances beyond his control. (Article 25)

Since then, a number of other human rights treaties have recognised the right to health. The most authoritative statement of the right to health is set out in the International Covenant on Economic, Social and Cultural Rights (ICESCR) (United Nations, 1966). Article 12 of the Covenant recognises 'the right of everyone to the enjoyment of the highest attainable standard of physical and mental health'. It sets out steps to be taken by state parties to achieve the full realisation of the right to health, which should include those necessary for: the reduction of the stillbirth rate and of infant mortality and the healthy development of the child; the improvement of all aspects of environmental and industrial hygiene; the prevention, treatment and control of epidemic, endemic, occupational and other diseases; and the creation of conditions which would assure access to all medical service and medical attention in the event of sickness. Furthermore, the obligation on states to respect the right to health recognises that health policies can be implemented in a way that violates human rights. Therefore, states should not deny or limit equal access – including for prisoners or detainees, asylum seekers and illegal immigrants – and should not impose discriminatory practices relating to women's health status.

The substantive obligations embodied within the right to health were clarified by the United Nations Committee on Economic, Social and Cultural Rights (CESCR, 2000) in legal guidance contained in General Comment 14. With regard to what is meant by 'highest attainable standard of health', the approach taken by CESCR is one of 'progressive realisation'. This recognises that the realisation of rights by states may only be achievable over time due to the limited availability of resources. Therefore, in determining what actions or omissions amount to a violation of the right to health under Article 12, a distinction will be made between the unwillingness and inability of a state party to comply (paragraph 47). This is not an opt-out for states and they are expected by the CESCR to 'move as expeditiously and effectively as possible towards that goal' (paragraph 9). The core obligations that states have to ensure include services that address the underlying determinants of health. For instance, irrespective of a state's available resources, it has to guarantee minimum essential food, basic shelter and education concerning the main health problems (WHO, 2016) – in short a floor below which states should not fall. Underlying factors also include gender equality and non-discrimination.

Other human rights instruments address the right to health in various ways, some with regard to the human rights of specific groups, others from a more general application (see Table 15.1). For example, the Convention on the Elimination of All Forms of Discrimination against

Table 15.1 Main international human rights instruments relating to the right to health

Universal Declaration of Human Rights (1948)	Article 25
International Convention on the Elimination of All Forms of Racial Discrimination (1965)	Article 5
(UN) International Covenant on Economic, Social and Cultural Rights (1976)	Article 12
(UN) International Covenant on Civil and Political Rights (1976)	Articles 6, 7 and 17
(UN) Convention on the Elimination of Discrimination against Women (1979)	Articles 12 and 14
(UN) Convention on the Rights of the Child (1989)	Article 24
(UN) Convention on the Rights of People with Disabilities (2006)	Article 25
European Convention on Human Rights (1950)	Article 8

Women (CEDAW) (United Nations, 1979), Article 12, complemented by Article 16, guarantees women the right to health, including sexual and reproductive health. Article 14 requires states to take all appropriate measures to eliminate discrimination against women in rural areas so that they can participate in and benefit from healthcare (and other services). The United Nations Convention on the Rights of the Child (United Nations, 1989) recognises the right of the child to the enjoyment of the highest attainable standard of health and to facilities for the treatment of illness and rehabilitation of health (Article 24). The right to health is, however, not guaranteed by the Convention for the Protection of Human Rights and Fundamental Freedoms – better known as the European Convention on Human Rights (Council of Europe, 1950) – but under the Convention states have a number of obligations impacting on healthcare policy and decisions. Article 8 of the Convention – the right to respect for private and family life – is the most relevant to health and social care and contains four rights: the right to respect for private life; the right to respect for family life; the right to respect for one's home; and the right to respect for correspondence (European Court of Human Rights, 2018). Within health and social care settings this could apply to issues such as the protection of patients' physical integrity, the right to autonomy and self-determination in a competent patient, and the right to confidentiality.

By ratifying these international treaties countries pledge to make sure their domestic laws and policies comply with them. The rights set out in them are universal and interdependent and governments cannot pick and choose what rights to offer citizens (Flanigan and Hosie, 2016). However, how rights are promoted and protected is up to individual member states. Debates about the right to health have often focused on the potential for generating rights at the level of national social policy or what has been argued to be unrealistic obligations placed on states (O'Neill, 2005). The lack of specificity about what states would be required to provide to meet obligations has also been raised as problematic, for example, in relation to the goal of universal health coverage (Chapman et al, 2018). Attempts have been made by the United Nations through the addition of General Comments to treaties and the appointment of UN Special Rapporteurs for Health to apply the treaties (see, for example, the Right to Health and Public Policy and the Right to Mental Health) (UN Special Rapporteur for Health, 2016).

Application of the human rights legislation to health and social care in the UK

The rights contained in the UN treaties are not directly legally enforceable in UK courts. However, in ratifying the treaties, the UK has pledged to make sure its domestic laws and policies comply with them. The Human Rights Act (1998) incorporates the European Convention on Human Rights into UK law and obliges all public authorities to ensure compliance with it. In addition to not breaching human rights there is an expectation that all public authorities will take proactive steps to protect people from human rights abuses (Dyer, 2015). Rights include: the right to life (Article 2), the prohibition of inhuman or degrading treatment (Article 3), the right to liberty and security (Article 5), the right to respect for private and family life (Article 8), freedom of thought, conscience and religion (Article 9), and the prohibition of discrimination (Article 14). There is no specific reference to health in the UK's Human Rights Act of 1998 similar to that contained in the Universal Declaration of Human Rights, for example. However, the Human Rights Act impinges on several areas of medical practice, including life-and-death issues, mental health, reproductive rights confidentiality, and access to treatment and care (Samanta and Samanta, 2005). The Act clearly encompasses National Health Service (NHS) institutions and agencies, regulatory and inspection bodies, and governance bodies such as research ethics committees. The human rights treaties and mechanisms have influenced discourse and domestic policy, and legislation in the UK. They have contributed to the strengthening of rights of autonomy and self-determination, dignity and access to care. The next section of this chapter looks at examples of human rights-based approaches in the UK, particularly in the areas of social care and reproductive rights.

Social care and human rights

Social care in the UK has historically lacked the universality of the NHS, with differences in access and entitlement across geographical boundaries and a much more extensive mixed economy of provision (Gray and Birrell, 2013). Authorities providing care have responsibilities under the treaties and legislation outlined earlier to protect and promote the human rights of people needing care. However, these have often been poorly understood and implemented. In social care settings people can face greater risks to their rights to dignity, to privacy and to being safe from degrading treatment. The Equality and Human Rights Commission is a non-departmental public body with responsibility to promote equality and diversity, eliminate unlawful discrimination, and protect and promote human rights in England, Scotland and Wales. In 2011, its report on older people's experiences of using home care services found serious, systematic threats to the human rights of older people (Equality and Human Rights Commission, 2011). These included inadequate support with food and drink resulting in weight loss and dehydration, neglect of older people because care workers did not have sufficient time to complete everything in the care plan, lack of respect for personal privacy when intimate tasks were carried out and a lack of control over when their care was provided. An inquiry by the Northern Ireland Human Rights Commission (2012) on the human rights of older people in nursing homes demonstrated how failure to place international human rights standards at the core of the legal and regulatory framework applicable to nursing homes undermined residents' human rights. A specific challenge in social care provision has been the limitation presented by the ambiguity around the interpretation of 'public authority'. This has been particularly important in a context of market-based commissioning of services from private and third sector providers. The Human Rights Act created a legal duty on 'public authorities' and those 'preforming public functions' to respect, protect and fulfil human rights. This recognised that public services were being increasingly contracted out. UN treaties have also attempted to clarify this. As early as 1994 the CESCR had noted that with regard to the treatment of people with disabilities:

> given the increasing commitment of Governments around the world to market-based policies, it is appropriate

in that context to emphasize certain aspects of States parties' obligations. One is the need to ensure that not only the public sphere, but also the private sphere, are, within appropriate limits, subject to regulation to ensure the equitable treatment of persons. (UN CESCR, 1994: paragraph 12)

However, in the UK a number of court interpretations had created ambiguity about who had obligations under the law, including a 2007 case (*YL v Birmingham City Council*) under the Human Rights Act in which private sector care homes were found not to fall within the public functions definition in the HRA (Ferrie, 2011). This meant that such service users had no direct legal remedy to hold their providers to account for abuse, neglect and undignified treatment. This loophole was partially closed by an amendment to the 2008 Health and Social Care Act whereby care homes providing services for people under the National Assistance Act (1948) were deemed to be exercising functions of a public nature under the HRA. Such protections did not apply to people cared for in their own home by a private or third sector agency, even if their care had been arranged by the local authority. This was eventually addressed under Section 73 of the 2014 Care Act (Department of Health, 2014), where people receiving care from a regulated provider and arranged by the local authority, whether they receive that care in a residential home or in their own home, will be covered by the HRA. However, limitations remain as this provision does not apply to people arranging and paying for their own care.

The failure to apply human rights obligations to social care has also been the subject of criticism from UN bodies. In 2015 the UN Committee on the Rights of Persons with Disabilities (CRPD) initiated an inquiry into the impact of the UK government's policies on the rights of disabled people under the Optional Protocol to the Convention (the first inquiry to be initiated under the Convention). It found that governmental reforms had led to 'grave and systematic' violations of the rights of disabled people. With regard to social care the report concluded that cuts to social care services negatively and disproportionately affect disabled people and obstruct their ability to live independently (Jones et al, 2017). It also referred to the tightening of eligibility criteria to access social care services and the reduction in personal care packages, claiming that individuals with disabilities are no longer receiving the level of care required. Change, even in the face of such strong conclusions and recommendations, has been limited. On 11 January 2019, the *New Statesman* carried the headline 'Why the social care crisis is a human rights issue'. It reported on a Human Rights Watch investigation on the impact of continuing cuts to social care funding and in particular with regard to how care assessments are carried out.

Access to reproductive healthcare rights in Northern Ireland

This section of the chapter examines the right to health through the issue of reproductive rights in Northern Ireland (NI). It discusses attempts to achieve reform of abortion law in NI through the international treaty mechanisms and CEDAW in particular. Abortion is legal in NI only in very restricted circumstances – to preserve a pregnant woman's life or to prevent permanent damage to physical or mental health. The 1967 Abortion Act, which made legal abortion available in England, Scotland and Wales, was never extended to Northern Ireland. This means that women in NI, a part of the UK, have never been able to access NHS abortions in the way that women in the rest of the UK have (Horgan and O'Connor, 2014). A number of CEDAW articles are relevant to abortion, in particular Article 12, which requires state parties to eliminate discrimination against women in healthcare, including in relation to family planning. General Recommendation 35 of the CEDAW Committee includes forced pregnancy and the criminalisation of abortion within the meaning of violence against women.

The CEDAW Committee has repeatedly challenged the UK government about non-compliance with the obligations of the Convention with regard to reproductive rights (in Concluding Observations in 1999, 2008, 2013 and 2019) and the implications for women's access to health services (O'Rourke, 2016). Following a complaint from non-governmental organisations (NGOs) in NI of grave and systemic violations of the Convention, the Committee undertook an inquiry under the Optional Protocol to CEDAW. The CEDAW Committee concluded (CEDAW, 2017) that the UK government had breached international standards concerning access to sexual and reproductive health, including access to safe abortions. It noted that policies affecting only women from exercising reproductive choice and resulting in women being forced to carry almost every pregnancy to full term involves mental and physical suffering constituting violence against women.

Other UN Treaty bodies have also made specific recommendations regarding the law on reproductive rights in NI. In 2016, the CRC recommended that the state decriminalise termination of pregnancy.

The CESCR took a similar position regarding decriminalisation of abortion in respect of cases of rape, incest and foetal abnormality. Women's rights with regard to this aspect of healthcare have also been tested in the UK courts. In 2013 the Northern Ireland Human Rights Commission (NIHRC) brought judicial review proceedings challenging the compatibility of the law on abortion in Northern Ireland with UK human rights commitments. The NIHRC argued that in three circumstances: sexual crime (rape or incest); cases involving fatal foetal abnormality; and cases involving serious malformation of the foetus, the prohibition of abortion is incompatible with rights to private and family life under Article 8 and Article 3 of the ECHR. The NI High Court (2015) ruled that incompatibility did exist but this decision was overturned by the Court of Appeal in 2016. The case was then taken to the Supreme Court by the NIHRC and in 2018 the Supreme Court added its views on the incompatibility of NI law with the UK's human rights obligations (NIHRC, 2018). It concluded that the NIHRC did not have the legal standing to take the case but a majority of the Court held that the criminal law on abortion was in breach of a woman's Article 8 right to private and family life, insofar as it prohibits termination of pregnancy on the grounds of rape, incest and fatal foetal abnormality. A minority of the Supreme Court found a violation of the right to freedom from torture, inhuman and degrading treatment under Article 3.

Guidance for healthcare professionals

Following lengthy litigation by the Family Planning Association, the Department of Health in NI has produced guidance on termination of pregnancy for healthcare professionals (Department of Health, 2016). This was a response to a court ruling that in order to comply with its statutory duty the Department needed to provide information and guidance to health professionals responsible for assessing whether the legal test for a termination is met. This guidance has, however, been criticised for its lack of clarity, with the CEDAW Committee recommending that the UK government: 'adopt evidence-based protocols for healthcare professionals on providing legal abortions particularly on the grounds of physical and mental health; and ensure continuous training on these protocols' (CEDAW, 2017: paragraph 15). With regard to the Department of Health guidelines, the CEDAW Committee also expressed concern about their 'chilling effect' and how lack of clarity regarding the situations in which abortion is legal, and references in the guidelines to criminal sanctions, discouraged women from exercising autonomy with regard to their right to healthcare and clinicians who might assist them – a point also made by the Supreme Court (2018).

In 2017, in response to ongoing criticism about women's access to healthcare rights in NI, the UK government legislated for women and girls to access free abortions on the NHS in England. However, the House of Commons Women and Equalities Committee (2019) found that doctors had not been provided with information from the Department of Health in NI about advising patients about the scheme and that patients were not getting the information they needed. It concluded that: 'there is uncertainty about the legality of doctors in Northern Ireland referring patients to the UK Government funded scheme providing free abortions in England and there can be a conflict between healthcare professionals' duties to their patients, and the law and guidance on abortion in Northern Ireland' (paragraph 110).

Devolution and UK state party obligations with regard to the right to health

The debate about access to reproductive healthcare rights has given rise to broader issues of where legislative responsibility lies in the context of devolution. Fegan and Rebouche (2003) discuss how opposition to abortion law reform has been framed as a 'cultural issue' which unites both sides of a divided society. In debates in the NI assembly there has been frequent reference to the public opposition to reform (O'Rourke, 2016) and the NI Secretary of State has frequently suggested that public opinion in NI may differ significantly from elsewhere in the UK, although empirical evidence does not support this (Gray, 2017). Given the contested nature of reproductive rights, the increasingly forceful statements from treaty bodies about how the right to healthcare is being breached, and a growing public debate, it is hardly surprising that the issue of where legislative responsibility lies has come to the fore. Under the devolution settlement responsibility for international treaties is considered an 'excepted' matter which remains the sole responsibility of the UK government. As noted by the NIHRC (2018), the CEDAW Committee dealt with the issue of the obligations of the state party with respect to a devolved administration in its Inquiry Report and in Concluding Observations. It noted:

> under international law of State responsibility, all acts of State organs are attributable to the State. The Vienna Convention on the Law of Treaties provides in article 27

that a party to a treaty may not invoke the provisions of its internal law as a justification for its failure to perform it. Moreover, the Committee's General Recommendation (GR) No. 28 (2010) on the core obligations of States parties reiterates that the delegation of government powers does not negate the direct responsibility of the State party's national or federal Government to fulfil its obligations to all women within its jurisdiction. (CEDAW, 2017)

In spite of this, the Secretary of State for NI has continued to argue that abortion is a devolved issue and the responsibility of the (non-functioning) NI government (House of Commons Women and Equalities Committee, 2019). In considering this issue, the Women and Equalities Committee concluded that there are specific obligations for the NI Assembly not to pass Acts that are contrary to the UK's international obligations and that internal laws cannot be used to justify a failure to comply with human rights standards.

Conclusion

The UK has not incorporated international economic, social and cultural rights standards into its domestic law. The Human Rights Act (1998) incorporates the rights set out in the European Convention on Human Rights, mostly political and civil rather than socio-economic rights. It has been argued that the approach of UK governments to international treaties has been to see them not as rights but as principles implemented through the domestic welfare state policies (Freeman, 2009). It could be argued, for example, that changes to the 2014 Care Act discussed earlier demonstrate this approach and that with regard to social care the residual model of provision suggests provision is a 'gift' to users rather than an entitlement. It could be argued that the UK has cautiously embraced the human right to health. A 2009 inquiry to assess the progress being made towards a culture of respect for human rights in Great Britain found that much remained to be done to give effect to international agreements (Equality and Human Rights Commission, 2009). This has been borne out by the findings of inquiries into the neglect and inhumane treatment of older people and people with a disability receiving health and social care services (Francis, 2013; Care Quality Commission, 2011; Commissioner for Older People NI, 2018).

The issue of access to reproductive health rights in NI and the NGO engagement with the human rights frameworks and institutions, and

CEDAW in particular, confirms the importance and value of its cultural work. It has been noted (O'Rourke, 2016) that none of the three NGOs that made the application for an Optional Protocol Inquiry to CEDAW saw human rights as their primary mandate – yet they perceived a value to engaging with local human rights institutions and international mechanisms in the face of domestic opposition. Although it could be argued that, while there has been very limited change in women's access to reproductive healthcare, the issue is now very prominent on the policy agenda in the UK.

References

Care Quality Commission (CQC) (2011) *Review of Compliance: Winterbourne View*, London: CQC.

Chapman, A.R., Forman, L. Lamprea, E. and Khanna, K. (2018) 'Identifying the components of a core health services package from a human rights perspective to inform progress toward universal health coverage', *Human Rights Quarterly*, 40(2): 342–368.

Commissioner for Older People NI (2018) *Home Truths: A Report on the Commissioner's Investigation into Dunmurry Manor Care Home*, Belfast: COPNI.

Convention on the Elimination of All Forms of Discrimination Against Women (CEDAW) (2017) *Report of the Inquiry concerning the United Kingdom of Great Britain and Northern Ireland under Article 8 of the Optional Protocol to the Convention on the Elimination of All Forms of Discrimination against Women*, New York: UN CEDAW.

Council of Europe (1950) *Convention for the Protection of Human Rights and Fundamental Freedoms and Optional Protocol*, Strasbourg: Council of Europe.

Department of Health (2014) *Care Act*, London: The Stationery Office.

Department of Health (NI) (2016) *Guidance for Health and Social Care Professionals on Termination of Pregnancy in Northern Ireland*, Belfast: DoH.

Dyer, L. (2015) 'Evidence of the impact of human rights-based approaches to health', *Health and Human Rights*, 17(2): 111–122.

Equality and Human Rights Commission (2009) *Human Rights Inquiry*, London: EHRC.

Equality and Human Rights Commission (2011) *Close to Home: An Inquiry into Older People and Home Care*, London: EHRC.

European Court of Human Rights (2018) *Guide on Article 8 of the European Convention on Human Rights*, Strasbourg: Council of Europe.

Fegan, E. and Rebouche, R. (2003) 'Northern Ireland's abortion law: the morality of silence and the censure of agency', *Feminist Legal Studies*, 11: 221–243.

Ferrie, J. (2011) 'Sociology and human rights: what have they got to say about care and dignity', in P. Hynes, L. Michele, D. Short and M. Waites (eds) *Sociology and Human Rights*, London: Routledge, pp 55–69.

Flanigan, D. and Hosie, A. (2016) 'Human rights and equality', in P. Alcock, T. Haux, M. May and S. Wright (eds) *The Student's Companion to Social Policy*, Chester: Wiley, pp 34–40.

Francis, R. (2013) *Report of the Mid Staffordshire NHS Foundation Trust Public Inquiry*, The Mid Staffordshire NHS Foundation Trust. London: HMSO.

Freeman, M. (2009) 'The right to health', in R. Morgan and B.S. Turner (eds) *Interpreting Human Rights*, London: Routledge, pp 44–67.

Gray, A.M. and Birrell, D. (2013) *Transforming Adult Social Care*, Bristol: Policy Press.

Gray, A.M. (2017) *Attitudes to Abortion in Northern Ireland*, ARK Research Update Ireland. Available from: www.ark.ac.uk/publications/updates/update115.pdf

Horgan, G. and O'Connor, J.S. (2014) 'Abortion and citizenship rights in a devolved region of the UK', *Social Policy and Society*, 13(1): 39–49.

House of Commons Women and Equalities Committee (2019) *Abortion Law in Northern Ireland*, HC 1584, London: House of Commons.

Jones, A., Wilson, W., Jarret, T., Kennedy, S. and Powell, A. (2017) *The UN Inquiry into the Rights of Persons with Disabilities in the UK. A Briefing Paper Number 07367*, London: House of Commons Library.

Northern Ireland Human Rights Commission (2012) *In Defence of Dignity: The Human Rights of Older People in Nursing Homes*, Belfast: NIHRC.

Northern Ireland Human Rights Commission (2018) *NIHRC Response to the Women and Equalities Committee Inquiry into Abortion Law in NI*, Belfast: NIHRC.

O'Neill, O. (2005) 'The dark side of human rights', *International Affairs*, 81(2): 427–439.

O'Rourke, C. (2016) 'Advocating abortion rights in Northern Ireland: local and global tensions', *Social and Legal Studies*, 25(6): 716–740.

Samanta, A. and Samanta, J. (2005) 'The Human Rights Act 1998 – why should it matter for medical practice?', *Journal of the Royal Society of Medicine*, 98(9): 404–410.

Supreme Court (2018) *In the Matter of an Application by the Northern Ireland Human Rights Commission for Judicial Review (Northern Ireland) Reference by the Court of Appeal in Northern Ireland pursuant to Paragraph 33 of Schedule 10 to the Northern Ireland Act 1998 (Abortion) (Northern Ireland)*. Available from: www.supremecourt.uk/cases/docs/uksc-2017-0131-judgment.pdf

United Nations (1948) *The Universal Declaration of Human Rights*, New York: United Nations.

United Nations (1966) *International Covenant on Economic, Social and Cultural Rights (ICESCR)*, New York: United Nations.

United Nations (1979) *Convention of the Elimination of All Forms of Discrimination Against Women*, New York: UN CEDAW.

United Nations (1989) *Convention on the Rights of the Child (CRC)*, New York: United Nations.

United Nations (2015) *Transforming our World: the 2030 Agenda for Sustainable Development*, New York: UN General Assembly.

United Nations Committee on CESCR (2000) *General Comment 14. The Right to the Highest Attainable Standard of Health*, Article 12, New York: UNCESCR.

UN Special Rapporteur for Health (2016) *Issues in Focus*. Available from: www.ohchr.org/EN/Issues/Health/Pages/IssuesFocus.aspx

World Health Organization (WHO) (1946) *Constitution of the World Health Organization*. Available from: http://apps.who.int/gb/bd/PDF/bd47/EN/constitution-en.pdf?ua=1

World Health Organization (2016) *Social Justice and Human Rights as a Framework for Addressing Social Determinants of Health: Final Report of the Task Group on Equity, Equality and Human Rights*, Copenhagen: WHO.

16

The right to housing

Dessie Donnelly, Joe Finnerty and Cathal O'Connell

This chapter describes the human rights approach to housing and analyses it from a critical social policy perspective. The first section outlines the importance of housing as a human right. The distinctiveness of housing is then explored and a third section provides a case study of a community advocacy group working in the area of housing rights. Finally, it discusses the prospects and limits of a human rights-based approach to housing, drawing on critical social policy perspectives.

Housing and human rights

Housing is a fundamental need, addressing the unavoidable and ongoing necessity for shelter and the basic requirement for a home (Ó Broin, 2019: 149–159; Kenna, 2011). As well as physical security and well-being, adequate housing contributes to psychological well-being by fulfilling a sense of personal space, autonomy and privacy. However, housing per se does not guarantee this, as in the case of domestic violence or child abuse (Hohmann, 2013). Housing, necessarily located in a particular geographical space, may both create and affirm a sense of social and cultural community. The links between (the right to) housing and (the right to) other 'goods' – for example, security and dignity, privacy, a family life, social inclusion, cultural diversity and health, and non-discrimination – are many and varied. For these reasons, a right to housing is seen as a crucially important human right.

Historically, key statements on the right to housing are contained in two documents authored by the United Nations. The United Nations' Universal Declaration of Human Rights (1948) states, in Article 25 (i), that everyone has the right to a standard of living adequate for health and well-being of themselves and their families, and includes housing as an example of what such an adequate standard of living would comprise. The United Nations' International Covenant on Economic, Social and Cultural Rights (ICESCR) (UN General Assembly, 1966) asserts, in Article 11 (1), the centrality of the right to adequate housing as a precursor to the enjoyment of all other economic, social and cultural rights. The UN Committee on Economic, Social and Cultural Rights (1991) goes on to set out seven essential components of adequate housing:

- Legal security of tenure against forced eviction and harassment.
- Availability of services such as safe drinking water, sanitation, heating and light, and refuse disposal.
- Affordability.
- Habitable housing that protects against health and structural hazards.
- Accessibility in relation to e.g. persons with disabilities.
- Location near to employment, shops, schools, etc.
- Housing that meets households' cultural expectations.

Thus, the essence of these statements is that all persons who are homeless or inadequately housed have a right to housing that fulfils these seven components. Under the ICESCR, a state must demonstrate that it is 'taking steps' to 'progressively realise' the right to housing using the 'maximum of its available resources', in the first instance centring on meeting 'minimum core obligations' to address extremely inadequate housing situations. Where states have signed up to the Optional Protocol of the International Covenant, individuals and groups may make complaints to the Committee on Economic and Social Rights (a body of independent experts set up in 1985) where they have failed to secure redress nationally for rights violations. A recent decision by the Committee, for example, found that an eviction in Spain without provision of alternative accommodation constituted a violation of the right to housing. However, the Committee does not have any powers to enforce its decisions on individual states (see Kenna, 2018; and De Schutter 2018 for detailed discussions of the various human rights mechanisms at European level).

Recent international reiterations of the right to housing include the New Urban Agenda (UN-HABITAT, 2016) and Target 11.1 of the United Nations' Sustainable Development Goals (2015). In some regional conventions, such as the African Charter on Human and Peoples' Rights (1981), or the American Convention on Human Rights (Organization of American States, 1969) – which do not contain an explicit right to housing – this right has been derived from rights to privacy, property and to protection of the family. The most systematic regional assertion of the right to housing is to be found in Europe. The Revised European Social Charter (1996) of the Council of Europe affirms a right to housing and obliges signatory states to take measures designed to promote access to affordable housing of an adequate quality, to prevent and reduce homelessness (Article 31). Relatedly, the prohibition of all forms of discrimination under Article 21 of the Charter of Fundamental Rights of the European Union (2012), has led to EU directives regarding national equality legislation protecting against discrimination in housing provision and services.

At national level, a law-based approach to vindicate the right to adequate housing may take two broad forms – via the country's constitution and/or via legislation. While the right to housing is recognised in the constitutions of 81 countries globally, in most cases these are merely aspirational statements with minimal legal force, one well-known exception being Section 26 of the Constitution of South Africa (Mercy Law Resource Centre, 2018), under which evictions leading to homelessness have been successfully challenged in the courts. The alternative approach is to enact the right to adequate housing in legislation and/or in housing strategies, with or without constitutional recognition (Farhi, 2018). Attempts to vindicate housing rights are then typically pursued via legal action against housing providers, undertaken by individuals or groups with sufficient resources, claiming their breach in some dimension. Legally enforceable rights to housing are rare, however, with France and the United Kingdom being among the few examples of countries where a specific group of persons suffering from inadequate housing, namely eligible homeless persons, must legally be offered some form of accommodation by the state.

There exist a wide variety of mechanisms to monitor developments in relation to the right to housing and related rights. At a global level, there is an increasingly important role being played by the UN Special Rapporteur on Housing Rights, producing annual reports to the United Nations General Assembly and undertaking country visits (see for example Farhi, 2016, 2017). States that have signed up to the ICESCR must produce country reports to the Committee every five years. Many NGOs and social movements play a role in monitoring and lobbying, and sometimes take direct action to effect change; with examples being the European Action Coalition for the Right to Housing and the City, and Participation and the Practice of Rights (PPR). The next section explores how housing is different from other 'goods' to which rights are claimed (Doling, 1997).

The distinctiveness of housing

In relation to the distribution of housing, 'housing tenure' refers to the arrangements under which the household occupies its accommodation. These tenure arrangements are underpinned by different sets of housing rights and obligations in relation to access, security of occupancy, cost and the quality of accommodation, any of which human rights approaches may attempt to modify. There are three main tenures identifiable across most housing systems, namely social rented housing, for-profit private renting and owner occupation (Kenna, 2011). Social rented housing is provided by a public or private not-for-profit body at below-market rents to people who cannot afford housing from their own resources. Private rented housing is owned by private landlords who rent it to tenants for a market rent. It is in these two rental tenures that precariously housed populations seek accommodation, and where issues of access, security of tenure, cost and quality are the subject of frequent contestation. Owner-occupied housing is owned by its residents, who may make a capital gain in the event that a dwelling is sold for more than it cost to buy. In addition, people may find shelter in the informal sector, including slums, squats and tent cities.

In terms of its production and consumption, housing is significantly different from other 'goods' to which rights may be claimed. The production of housing (apart from informal dwellings) requires front-loaded capital spending on land, materials, labour and developer margins, unlike other 'goods' such as health and education, where much more of the budget is on current spending such as staffing and materials. Financing the production of housing is therefore much more onerous than financing the production of other 'goods'. The consumption of housing is strongly individualised, typically occurring within individual accommodation units (by contrast with education or health, which are accessed for generally limited periods of time in collective settings such as schools or hospitals). Paying for housing (rent or mortgage repayment) is usually the highest outgoing from a household budget. Even in subsidised rental accommodation, households are still required to pay a rent contribution. The consumption of housing is of continuous duration throughout the lifecycle, again by contrast with other goods, with housing costs being correspondingly long-term, enduring, and generating an income stream for housing suppliers and financiers.

Finally, housing is also distinctive in that it is increasingly governed by private for-profit actors in its finance, production and distribution (Ó Broin, 2019: 149–150; Iglesias, 2012). Social housing is a minority tenure in most countries and is increasingly subject to influence from private finance.

Case study: Participation and the Practice of Rights

In 2001 a fledgling coalition of trade unions, community organisations, civil liberties and human rights NGOs from across Ireland began exploring how human rights practice on the island could be transformed from a relative specialism into popular tools for change, of immediate and practical use for marginalised communities experiencing socio-economic inequality. The coalition, convened by Inez McCormack as the first female president of the Irish Congress of Trade Unions (ICTU), understood the disconnect between 'those who know' and 'those who need to know' about human rights, and sought to pilot approaches which placed their institutional expertise and influence at the service of grassroots rights-based campaigns.

Since it began organising in Belfast and Dublin in 2006, PPR (the organisation that grew out of this coalition) has supported a broad range of rights to housing and accommodation campaigns, to mount effective challenges to state policies and secure significant progress – measured as tangible improvements in people's housing status and conditions, changes to the distribution of state resources and increased rights-based activism within marginalised communities (PPR, 2019). The distinctive methodology developed by PPR centres on what is considered to be the critical weakness in economic and social rights legislation – 'progressive realisation'. Unlike many civil and political rights, such as the right to due process, which are immediately realisable and justiciable, under international law, social and economic rights are considered over time with the state committing to:

> take steps, individually and through international assistance and co-operation ... to the maximum of its available resources, with a view to achieving progressively the full realization of the rights recognized in the present Covenant ... without discrimination of any kind as to race, colour, sex, language, religion, political or other opinion, national or social origin, property, birth or other status. (Article 2 of the ICESCR, UN General Assembly, 1 January 2019)

Arguably, such a formulation can serve to devalue fundamental rights and legitimise inequality: mostly legally unenforceable, social and economic rights are relegated to being another lobbying tool for NGOs in the policy development processes.

PPR's approach, however, has been used by diverse groups such as the Travellers of North Cork, Galway Traveller Movement, residents of the Seven Towers in the republican New Lodge and loyalist Lower Shankill estates of Belfast, families from Dolphin's House in Dublin, homeless and destitute asylum seekers, to turn 'progressive realisation' from a vague promise of change into a pressurised timetable for measurable change. The approach exemplifies how a human rights framework – incorporating elements of community, labour and feminist organising, strategic litigation, action research, human rights advocacy and coalition-building – can be effectively used to build power and secure change:

- Grassroots human rights indicators and benchmarks are developed to monitor progressive realisation, enabling marginalised communities to evidence the outcomes of state programmes and expenditure at the local level and reveal the human impact.
- Periodic monitoring reports are submitted to regional and international human rights authorities, their findings publicised and popularised to pressurise decision-makers and build public concern and consensus around housing rights abuses.
- Duty-bearers with obligations to take action are held accountable through Parliamentary Questions and Committees, Freedom of Information requests, media, petitions, lobbies, protests and social media campaigns. Actions are taken following sophisticated power analyses assessing the relative strengths and weaknesses of those for and against change.
- Coalitions are built with economists, architects, academics, lawyers and NGOs.
- Politicians are lobbied and encouraged to exercise their power in support, but forms of direct action are used to maintain control over the momentum and direction of the campaign.

Housing rights violations are not unintended outcomes of state policy resolvable through administrative remedies. Homelessness and housing inequality are democratic problems revealing whose voices are elevated and whose interests are prioritised in decisions about how public resources are expended. Therefore, conventional forms of public involvement in state policy, for example, consultations or partnerships which do not afford people the rights required for effective and meaningful participation (such as information, transparency, technical support) are tactically ignored, circumvented or subverted. Complaints processes and other remedial administrative procedures are engaged and exhausted to secure both immediate relief for individuals experiencing rights abuses, while constantly exposing the limitations of these systems and the need for deeper, structural change. In 2015, one of the PPR campaigns, Equality Can't Wait, supported 82 families to secure almost 3,000 additional points on the housing waiting list following challenges to their initial assessments, with 24 families to be re-housed into appropriate accommodation and 12 families gaining reduced rent arrears. PPR housing rights campaigns have triggered multi-million pound investments into deprived communities, addressing persisting inequalities, including: rehousing 60 families with young children out of high-rise accommodation and into appropriate housing; new sewage systems being installed into seven high-rise towers; the forced withdrawal of development plans for the Lower Shankill estate in Belfast and the securing of the first social housing development (39 new units) in over 20 years. The PPR model and approach has been utilised by tenants in Dublin and Edinburgh to help secure improvements costing €26m and £2.3m respectively.

The general non-justiciable nature of socio-economic rights has meant that litigation strategies have not been central to PPR's approach. Domestic legislation which gives effect to, or reinforces, international standards – such as the equality provisions under section 75 of the Northern Ireland Act (1998) – are instead popularised to frame the state's powers and obligations. Community monitoring supplements this framing by producing a robust evidence base, demonstrating the failure of the state to use its powers or honour its obligations. The use of law in this fashion means that while the potential for litigation is always possible, it is primarily a tool for constructing a public narrative, recruiting allies, triggering interventions from statutory commissions and regional or international rights bodies, and compelling political action.

For marginalised communities, participation becomes an exercise in asserting rights to build pressure for change, not engaging with the state or partners to make a case for the need for change, or building a persisting organisation or structure. The monitoring framework, requiring regular peer-to-peer research, ensures campaign objectives emerge from and reflect conditions in marginalised communities. The activities involved (surveys and canvassing, murals, public speaking, media interviews, negotiations, rights clinics and protests) facilitate the building of communities, development of skills and strategic capacity. Traditional committee or organisational structures are avoided to promote flexible and organic leadership, staying focused on pressure tactics and strategies.

Transforming housing systems using a rights-based approach

Clearly, having a right to housing in a country's constitution or legislation, or committing to in an internationally binding treaty, does not immediately translate into implementation machinery and strategies, or adequate access to justice, let alone into outcomes in the form of adequate housing for all. Human rights statements are normative claims about what ought to be, rather than descriptions of what exists. While housing problems evidently differ from country to country, with poorer countries often having poorer quality of housing and large slum areas, problems of affordability, precarity and growing homelessness exist in many economically developed countries (Abbe Pierre and FEANTSA, 2018). This persisting and often worsening gap between lofty aspirations and grim realities has prompted four critical responses to the housing rights approach, centring on its alleged lack of clarity, its minimalism/maximalism, its lack of realism, and the lack of political support for this approach.

The first criticism relates to the alleged lack of clarity around what concretely the right to housing means, what obligations the right specifically imposes on rights bearers, and how this right relates to other rights (Fitzpatrick et al, 2014). The charges of lack of clarity have to some extent been addressed by a series of annual reports by the United Nations Special Rapporteur on Housing in recent years, for example, in relation to the role of housing strategies in advancing the right to housing (Farhi, 2018). The abstractness of housing rights has been defended as striking a balance between universal norms and flexibility on local conditions (UN Committee on Economic Social and Cultural Rights, 1991). Indeed, given that a more general language of housing rights is often used without reference to universal human rights, as in the Scottish homelessness legislation or the European Action Coalition platform, and given the constructively ambiguous role of 'progressive realisation', as illustrated by the PPR case study, such openness to interpretation may be expected to remain a feature of housing rights discourse (Hohmann, 2013).

A second related criticism is that housing rights have been typically interpreted in either a minimalist or maximalist manner. In the minimalist version, only 'minimum core obligations' – the most extreme symptoms of inadequate housing – are seen as covered by the right to housing. Jessie Hohmann in *The Right to Housing* (2013), however, insists on the radical potential of the right to housing and argues that, for example, ICESCR guidelines on forced evictions must not ignore root causes of tenure insecurity such as land rights and gender inequality. Likewise, the UN Special Rapporteur has forcibly argued that the right to housing needs to be radicalised and that the link with other rights be reaffirmed in policy and practice:

> Lived experience illustrates that adequate housing, dignity, security and life are so closely intertwined as to be essentially inseparable. The same is true in international human rights law. The right to life cannot be separated from the right to a secure place to live, and the right to a secure place to live only has meaning in the context of a right to live in dignity and security, free of violence. (Farhi, 2016: 11)

In the maximalist version of this criticism, conversely, the right is caricatured as 'free housing' with a range of potentially negative effects on welfare state expenditure, on property rights and on the balance between the political executive and the judiciary. However, the experience of countries which have a constitutional right to housing enforced by the courts, such as South Africa or Finland, shows no sign of judicial 'overreach' (Mercy Law Resource Centre, 2018). Moreover, as the UN Special Rapporteur points out, the housing rights approach has involved establishing a basic floor of protection for specific groups: homeless persons, persons living in informal settlements, many migrants, people displaced by natural disasters, those living in post-conflict situations, those impacted by financial and housing crises and underinvestment in social housing, women and children escaping domestic violence, and many people with disabilities (Farhi, 2016).

A third criticism relates to the alleged lack of realism regarding attempting to secure a right to housing in increasingly adverse housing contexts. A key trend in social housing policy has been the increasing reliance on market-based approaches, involving a switch from direct bricks and mortar provision to a cash subsidy towards rental payments, an associated reliance on private (and usually for-profit) suppliers, and the sale of social housing stock to private companies. This relates to a broader shift towards the financialisation of housing, and to treating housing as 'a commodity like any other' (Aalbers, 2016), to which housing is particularly susceptible due to its requirement for front-loaded capital funding and to its provision of a long-term income stream in the form of rents and mortgage repayments. Corporate finance is increasingly linked with housing, whether direct investment or through using housing as security for financial instruments. This process makes housing in central areas of global cities increasingly unaffordable, drives the displacement of informal settlements in cities in the Global South, and increases precarity for households worldwide (Farhi, 2017). The UN Special Rapporteur laudably calls on states:

> to reclaim the governance of housing systems from global credit markets and, in collaboration with affected communities and with cooperation and engagement by central banks and financial institutions, redesign housing finance and global investment ... around the goal of ensuring access to adequate housing for all. (Farhi, 2017: 21)

Farhi also calls on stakeholders to engage around the right to adequate housing. However, as Kollocek (2013) notes, most of the powerful housing stakeholders in the finance, production and delivery of housing are for-profit businesses.

The most radical variant of this 'lack of realism' criticism asserts that inadequate housing is an endemic feature of capitalism, and that a more radical break with the economic system that encases housing systems is required (see Friedrich Engels' *The Housing Question*, 1872, for an early elaboration). However, more policy-oriented and politically engaged variants of these radical approaches do propose reforms and advocate change within (or against) the existing system, for example, in relation to laws concerning the quality of accommodation in specific tenures – as illustrated in the PPR case study.

A fourth criticism relates to the varying political will to implement and enforce a housing rights approach in constitutions, laws and in budgetary decisions (Mercy Law Resource Centre, 2018). At national level, in these cases where a right to housing exists only in the country's constitution, these are rarely legally enforceable rights. At EU level, some states have not yet ratified the revised version of the European Social Charter, and other states have not signed up to all of its provisions (De Schutter, 2018). Even where findings have been made against states for being in breach of housing rights under the ICESCR, effective sanctions do not exist to remedy this breach. Lack of political will often reflects discrimination against ethnic minorities or migrants, expressed in the denial of housing rights to 'outsiders' of various kinds (Abbe Pierre and FEANTSA, 2018).

Conclusion

The domination of housing systems by market actors, processes and ideologies, the varying political will to effect change, and 'maximalist' caricatures of what the right to housing involves, pose significant challenges to attempts to move beyond 'minimalist' rights-based changes to housing systems. These challenges are clearly linked to the distinctive features of the production and consumption of housing. However, this pessimistic outlook is tempered by alternative models, such as that designed by PPR, and as suggested by Hohmann, Farhi and Kenna. The range of PPR approaches within the housing rights framework suggests a mix of tactics and strategies: while one singular approach – be it community development, electoral campaigns, referenda, exercising government power, policy advocacy, strategic litigation, and so on – is unlikely to be capable of generating structural change on its own, a mixture of approaches that reinvigorate what a right to housing is and how it may be fought for is capable of pushing housing systems closer to the goal of the human right to housing.

Thus, human rights-based approaches to housing may take a variety of forms. For politicians, it can mean trying to establish forms of governance which translate international commitments into policy. For campaigners, it can be a tool to criticise state policy, raise public expectations and provide a series of accountability tools to mobilise people and create pressure (not always based in legal appeals) for change. For civil society coalitions, it can provide a common language through which to articulate broader policy demands. For lawyers, it can provide a set of codified norms which can be used to protect and, on occasion, expand rights through strategic litigation. Moreover, given the recent calls from the UN Special Rapporteur on Housing for a more radical interpretation of the human right to housing, and in the context of combating discrimination, attempts to vindicate housing rights, whether interpreted narrowly or broadly, will increasingly occur via wider economic, social and cultural struggles operating within radical democratic, or socialist, political paradigms.

References

Aalbers, M. (2016) *The Financialization of Housing: A Political Economy Approach*, London: Routledge.

Abbe, Pierre and FEANTSA (2018) *Third Overview of Housing Exclusion in Europe*. Available from: www.feantsa.org/download/chapter-36058619871081580298.pdf

De Schutter, O. (2018) *The European Pillar of Social Rights and the Role of the European Social Charter in the EU Legal Order*. Available from: https://rm.coe.int/study-on-the-european-pillar-of-social-rights-and-the-role-of-the-esc-/1680903132

Doling, J. (1997) *Comparative Housing Policy*, Basingstoke: Macmillan.

Engels, F. (1872) *The Housing Question.* Available from: www.marxists. org/archive/marx/works/download/Marx_The_Housing_Question. pdf

Farhi, L. (2016) *Report of the Special Rapporteur on Adequate Housing as a Component of the Right to an Adequate Standard of Living, and on the Right to Non-discrimination in this Context.* Available from: https:// documents-dds-ny.un.org/doc/UNDOC/GEN/N16/253/02/ PDF/N1625302.pdf?OpenElement

Farhi, L. (2017) *Report of the Special Rapporteur on Adequate Housing as a Component of the Right to an Adequate Standard of Living, and on the Right to Non-discrimination in this Context.* Available from: https:// documents-dds-ny.un.org/doc/UNDOC/GEN/G17/009/56/PDF/ G1700956.pdf?OpenElement

Farhi, L. (2018) *Report of the Special Rapporteur on Adequate Housing as a Component of the Right to an Adequate Standard of Living, and on the Right to Non-discrimination in this Context.* Available from: www. undocs.org/A/HRC/37/53

Fitzpatrick, S., Bengtsson, B. and Watts, B. (2014) 'Rights to housing: reviewing the terrain and exploring a way forward', *Housing, Theory and Society*, 31(4): 447–463.

Hohmann, J. (2013) *The Right to Housing: Law, Concepts, Possibilities*, Oxford: Hart.

Iglesias, T. (2012) 'Housing paradigms', in S.J. Smith, M. Elsinga, L.F. O'Mahony, O.S. Eng, S. Wachter and R. Ronald (eds) *International Encyclopedia of Housing and Home*, Volume 3, Oxford: Elsevier, pp 544–549.

Kenna, P. (2011) *Housing Rights, Law and Policy*, Dublin: Clarus Press.

Kenna, P. (2018) 'Introduction', in P. Kenna, S. Nazarre-Aznar, P. Sparkes and C.U. Schmid (eds) *Loss of Homes and Evictions Across Europe*, Cheltenham: Edward Elgar, pp 1–65.

Kolocek, M. (2013) 'The human right to housing in the 27 member states of the European Union', *European Journal of Homelessness*, 7(1): 135–54.

Mercy Law Resource Centre (2018) *The Right to Housing in Comparative Perspective*, Dublin: MLRC.

Ó Broin, E. (2019) *Home: Why Public Housing is the Answer*, Dublin: Merrion Press.

Organization of American States (1969) *American Convention on Human Rights.* Available from: www.oas.org/dil/treaties_B-32_American_ Convention_on_Human_Rights.pdf

UN Committee on Economic, Social and Cultural Rights (1991) *General Comment No 4: The Right to Adequate Housing.* Available from: www.refworld.org/docid/47a7079a1.html

PPR (2019) 'Right to Housing'. Available from: www.pprproject. org/right-to-housing

UN General Assembly (2019) *Transforming our World: The 2030 Agenda for Sustainable Development.* Available from: www.un.org/ga/search/ view_doc.asp?symbol=A/RES/70/1andLang=E

UN General Assembly (1966) *International Covenant on Economic, Social and Cultural Rights*, 16 December 1966, United Nations, Treaty Series, 993(3). Available from: www.refworld.org/docid/3ae6b36c0.html

UN-Habitat (2016) *New Urban Agenda.* Available from: http://habitat3. org/the-new-urban-agenda.

17

Children's rights and social policy

Fiona Donson

The global embracing of children's rights, at least in theory, is illustrated by the almost global ratification over the past few decades of the United Nations Convention on the Rights of the Child (UNCRC). The UNCRC has undoubtedly established a strong foundation for the development of child rights at national, regional and international levels. Children's rights operate at the legal, policy and advocacy level creating enforceable legal claims, rights-based programmes and policy, and a space to recognise children as rights holders, with views that need to be heard and agency to make decisions. However, despite the substantial developments over the past 30 years, there remain significant limits as to the extent to which children are genuinely recognised as full human beings deserving of the same rights as adults. As Baroness Hale, President of the UK Supreme Court, recently noted: '[t]he law still has trouble seeing children as real people' (Hale, 2018).

This chapter critically assesses existing international human rights mechanisms and in particular the UN Convention on the Rights of the Child, in relation to the promotion of the rights and welfare of children. In doing so it examines such mechanisms in a world of social, economic, cultural, ideological and political diversity, different levels of 'peace', stability, governmental organisation and conflict, and changing contexts and circumstances. It reflects on the inability of some states (such as the USA) to ratify the UN Convention, and on issues of enforceability and realisability in others which have. Finally, it discusses contemporary attempts by NGOs and other campaigning organisations to promote the recognition and realisation of universal rights for children.

UNCRC: a children's rights framework

The development of approaches to 'saving children' from work, poverty and other social harms first coalesced in the context of the 'child-saving movement' (Platt, 1969) in the nineteenth century. Today's children's rights approach has moved a long way from a paternalistic and charitable desire to protect children. While a discussion of what children's rights are conceptually founded on, what they include and how to prioritise them is beyond the scope of this chapter (Hanson, 2012: 63–79), certain underlying elements can be highlighted:

> [T]he Convention on the Rights of the Child is concerned with the four 'P's: the participation of children in decisions affecting their own destiny; the protection of children against discrimination and all forms of neglect and exploitation; the prevention of harm to children; and the provision of assistance for their basic needs. (Van Bueren, 1998: 15)

Given that childhood is understood to be multi-varied, the UNCRC delivers a general rights framework highlighting certain groups identified as requiring particular attention, for example child workers (Article 32). The provisions are broadly described by UNICEF as providing for a realisation for children to 'develop their full potential free from hunger and want, neglect and abuse' (UNICEF, nd). However, children do not have rights *only* as a way of allowing them to evolve into 'good adults'; the convention recognises children as independent rights holders. This focus on seeing children as active participants in defending and facilitating their own rights is supported by Article 12 (UNCRC) and has had significant impact in practice (Parkes, 2013). For example, in Ireland the Department of Child and Youth Affairs' (DCYA) National Strategy on Children and Young Person's Participation in Decision-Making (2015–20) includes specific commitments to ensure participation, including: 'Mainstreaming the participation of children and young people in the development of policy, legislation and research' (Objective 7) (DCYA, 2015a: 4). However, this commitment is inconsistently realised, despite the strong attempt to include 'seldom heard children' (DCYA, 2015b). In the UK, Children's Commissioners, established in all four devolved administrations, play a vital role in supporting participation.

The children's rights provided in the UNCRC are broad in nature and reflect the drafting process, which was influenced by NGOs seeking to bring 'together the rights that were scattered throughout a range of instruments that were so wide as to render them almost inoperative as a basis for coherent, comprehensive advocacy and meaningful responses to violations' (Cantwell, 2011: 41). Begun in 1979 – the International Year of the Child – drafting took nearly ten years, with the UNCRC being adopted by the UN General Assembly in 1989.

The UNCRC designates children as aged under 18 (Article 2); however, despite this clear delineation between child/adult at a general level in the Convention, specific measures demonstrate that definitional tensions can arise. Thus Article 38 uses a lower age – 15 – as the minimum for recruitment or participation in armed conflict while the Optional Protocol to the Convention on the Rights of the Child on Involvement of Children in Armed Conflict (2000) allows states to accept 16-year-olds as volunteers to their armed forces (Article 3). These reduced age limits operate despite the fact that child soldiers were identified as a group particularly in need of protection, and that children's rights are committed to ensuring childhood, as far as possible, be a 'violence free space' (Kononenko, 2016).

The rights within the Convention operate across civil, political, social, economic and cultural rights, reflecting the overriding focus on *children* rather than on specific groups of rights. Central to the Convention is the interplay between rights, operating on a holistic basis requiring that they are interpreted as a whole rather than individually. At the heart of the Convention are four central pillars: non-discrimination (Article 2); the best interests principle (Article 3); the child's right to development (Article 6); and child participation (Article 12). Article 6, establishing the right of the child to survival and development, has, in combination with the other UNCRC rights, provided for the development of a 'normative framework to understand child well-being' (Ben-Arieh, 2008), an approach which emerged from the 'new' sociology of childhood. In this area of social policy this has been a useful mechanism for focusing attention and assessing progress in improving the lives of children.

A right to well-being not only provides a framework by which policy and progress on child well-being can be assessed, but also allows for positive claims to children's rights to be made. This has been particularly important in the context of socio-economic rights which engage resource allocation questions. However, it is important to note that in relation to economic, social and cultural rights Article 4 UNCRC requires states parties to 'undertake such measures to the maximum extent of their available resources', requiring a progressive realisation of rights specifically in relation to these three categories. Khadka expresses concern at the difficulties in implementing economic and social rights in a context where the complex (and) structural issues that give rise to rights violations are not addressed either at the broader policy level (nationally and internationally), or the practical level (Khadka, 2013).

For example, policies drafted to reduce child labour in developing countries need to reflect on the deeper economic crises families face in just surviving without children contributing to the family income (Armin et al, 2004). Children's rights operate within these complex situations as a component, a positive claim to policy, law and practice that conceptualises children as rights holders, with agency and voice, who can make claims against the state and demand change. However, this needs to be done within a space that engages directly with the multiplicity of economic and social challenges that are often at the heart of these problems. In this way, rights are an invaluable tool, but not a sole solution.

As an international treaty the impact of the UNCRC is reliant upon states parties' implementation at the domestic level. However, the UN Committee on the Rights of the Child (ComRC) is a key body made up of experts which monitors its implementation and provides clarification on its meaning through General Comments. The Committee's influence is important, although change can take time. For example, it took 12 years for Ireland to amend its Constitution following a recommendation to that effect by the Committee in 1998. States report to the ComRC on their progress under the UNCRC on a rolling basis, and these have become invaluable opportunities for NGOs to leverage influence which may be absent at the national level. NGO shadow country reports and cooperation have all been seen to effect change in practice (Hart and Thetaz-Bergman, 1996).

The United States: absent a child rights framework

The United States is the one country not to ratify the UNCRC despite being heavily involved in its drafting (Cohen, 2006). Explanations include the idea that the convention 'interferes with the independence of the parent–child relationship' (Cohen, 2006: 195). However, US mistrust of the UN and international rights frameworks more generally is also significant: '[T]he administration's main reservations center on states' rights issues and a constitutional question of whether basic human rights in this country can be guaranteed by an international treaty' (Nauck, 1994: 677). The US is typically resistant to the imposition of positive duties/responsibilities, preferring to view them more as limitations on states' interferences with citizen's action.

Ultimately, the US has shown little enthusiasm at government level to ratify the UNCRC. Even President Obama, who in 2008 had described the non-ratification as 'embarrassing', took no action. Some argue that the issue is overstated and the adoption of the UNCRC would make no difference in practice to the current status of children's rights because it would require positive implementation to come into force (Ku, 2014: 1).

In the US, children's rights are recognised through federal and state-level legislation. However, the lack of a mechanism for holding the overarching system of law and policy to account through adopting a clear children's rights framework can have significant practical effect. Beyond the 'embarrassment' factor of being an 'outlier' by refusing to ratify the treaty, Mehta notes that the US needs to 'confront some hard truths about the exceptionally bad way we treat children' (Mehta, 2015). Issues such as punitive immigration policies leading to parent–child separation (Gharabaghi and Anderson-Nathe, 2018) and a failure to systematically adopt and promote children's well-being in health programmes (Huntington and Scott, nd), are seen by some as indicative of a country that does not prioritise children's rights.

The European Union (EU): regional approaches

Children's rights were not traditionally regarded as being within the purview of the EU, resulting in, as Stalford notes, 'a somewhat haphazard, half-hearted manner' of engagement (Stalford, 2012: 15). However, this has changed as the EU has changed:

> Child-related provision was enacted from the late 1960s onwards, primarily with a view to encouraging the migration of EU workers between Member States. This body of law has been heavily criticised for its instrumental approach insofar as it endowed children with merely "parasitic rights" that were highly dependent on and vulnerable to the decisions of their parents. (Stalford, 2012: 16; McGlynn, 2006; Ackers and Stalford, 2004)

Children's rights therefore developed to fill needs that arose as a result of broader EU policies. Typically, this did not engage directly with social policy or with children's rights or needs as a primary concern. However, as the EU became more concerned with questions of social exclusion in the context of unemployment and poverty, consideration of how this affected children was pushed further up the agenda. When the EU adopted child poverty as a key priority in its social inclusion agenda – agreed as part of the Lisbon Process – a significant change began (Frazer, 2010). Child well-being, in this context, became important to the adoption of child poverty strategies, with 2007 being declared a year focusing on child poverty and well-being, which included the establishment of the EU Task Force on Child Poverty and Child Well-Being (Tarki Social Research Institute, 2010).

However, while the concept of child well-being is significant in the development of broader social policy in the EU, other developments around the same time provided a clearer framework for the advancement of rights, not least the introduction of the European Charter of Fundamental Rights (2000). While addressing a broad array of rights, the Charter specifically makes reference to children in Article 24, stating that they: 'shall have the right to such protection and care as is necessary for their well-being'; that their 'views shall be taken into consideration on matters which concern them in accordance with their age and maturity'; that 'the child's best interests must be a primary consideration'; and that every child has the 'right to maintain on a regular basis a personal relationship and direct contact with both his or her parents, unless that is contrary to his or her interests' (European Union, 2000).

The Charter was formally adopted into the EU Constitution by the Lisbon Treaty (2009). Placing rights on a constitutional and legally enforceable basis can be a game changer in achieving substantial change in practice. The elevation of the Charter meant that it had the same legal status as EU Treaties, making it legally binding and allowing for EU institutions and member states alike to be held legally accountable for any failure to comply with it (Stalford, 2012: 18).

In the context of social policy, Stalford highlights the powerful nature of the inclusion of broad children's rights commitments in the EU constitutional framework, noting that it acts as a 'hook' upon which to hang initiatives 'aimed at promoting or protecting the rights of the child (Stalford, 2012: 18). Given the impact of EU law and policy at member state government level, the recognition of the importance of children's rights by the EU is an extremely important step. However, the EU only has a remit in certain areas of action and it remains the case that the most important policy-making powers relating to children remain within the remit of member states. In addition, there has been criticism of the EU agenda and the more general rights framework for lacking a coherent approach to children's rights along the lines of the UNCRC – a concern that is voiced by organisations working in support of children's rights on the ground.[1] However, Stalford notes that the vague nature of the rights provisions does not remove their power, while other EU treaties provide for engagement on the social policy front: 'EU action to address child poverty finds its legal basis on a much broader treaty reference to "combating social exclusion"' (Stalford, 2012: 20).[2]

The Council of Europe/European Convention on Human Rights

While the European Convention on Human Rights (ECHR) provides an enforceable rights framework in relation to state parties, it makes no direct reference to children. However, Article 1 of the Convention requires member states to secure convention rights for 'everyone' within their jurisdiction, underlining that the Convention applies to children and adults alike. The only direct engagements with children's rights are found in Article 5(1), on educational detention, Article 6, on juvenile detention, and Article 2 of Protocol 1, on the right to education. In addition, Article 8 raises clear child rights elements in the context of the right to family life. Despite this, the Convention has in practice had a significant impact on children's rights in Europe (Kilkelly, 1999, 2001, 2015).

The structure of the ECHR has a distinct implementation advantage over the UNCRC through the creation of the European Court of Human Rights (ECtHR). This regional court provides a judicial forum for case resolution brought by state parties and more often by affected individuals. Operationally, the ECtHR has adopted a practice in recent years of making use of the UNCRC to help interpret its own Convention in the context of children's rights. An extensive body of case law has produced a more nuanced and effective regional system of child rights protection, stretching far beyond the specific wording of the Convention itself. This illustrates the value of a judicially enforceable regional framework, as well as the willingness of those judges to draw on other sources to support the expanding nature of children's rights, reflecting in turn the changing world of rights protections. However, as Kilkelly and Nolan highlight, 'the ECtHR has rarely relied directly on the [UN]CRC in its judgments'; rather, the court has been influenced in a more indirect way (Nolan and Kilkelly, 2016: 313).

The power of litigation to ground national and regional change in the area of children's rights is significant and is supported by cases brought by NGOs or others that act as test cases. For example, in *Centre of Legal Resources on behalf of Valentin Câmpeanu v Romania* (2014) the court accepted an application from an NGO representing the deceased, a child who had been suffering from HIV and intellectual disabilities. The ECtHR found that domestic authorities had violated the right to life of the deceased (Article 2) because they had placed him in an institution where he died from a lack of adequate food, accommodation and medical care. While in *O'Keefe v Ireland* (2014), a case brought by a woman who had been the victim of sexual abuse in the Irish school system in the 1970s, the court found against Ireland, holding that states have a positive duty to take steps to protect children from ill-treatment – including sexual abuse under Article 3 (prohibition on torture, and inhumane and degrading treatment). The impact of these cases can often go beyond the specific parties, creating foundations for change at a domestic law level.

Finally, it should be highlighted that the Council of Europe (CoE), which created and oversees the ECHR, is generally guided by the UNCRC and takes note of ECtHR decisions. Thus CoE human rights instruments such as the Convention on Action against Trafficking in Human Beings and its Recommendation on children's rights and social services friendly to children and families directly reference the UNCRC and set the definition of a child as 'any person below the age of 18'. Overall, the CoE has in recent years been actively engaged with a child rights agenda and is currently on its third children's rights strategy (2016–21).[3]

African Charter on the Rights and Welfare of the Child

Whereas the ECHR was drafted prior to the widespread adoption of children's rights leading to little direct reference, the African regional rights regimes are much more explicitly engaged. In 1990, the African Charter on the Rights and Welfare of the Child (ACRWC) was adopted, sharing many key elements of the UNCRC, including a broad approach covering a wide range of civil, political, economic, social and cultural rights (Organization of African Unity, 1990; Chirwa, 2002). At the time of writing, 41 states have ratified the Charter, nine have signed but not ratified and four have not signed.

Despite the similarities with the UNCRC, there are differences. While the best interests of the child is prioritised in both regimes, it is accorded a higher status in the ACRWC: 'In all actions concerning the child undertaken by any person or authority the best interests of the child shall be *the* primary consideration' (Article 4). Alternatively, Article 3 of the UNCRC places it as *a* primary consideration. Also, while the UNCRC Article 4, discussed earlier, provides a clear reference to resource allocation relating to economic, social and cultural rights, the ACRWC does not distinguish between any of the types of rights set out, although in practice the latter rights are emphasised, subject to availability of resources (Nolan and Kilkelly, 2016: 299).

Conclusion

The UNCRC has had a significant role globally in setting the approach to children's rights, development and understandings. So much so at times that it seems to be ever present in policy, law and practice developments. In England, for example, Lyon questions why the UNCRC seems to be more often referenced in policy documents than the ECHR, despite the latter having legal effect under the Human Rights Act 1998. Tellingly, she describes the UNCRC as being viewed as the 'aspirant gold standard by which the laws and policies made by the UK Government, which govern children's lives, "should be judged"' (Lyon, 2007: 148). Consequently, the negative media and political attitudes towards the ECHR in that jurisdiction potentially limit the power of that rights framework (Farrell et al, 2019). In Ireland, too, the UNCRC has had a significant impact on the institutions of government and the development of policy – the establishment of the Department for Children and Youth Affairs, and the Ombudsman for Children have focused government attention on children's issues and, as noted earlier, the children's rights framework of the UNCRC in areas such as child participation has been directly embraced in the policy-making structure.

More generally, the focus on child well-being through Article 6 of the UNCRC has provided for a dialogue that addresses children as rights holders both in their current lives and as future adults. However, in practice there can remain significant disconnects at fundamental social policy level between the rhetoric of well-being and the implementation of economic and social welfare policies. For example, current concerns regarding child and young person homelessness in Europe following widespread implementation of austerity measures, and a lack of future investment in social supports, indicates how that disconnect develops when there is a failure to connect child rights with broader economic well-being. The 2017 FEANTSA Report on European homelessness highlights how such a problem is seen as a *housing problem*, rather than a child policy issue, child rights issue or social inclusion issue at least at the operational and policy level (Baptista et al, 2017). This separation of children's rights from broader problems that in reality directly impact on child well-being prevents a holistic approach being adopted in practice.

Children's rights offer an important tool in supporting legal and policy change through the adoption of a positive framework of entitlements. This is particularly important in the social policy sphere where fundamental rights claims, such as the right to child well-being, can be used to leverage social and economic change to improve the lives of marginalised, vulnerable and often forgotten groups. When we add to this the requirement to hear the voice of the child, this has the potential to drive powerful change in social policy and practice.

Notes

[1] https://eurohealthnet.eu/health-gradient/early-child-development/childrens-rights

[2] Referencing Article 153 of the Treaty on the Functioning of the European Union, European Union, *Consolidated Version of the Treaty on the Functioning of the European Union*, 13 December 2007, 2008/C 115/01, available from: www.refworld.org/docid/4b17a07e2.html

[3] Strategy for the Rights of the Child (2016–21), adopted in Sofia in 2016. More information can be found at: www.coe.int/en/web/children/children-s-strategy

References

Ackers, H.L. and Stalford, H. (2004) *A Community for Children? Children, Citizenship and Migration in the European Union*, Aldershot: Ashgate.

Armin, S., Quayes, M. and Rives, J. (2004) 'Poverty and other determinants of child labor in Bangladesh', *Southern Economic Journal*, 70(4): 876–892.

Baptista, I., Benjaminsan, L. and Pleace, N. (2017) *Family Homelessness in Europe*, Brussels: FEANTSA.

Ben-Arieh, A. (2008) 'The child indicators movement: past, present, and future', *Child Indicators Research*, 1(1): 3–16.

Cantwell, N. (2011) 'Are children's rights still human?', in A. Invernizzi and J. Williams, *The Human Rights of Children: From Visions to Implementation*, Abingdon: Routledge.

Chirwa, D.M. (2002) 'The merits and demerits of the African Charter on the Rights and Welfare of the Child', *International Journal of Children's Rights*, 10(2): 157.

Cohen, C. (2006) 'The role of the United States in the drafting of the Convention on the Rights of the Child', *Emory International Law Review*, 20: 185–198.

Council of Europe (1950) European Convention for the Protection of Human Rights and Fundamental Freedoms, as amended by Protocols Nos 11 and 14, 4 November, ETS 5. Available from: www.refworld.org/docid/3ae6b3b04.html

Council of Europe (2005) *Council of Europe Convention on Action Against Trafficking in Human Beings*, 16 May, CETS 197. Available from: www.refworld.org/docid/43fded544.html

Council of Europe (2011) Recommendation CM/Rec(2011)12 of the Committee of Ministers to Member states on children's rights and social services friendly to children and families, 16 November. Available from: http://rm.coe.int/CoERMPublicCommonSearch Services/DisplayDCTMContent?documentId=090000168046ccea

Department of Children and Youth Affairs (2015a) *National Strategy on Children and Young People's Participation in Decision-making 2015–2020*, Dublin: DCYA.

Department of Children and Youth Affairs (2015b) *A Practical Guide to Including Seldom-heard Children and Young People in Decision-making*, Dublin: DCYA/Barnardos.

European Union (2012) *Charter of Fundamental Rights of the European Union*, 26 October, 2012/C 326/02. Available from: www.refworld. org/docid/3ae6b3b70.html

Farrell, M., Drywood, E. and Hughes, E. (2019) *Human Rights in the Media: Fear and Fetish*, Abingdon: Routledge.

Frazer, H.M. (2010) 'Child poverty and social exclusion', in H.M. Frazer, *A Social Inclusion Roadmap for Europe 2020*, Antwerp: Garant, pp 34–95.

Gharabaghi, K. and Anderson-Nathe, B. (2018) 'Dismantling children's rights in the Global North', *Child and Youth Services*, 39(1): 1–3.

Hale, B. (2018) 'All human beings? Reflections on the 70th anniversary of the Universal Declaration on Human Rights', *Society of Legal Scholars*. Available from: https://www.supremecourt.uk/docs/speech-181102.pdf

Hanson, K. (2012) 'Schools of thought in children's rights', in M. Liebel (ed.) *Children's Rights from Below*, London: Palgrave Macmillan, pp 63–79.

Hart, S. and Thetaz-Bergman, L. (1996) 'The role of non-governmental organizations in implementing the Convention on the Rights of the Child', *Transnational Law and Contemporary Problems*, 6: 373–392.

Huntington, C. and Scott, E. (nd) 'Children's health in a legal framework', *The Future of Children*, 25(1): 177–197.

Khadka, S. (2013) 'Social rights and the United Nations – Child Rights Convention (UN-CRC): is the CRC a help or a hindrance for developing universal and egalitarian social policies for children's wellbeing in the "developing world"?', *International Journal of Children's Rights*, 21: 616–628.

Kilkelly, U. (1999) *The Child and the ECHR*, Aldershot: Ashgate.

Kilkelly, U. (2001) 'The best of both worlds for children's rights – interpreting the European Convention on Human Rights in the light of the UN Convention on the Rights of the Child', *Northern Ireland Human Rights Quarterly*, 23: 308–326.

Kilkelly, U. (2015) 'The CRC in litigation under the ECHR', in T. Liefaard and E. Jaap Doek (eds) *Litigating the Rights of the Child*, Dordrecht: Springer, pp 193–209.

Kononenko, J. (2016) 'Prohibiting the use of child soldiers: contested norm in contemporary human rights discourse', *Nordic Journal of Human Rights*, 34(2): 89–103.

Ku, K. (2014) 'So it turns out US ratification of the Convention on the Rights of the Child would be pointless', 25 November, *OpinioJuris*. Available from: http://opiniojuris.org/2014/11/25/turns-us-ratification-convention-rights-child-pointless/

Lyon, C. (2007) 'Interrogating the concentration on the UNCRC instead of the ECHR in the development of children's rights in England?', *Children and Society*, 21: 147–153.

McGlynn, C. (2006) *Families and the European Union: Law, Politics and Pluralism*, Cambridge: Cambridge University Press.

Mehta, S. (2015) 'There's only one country that hasn't ratified the Convention on the Rights of the Child', ACLU, 20 November. Available from: www.aclu.org/blog/human-rights/treaty-ratification/theres-only-one-country-hasnt-ratified-convention-childrens

Nauck, B. (1994) 'Implications of the United States ratification of the United Nations Convention on the Rights of the Child: civil rights, the constitution and the family', *Cleveland State Law Review*, 42: 675–703.

Nolan, A. and Kilkelly, U. (2016) 'Children's rights under regional human rights law – a tale of harmonisation?', in C. Buckley, A. Donald and P. Leach (2016) *Towards Convergence in International Human Rights Law*, Leiden: Brill, pp 296–322.

Organization of African Unity (OAU) (1990) *African Charter on the Rights and Welfare of the Child*, 11 July, CAB/LEG/24.9/49. Available from: www.refworld.org/docid/3ae6b38c18.html

Parkes, A. (2013) *Children and International Human Rights Law: The Right of the Child to be Heard*, Abingdon: Routledge.

Platt, A. (1969) *The Child Savers: The Invention of Delinquency*, Chicago: University of Chicago Press.

Stalford, H. (2012) *Children and the European Union: Rights, Welfare and Accountability*, Oxford: Hart Publishing.

Tarki Social Research Institute (2010) *Child Poverty and Child Well-being in the European Union*, Brussels: European Commission.

UN General Assembly (2000) *Optional Protocol to the Convention on the Rights of the Child on the Involvement of Children in Armed Conflict*, 25 May. Available from: www.refworld.org/docid/47fdfb180.html

UNICEF (2003) *Guide to the Optional Protocol on the Involvement of Children in Armed Conflict*. Available at: www.unicef.org/protection/option_protocol_conflict.pdf

UNICEF (nd) Available from: www.unicef.org/crc/index_protecting.html

Van Bueren, G. (1998) *The International Law on the Rights of the Child*, Leiden: Martinus Nijhoff.

Cases

Centre of Legal Resources on behalf of Valentin Câmpeanu v Romania, [2014] ECHR 789, 47848/08.

O'Keeffe v Ireland, [2014] ECHR 96, 35810/09.

18

The rights of people with disabilities

Charles O'Mahony and Shivaun Quinlivan

The rights-based perspective on disability is a relatively new approach that moves away from medical and charity-based approaches (Stein, 2007: 75–122). It is estimated that 15 per cent of the world's population live with a disability. Persons with disability have been described by the United Nations (UN) as the world's largest minority, the majority of whom live in developing countries. Women and persons with lower educational attainment are more likely to live with a disability. The UN has recently collated research on people with disabilities which highlighted that they are amongst the most disadvantaged groups in society. Indeed, children with disabilities are significantly less likely to be educated; the global literacy rate for adults with disabilities is 3 per cent; people with disabilities are more likely to be unemployed or underemployed; persons with disabilities are more likely to be victims of violence or rape and less likely to obtain police intervention, legal protection or preventive care; women and girls with disabilities are particularly vulnerable to abuse; and it is estimated that violence against children with disabilities occurs at least 1.7 times more than for their non-disabled peers (United Nations, 2019). From this it is evident that human rights principles have an obvious relevance for persons with disability, yet historically the legal response has been a mix of charity, paternalism and social policy rather than a human rights approach. Consider, as an example, education policies for children with disabilities: the focus is often on specialised and segregated provision, determined on the basis of a person's disability – for example, a school for the deaf. Thus, it is the very condition of disability that separates. 'In a way the "natural" distribution of human capacities was seen separating persons with disabilities. It was as if the disability was seen as eroding rather than simply complicating human existence' (O'Mahony and Quinn, 2017).

That historical position has been difficult to overcome. One significant contribution of the United Nations Convention on the Rights of Persons with Disabilities (CRPD) is that it offers an international human rights instrument that questions and challenges these previously unquestioned presumptions. It should be unquestionable that human rights principles are universal in their application. The Universal Declaration of Human Rights declared: 'All human beings are born free and equal in dignity and rights'. Why then was there a need for a disability-specific convention? Degener and Quinn, in a 2002 report, showed that existing human rights conventions were not responding or responsive to the needs of persons with disability. UN treaty bodies publish their interpretation of different provisions in the form of a General Comment. Up until 2002 only one General Comment referred to disability; country reports from states parties to the various treaty bodies rarely referred to disability issues and concluding observations of most treaty bodies were largely silent on the issue of disability rights (Degener and Quinn, 2002). It was therefore necessary to highlight the human being behind the disability and extend the protection of the law to all human beings, and not just to some or even to most. The value added by the CRPD has to do with treating persons with disabilities as human beings with full legal personhood as opposed to objects to be merely managed, pitied and cared for.

The CRPD is the most important and exciting development to take place in the disability field for many decades. It has clarified the application of international human rights law for persons with disabilities and serves as a driver for law reform and to inform social policy. This chapter sets out why the CRPD is such a ground-breaking Convention and provides a case study on the impact of that Convention on the disability policy of the European Union (EU).

The CRPD

The CRPD is a novel Convention for a number of reasons. It ensures the participation and inclusion of persons with disabilities, not just in the drafting of the CRPD but also in its future implementation. It represents a fundamental change in underlying assumptions in respect of persons with disabilities and reinvigorates, and gives substance to, the right to equality. Also, it highlights the artificial dichotomy between civil and political rights and socio-economic rights. With this in mind, it is worth briefly amplifying each of these reasons in turn.

Social policy and the inclusion of persons with disabilities

One of the striking features of the CRPD is the emphasis in its drafting on inclusion and full participation of persons with disabilities. The motto from the drafting of the CRPD was 'Nothing about us without us'. The participation and involvement of persons with disabilities in the negotiation of the CRPD was unique in many ways in terms of an international human rights treaty. The involvement of persons with disabilities transcended the treaty process. Specifically, Article 4(3) requires that state parties, in the development and implementation of legislation and policies to implement the Convention, are required to closely consult with and actively involve persons with disabilities (including children).

The focus on the involvement and participation of persons with disabilities throughout the CRPD is aimed at empowering persons with disability to be included in political and social decision-making. Many of the Articles in the CRPD require the involvement of persons with disabilities in the formulation of policies that affect them. This reflects a social model of disability that strives to break down barriers that prevent persons with disabilities participating as members of the community at all levels.

Move to human rights model

Historically people with disabilities have been viewed as objects of charity, people who evoke sympathy. They have been considered to be in need of protection or as burdens on their family or society. The introduction of the CRPD has ensured that the concept of disability has undergone a 'paradigm shift' (Kayess and French, 2008). Traditionally, the response to disability has been to focus on what is 'wrong' with the person and the 'problem' caused by a particular impairment or condition. This shift in thinking is encapsulated in the move from the 'medical model' to the 'social model' (Kayess and French, 2008) and now to the 'human rights model' of disability (Degener, 2016: 35).

The medical model assumes that any reduction in the quality of life or the ability to participate in society is as a result of a medical condition intrinsic to the individual. Therefore, the focus of the medical model is on medical solutions such as healthcare and related services. The focus is on addressing the functionality of the individual to allow them to live a more 'normal' life; in other words, all the failings are with the individual (Quinlivan, 2012). This has resulted in a number of assumptions – for example, that people with disabilities need to be minded and protected, or are not capable or able. These assumptions have led to the development of segregated or separate laws and social policies such as mental health and guardianship laws, special schools and institutions.

In contrast, the social model of disability 'focuses on how society and societal constraints and barriers seek to limit or inhibit full participation by, and inclusion of persons with disabilities in society' (Quinlivan, 2012: 74). Those barriers to inclusion could be legal, physical or attitudinal, but they all serve to exclude an individual with a disability. This model differentiates between impairment and disability, where impairment relates to a condition whether it is physical, mental or sensory; a disability, on the other hand, is the consequence of a discriminatory response by society to that impairment. Therefore, for example, it is the failure to ensure the accessibility of a polling station by means of a ramp or lift that excludes those with mobility impairments from accessing the right to vote, not the person looking to vote.

The social model requires society to respond to a person with a disability by removing discriminatory barriers. It is not for that individual to mould themselves to a system not designed with their needs in mind. The social model influenced the CRPD but arguably it 'goes beyond the social model of disability and codifies the human rights model of disability' (Degener, 2016: 35). The human rights model provides a value-driven foundation for disability policy. This is established at the outset of the CRPD. Article 1 provides that '[t]he purpose of the present Convention is to promote, protect and ensure the full and equal enjoyment of all human rights and fundamental freedoms by all persons with disabilities, and to promote respect for their inherent dignity'.

This approach is reinforced through the general principles in Article 3, which contain the express values upon which the Convention is built. They include dignity, individual autonomy, non-discrimination, full and active participation and inclusion, respect for difference, equality of opportunity, accessibility, equality between men and women, and respect for the evolving capacities of children with disabilities. Degener argues that the human rights model is the logical development of the social model, one that offers a roadmap for change (Degener, 2016).

The social model, in its challenge to the medical model of disability, naturally concentrated on barriers as opposed to impairment. In fact, impairment is important and does impact on the lives of persons with disabilities. It can result in pain, fatigue and discomfort. The human rights model of disability 'acknowledges these life circumstances and demands they be considered when social justice theories are developed' (Degener, 2016). The human rights model does not require the absence of impairment; instead it requires a response to that impairment and is therefore more demanding than the social model. For example, access to education is not just about removing the barriers to participation but the imposition of a duty to provide supports to enable the full and effective participation of persons with disabilities. Article 24(2) on the right to education requires reasonable accommodation, provision of support within the general education system to facilitate their effective education and effective individualised support measures. The social model by necessity is focused on the discriminatory nature of the barriers to participation, in itself a very valid concern. However, the human rights model injects a more proactive and comprehensive response. The injection of that positive duty is most evident when we consider rights traditionally considered to be negative in character – such as that contained in Article 5 CRPD on equality and non-discrimination.

Equality

Article 1 of the CRPD sets the goal of equality as its purpose. The concept of equality envisaged goes beyond formal and substantive equality to include a duty to act via the duty to provide 'reasonable accommodation'. A non-discrimination provision must be robust enough to overcome historical barriers that isolated and segregated persons with disabilities in order to sufficiently address disability discrimination. The concept of equality and the duty to reasonably accommodate underpins the entire CRPD. Article 5(3) provides that 'in order to promote equality and eliminate discrimination, States Parties shall take all appropriate steps to ensure that reasonable accommodation is provided'.

It is evident that the duty to promote equality 'imposes positive obligations to identify barriers in the way of a disabled person's enjoyment of their human rights and to take appropriate steps to remove them' (Lawson, 2009: 109). The duty to provide reasonable accommodation is an 'individualised reactive duty' (Quinlivan, 2019: 176). The provision requires the 'modification and adjustment' of barriers in 'a particular case' to enable a person with a disability to fully exercise their human rights on an equal basis with others. It is therefore responsive to the needs of the individual and each accommodation must be appropriate to that individual. The duty to provide reasonable accommodation is limited by the need to avoid imposing a 'disproportionate and undue burden' (UN General Assembly, 2006). The limit to the duty to provide reasonable accommodation is also a reactive limit, as it responds to the needs of the duty bearer. So, for example, what would be considered a disproportionate and undue burden for a small employer may differ considerably from that appropriate to a public sector employer. The very personalised nature of this legal obligation is arguably what makes it so effective.

A notable element of the imposition of a duty to provide reasonable accommodation within the CRPD is that private actors are in fact engaged in the enforcement of the Convention. In order to implement this duty, states should 'ensure that non-discrimination legislation extends to the private and public spheres, covers areas including education, employment, goods and services and tackles disability-specific discrimination' (UN CRPD Committee, 2018: 73). Traditionally, human rights treaties are addressed to states parties and require those states parties to undertake certain actions to realise the human rights of a particular group. Mégret and Msipa note that: '[i]t is almost as if the CRPD, through state's accession, spoke directly past the sovereign to the various non-state actors that in practice will have to do much of the work of reasonable accommodation' (Mégret and Msipa, 2014).

Thus, the non-discrimination duty contained in the CRPD is expansive. This is reinforced by virtue of the fact that some rights within the Convention are considered to be cross-cutting rights, that is rights that apply to all other rights within the Convention. The duty not to discriminate is one that is considered capable of immediate enforcement and thus the inclusion of reasonable accommodation within that concept has significant potential. Lawson describes it as playing a 'peculiar bridging role' in the context of human rights (Lawson, 2009: 104). She notes that the duty to provide reasonable accommodation can legitimately be considered a non-discrimination measure, thus situating it firmly in the category of civil and political rights. But the function of the duty to reasonably accommodate is to inject an element of positive duties to ensure that human rights become available to persons with disabilities. The imposition of positive duties has traditionally been associated with socio-economic rights. Therefore, the obligation to provide reasonable accommodation highlights the artificial dichotomy and challenges the very divergence of both sets of rights.

Indivisibility and interdependence

Traditionally there has been a distinction between civil and political rights on the one hand and economic, social and cultural rights on the other hand (Lawson, 2009; Flóvenz, 2009). This traditional dichotomy has been increasingly eroded in academic discourse, but nonetheless is worth a brief mention here (Koch, 2009). This distinction assumes that civil and political rights are definite, negative in character, immediate and justiciable. Economic, social and cultural rights, in contrast, are more programmatic, vague, positive in character and costly. The traditional distinction between civil and political rights and socio-economic rights conceivably aggravates the experience of exclusion for people with disabilities. Mégret suggests 'that the fractured, disaggregated nature of much human rights law is itself what requires reinvention if the rights of persons with disabilities are to be fully respected' (Mégret, 2008: 264). He goes on to note that this is what the CRPD has done, by ignoring, reinventing or transcending those traditional divisions.

The ability, in practice, of a person with a disability to be able to exercise their rights may often be more complex than overcoming a denial of access to a particular right. For example, a provision that denies a woman the right to vote can be addressed by removing that legal barrier. The same actions for a person with a disability may not actually enable that person to vote – a polling station could be inaccessible to a person with mobility impairment or the ballot paper may be inaccessible to a visually impaired person. It is therefore entirely conceivable to give full civil and political rights to persons with disabilities, while simultaneously disenfranchising and excluding that individual from exercising that right. Therefore, something more is needed to ensure that a person with a disability is enabled to exercise that right. The CRPD has muddied the lines between both sets of rights by injecting positive legal obligations into rights traditionally considered to be civil and political rights. For example, Article 12 gives the right to equal recognition before the law (legal capacity) and requires state parties to provide support if a person with a disability requires it in order to exercise their decision-making. Similarly, a proactive non-discrimination duty exists in respect of rights traditionally considered to be economic, social and cultural – such as Article 24 on the right to education. The following case study outlines the impact of the CRPD as a tool in driving disability policy reform.

Case study

All member states of the EU have ratified the CRPD. The EU's accession to the CRPD was historic and it was the first human rights treaty to be ratified by a regional organisation. This case study highlights the impact of the CRPD on social policy throughout Europe as it applies to persons with disabilities. The case study considers the misuse of European Structural and Investment Funds (Structural Funds) in member states to build new, or renovate existing, long-stay institutions for persons with disabilities and how the CRPD was used to challenge this practice.

The ratification of the CRPD by the EU means that it is responsible for implementation of the Convention to the extent of its competences (Council Decision, 2010/48/EC). The EU has committed itself to complying with the obligations in the Convention and to ensure that its laws and policies are reviewed and compliant with the CRPD. This is perhaps most evident in respect of the EU's obligations to realise the de-institutionalisation of persons with disabilities across the EU (OHCHR, 2012). Structural Funds account for more than 50 per cent of EU funding and are the main financial tool used by the EU to invest in employment and the creation of a sustainable and healthy European economy and environment (European Commission, 2019). The EU's accession to the CRPD provided an opportunity for non-governmental organisations, disabled persons' organisations and other stakeholders to critique its record on disability law and policy. A major criticism was the use of Structural Funds to support the institutionalisation of persons with disabilities in contravention of the CRPD (Quinn and Doyle, 2013). The EU's accession allowed space for critical reflection on the use of these funds and put pressure on the EU to ensure the funds were used to develop community-based services in a manner compliant with Article 19 of the CRPD (the right of persons with disabilities to live and be included in the community) (Parker and Clements, 2012: 95–116).

The criticism, advocacy and campaigning surrounding the misuse of Structural Funds proved highly impactful. The regulation governing Structural Funds for the period 2014–20 specifically provides that the Structural Funds could only be used to support de-institutionalisation. The regulation provides that the funds:

> should support the fulfilment of the Union's obligation under the UN Convention on the Rights of Persons with Disabilities with regard *inter alia* to education, work, employment and accessibility. The ESF should also promote the transition from institutional to community-based care. The ESF should not support any action that contributes to segregation or to social exclusion. (European Commission, 2015: 222)

This was a significant victory for civil society organisations and disabled persons' organisations. The commitment to de-institutionalisation, as provided for in the Structural Funds regulation, is set out as an '*ex ante* conditionality' which must be met before funds can be disbursed (European Commission, 2014: 259). EU member states are required to demonstrate that their national policies on poverty reduction specifically include measures that make the move from institutional to community care (Regulation (EU) 1303/2013).

Despite the introduction of these measures to address the misuse of Structural Funds, significant concerns persist in that they continue to be used to support institutionalisation (EU Fundamental Rights Agency, 2017). Disabled persons' organisations and others used the opportunities presented by the monitoring mechanism created in Articles 34–39 of the CRPD to highlight these concerns. The EU submitted its report to the CRPD Committee (the Committee) in 2014. In its report the EU asserted that its disability strategy promoted: 'the use of EU Structural Funds to assist Member States in the transition from institutional to community-based services and to raise awareness of the situation of people with disabilities living in residential institutions' (EU, 2014).

The Committee concluded that the right under Article 19 of the CRPD was not a reality for thousands of persons living in institutions rather than the community across the member states of the EU (United Nations, 2015). The Committee noted that the EU had made a number of changes to the regulations governing Structural Funds to promote their use for community living. However, the Committee was critical of the continued use of these funds by a number of member states 'for the maintenance of residential institutions rather than for the development of support services for persons with disabilities in local communities' (United Nations, 2015: 50). In effect, the Committee recommended that the EU do more to promote de-institutionalisation and to strengthen the monitoring of the use of Structural Funds to ensure that they were strictly used to develop community services. The Committee also recommended that the EU suspend, withdraw and recover payments if the obligation to respect fundamental rights, as provided for in the CRPD, was breached. The Committee expressed concern about the number of children with disabilities living in institutional settings in the EU (United Nations, 2015: 22–23), noting that children with disabilities experienced restricted access to mainstream, inclusive, quality education. They also highlighted the adverse impact of austerity measures on the availability of support services in local communities. The Committee recommended that the EU use Structural Funds and other funding streams to develop support services for children with disabilities and their families in local communities, facilitate de-institutionalisation, prevent any new institutionalisation and promote social inclusion and access to mainstream, inclusive, quality education.

Despite the ongoing concerns about the misuse of Structural Funds at national level, this case study highlights the effectiveness of the CRPD in promoting the move from institutional to community-based services for persons with disabilities across the EU. The Committee's recommendations are of note as they set out both negative and positive obligations for the EU in ensuring the move to community-based services for persons with disabilities. Not only is the EU now required to ensure that the funds are not used to build or maintain institutions, the EU is also required to use the Structural Funds to develop community-based services. The CRPD has been utilised to ensure that the EU effectively grounds the right to live independently for persons with disabilities in its law and policy, and has prodded the EU to be significantly more proactive in ensuring the Structural Funds are used in a manner that complies with its obligations under international human rights law.

Conclusion

The CRPD has been driving a law reform agenda globally since 2007. The Convention is undoubtedly a tool that can be used effectively to advocate for the realisation of the rights of persons with disabilities. Perhaps its greatest strength is that it challenges perceived wisdom as it applies to persons with disabilities, insisting that persons with disabilities are entitled to be treated on an equal basis with others and to be fully included in society. This participation is further strengthened by the requirement to involve people with disabilities in the enforcement and implementation of the CRPD. States parties must adopt proactive equality norms and provide positive supports for persons with disabilities. The potential of the CRPD as a tool for social policy reforms is aptly illustrated with reference to its use to impact EU policy in order to accelerate the de-institutionalisation and de-segregation of persons with disabilities across the EU.

References
Degener, T. (2016) 'Disability in a human rights context', *Laws*, 5(3): 1–24.
Degener, T. and Quinn, G. (2002) *Human Rights and Disability: The Current Use and Future Potential of United Nations Human Rights Instruments*, New York: United Nations.

European Commission (2014) *Guidance on Ex Ante Conditionalities for the European Structural and Investment Funds: Part 2*, Brussels: European Commission.

European Commission (2015) *European Structural and Investment Funds 2014–2020: Official Texts and Commentaries*, Brussels: European Commission.

European Commission (2019, 11 February). Available from: https://ec.europa.eu/info/funding-tenders/funding-opportunities/funding-programmes/overview-funding-programmes/european-structural-and-investment-funds_en

European Union (2014) *European Union Report to the Committee on the Rights of Persons with Disabilities*, CRPD/C/EU/1.

EU Fundamental Rights Agency (2017) *From Institutions to Community Living*, Brussels: European Commission.

Flóvenz, B.G. (2009) 'The implementation of the UN Convention and the development of economic and social rights as human rights', in O.M. Arnardóttir and G. Quinn (eds) *The UN Convention on the Rights of Persons with Disabilities: European and Scandinavian Perspectives*, Leiden: Martinus Nijhoff, pp 257–278.

Kayess, R. and French, P. (2008) 'Out of darkness into light? Introducing the Convention on the Rights of Persons with Disabilities', *Human Rights Law Review*, 8(1): 1–34.

Koch, I.E. (2009) 'From invisibility to indivisibility: the International Convention on the Rights of Persons with Disabilities', in O.M. Arnardóttir and G. Quinn (eds) *The UN Convention on the Rights of Persons with Disabilities: European and Scandinavian Perspectives*, Leiden: Martinus Nijhoff, pp 67–80.

Lawson, A. (2009) 'The UN Convention on the Rights of Persons with Disabilities and European disability law: a catalyst for cohesion?', in O.M. Arnardóttir and G. Quinn (eds) *The UN Convention on the Rights of Persons with Disabilities: European and Scandinavian Perspectives*, Leiden: Martinus Nijhoff, pp 81–110.

Mégret, F. (2008) 'The Disabilities Convention: towards a holistic concept of rights', *International Journal of Human Rights*, 12(2): 261–278.

Mégret, F. and Msipa, D. (2014) 'Global reasonable accommodation: how the Convention on the Rights of Persons with Disabilities changes the way we think about equality', *South African Journal on Human Rights*, 30(2): 252–274.

O'Mahony, C. and Quinn, G. (2017). *Disability Law and Policy: An Analysis of the UN Convention*, Dublin: Clarus Press.

Office of the High Commissioner for Human Rights (OHCHR) Regional Office for Europe (2012) *Getting a Life: Living Independently and Being Included in the Community*. Brussels: OHCHR.

Parker, C. and Clements, L. (2012) 'The European Union structural funds and the right to community living', *Equal Rights Review*, 9: 95–116.

Parker, C. and Clements, L. (2015) *The European Union and the Right to Independent Living: Structural Funds and the European Union's Obligations under the Convention on the Rights of Persons with Disabilities*, New York: Open Society Foundations.

Quinlivan, S. (2012) 'The United Nations Convention on the Rights of Persons with Disabilities: an introduction', *ERA Forum*, 13(1): 71–85.

Quinlivan, S. (2019) 'Reasonable accommodation: an integral part of the right to education for persons with disabilities', in G. de Beco, S. Quinlivan and J.E. Lord (eds) *The Right to Inclusive Education in International Human Rights Law*, Cambridge: Cambridge University Press.

Quinn, G. and Doyle, S. (2013) 'Marrying principle with power in the EU: the test case of the EU structural funds negotiations: update', *Equal Rights Review*, 11: 61–66.

Stein, M.A. (2007) 'Disability human rights', *California Law Review*, 95(1): 75–122.

UN CRPD Committee (2018) 'General Comment No 6: equality and non-discrimination': 73(c). New York: United Nations.

UN General Assembly (2006) *Convention on the Rights of Persons with Disabilities*, A/RES/61/106, Article 2.

United Nations (2015) *Concluding Observations on the Initial Report of the European Union*. CRPD/C/EU/CO/1.

United Nations (2019) *Disability: Factsheet on Persons with Disabilities*. Available from: https://www.un.org/development/desa/disabilities/resources/factsheet-on-persons-with-disabilities.html

19

The right to development

Stephen McCloskey

The rights most firmly associated with international development – social, economic and cultural rights – were to a large extent victims of the Cold War, when they were viewed by some as either too closely associated with the goals of Soviet socialism in the Eastern bloc or relegated to the primary goal of economic liberalisation in the West. It was only with the thawing of the Cold War in the 1980s that these rights, as Amnesty International (2014: 25) put it, began to be reclaimed and restored to a lineage that dated back to declarations of national rights in France and the United States in the late eighteenth century. These rights include: the right to work and to join a trade union; the right to education; the right to food, clothing and housing; the right to healthcare and social services; and the right to participate in cultural and scientific life (2014: 25).

Many of these rights are enshrined in United Nations (UN) resolutions and declarations, including: the Right to Development (UNGA 1986); the Convention on the Elimination of All Forms of Discrimination Against Women (1979); the Convention on the Rights of the Child (1989); and the International Covenant on Civil and Political Rights (1976). Since the mid-1960s, human rights provisions have been agreed in relation to 'a range of racial and ethnic groups, women, indigenous peoples, children, migrant workers, and people with disabilities' (Amnesty International, 2014: 26). This has helped to provide a legal framework for human development. As the *Human Development Report* states: 'human rights lend moral legitimacy and the principle of social justice to the objectives of human development' and, for its part, human development 'brings a dynamic long-term perspective to the fulfilment of rights. It directs attention to the socio-economic context in which rights can be realized – or threatened' (UNDP, 2000: 2).

This chapter considers the contrasting approaches of two rights-driven development agendas that emerged in the 1980s. The first is the idea of human development as the enhancement of human rights, civil liberties and individual freedoms as encapsulated in the United

Nations' *Human Development Report* (UNDP, 2000) and economist Amartya Sen's *Development As Freedom* (1999). This approach was counterpointed by, second, neoliberalism's economic instrumentalism and its determination that human development, economic and social rights would directly result from the unfettered activities of the market (Monbiot, 2016). The chapter argues that the 2008 global financial crisis and resurgent ethnic and nationalist populism has negatively impacted the international non-governmental development sector, and as Khoo (2017) suggests, has 'shattered' the minimum floor of humanitarian norms. The chapter discusses the correlation between neoliberalism, austerity and a weakening of social and economic safeguards and development practice. It concludes by asking if the Sustainable Development Goals (SDGs) can help to push back the neoliberal economic model that undermines rights and impedes development.

Human rights and human development

Human rights and human development are often invoked as two sides of the same coin. Thus, Isoh comments that:

> Human rights could best be protected by adopting a rights-based approach to development. It is a framework that integrates the norms, principles, standards and goals of the international human rights system into the plans and processes of development. It requires that all stakeholders be included and reinforces capacities of duty bearers (usually governments) to respect, protect and guarantee these rights. (Isoh, 2013)

Similarly, the *Human Development Report* (2000) states that: 'human rights and human development share a common vision and a common purpose – to secure the freedom, well-being and dignity of all people everywhere' (UNDP, 2000: 1). This view of development has been manifested in development practice through the work of Dóchas, the Irish association of non-government development organisations, which argues that:

> Using the prism of Human Rights to look at development, means redefining problems and the corresponding solutions, away from the provision of services and goods, towards an approach that addresses the different dimensions of

poverty (powerlessness; social exclusion; lack of protection, participation and access to/control over resources), on multiple levels, and in a participatory way. (Dóchas, 2003: 3)

This rights-based approach to development resulted from the convergence of civil and political rights on the one hand and economic and social rights on the other in the post-Cold War era (UNDP, 2000: iii). Khoo identified contrasting rights-based routes to development in this period that appeared to integrate human rights and development (Khoo, 2017: 37). The first is the 'Right to Development', which is based on an approach to development as a collective right and was first recognised in the 1981 African Charter on Human and People's Rights. A Declaration on the Right to Development was subsequently adopted as a resolution by the UN General Assembly in 1986, affirming 'the right of peoples to self-determination, by virtue of which they have the right freely to determine their political status and to pursue their economic, social and cultural development' (UNGA, 1986).

More widely adopted by Western governments and NGOs is the human rights-based approach (HRBA) to development which focused on enlarging the freedoms and rights of the individual rather than collective rights (Sen, 1999). Thus, the *Human Development Report* (2000) stipulates that: 'A human right is realized when individuals enjoy the freedoms covered by that right and their enjoyment of the right is secure' (UNDP, 2000: 16). Heavily influenced by Sen's *Development as Freedom* (1999), the HRBA is described by the UNDP as 'expanding people's choices and capabilities but above all is about the empowerment of people to decide what this process of expansion should look like' (UNDP, 2002). However, it does have its critics. Denis O'Hearn considers Sen's economic vision as development 'driven by capitalism laced with good values' (O'Hearn, 2009: 12). He is critical of Sen's frequent recourse to Adam Smith's limiting role of the state in social welfare and Friedrich Hayek 'for championing liberties and freedoms as a foundation of economic progress' (O'Hearn, 2009: 11–12). O'Hearn argues that:

> Having stated the prerequisites of freedom and capability
> in individual terms, Sen never attempts to derive the social
> origins of ethics, or their historical or cultural specificity, or
> the ways in which some kinds of capability may be socially
> organized rather than just a sum of individual capacities.
> (O'Hearn, 2009: 10)

The near-universal acclaim of Sen's economic vision is, according to O'Hearn, based on his adherence to Western individualism, the limiting role of the state, the assertion of individual rights over the collective, and his lack of criticism of Western institutions and states (O'Hearn, 2009: 13–14).

Khoo suggests that 'the expansion of human rights and human development in the 1990s offered potentially powerful counterpoints to neoliberalism's economic instrumentalism and implicit authoritarianism' (Khoo, 2017: 37). However, she believes that the 'tensions between neoliberalism and rights have never been resolved' with many regarding 'human rights as being fundamentally irreconcilable with neoliberalism' (Khoo, 2017: 38). The adherence of most industrialised nations to the neoliberal model of economic development therefore threatens to undermine the human rights approach to development asserted in the 1980s and 1990s. For example, in the wake of the 2008 global financial crisis, 860,000 families in the United States lost their homes when a recklessly deregulated financial sector imploded 'as risky subprime mortgages proved unsustainable' (Clark, 2009). By 2016, more than 500,000 people were homeless in the US, many of them living in official and unofficial tent cities (Taylor, 2016), reflecting the extent to which social and economic rights had been compromised by a casino-like capitalism.

The state of development

The UN rightly points to the considerable strides that were made in the last century in advancing rights and human liberties. 'In 1900 more than half the world's people lived under colonial rule, and no country gave all its citizens the right to vote'. However, by the end of the century, 'some three-quarters of the world lived under democratic regimes' (UNDP, 2000: 1). Despite this progress, stubbornly high levels of poverty persisted in the Global South, particularly in Sub-Saharan Africa, largely as a result of unfair trade rules which favoured so-called 'developed countries' and the debt crisis which enveloped the Global South in the 1970s as a result of reckless lending by banks, governments and multilateral development bodies in the Global North (Bello, 1998; George, 1990). These persistent levels of poverty meant that the United Nations and its member states had to launch a new anti-poverty initiative in 2000, the Millennium Declaration, with eight targets to address the most pressing development problems at the turn of the century. The eight Millennium Development Goals (MDGs) had the overarching target of 'reducing by half the proportion of people whose income is less than one dollar a day' by 2015 (UNGA, 2000: 5). When the goals reached their end point, the former UN Secretary-General, Ban Ki-Moon, claimed that the MDGs had lifted more than a billion people out of extreme poverty and yet he admitted that 'inequalities persist and that progress has been uneven' (UN, 2015: 3). The extent of these inequalities was outlined in the data presented in the 2016 *Human Development Report*, which revealed that: 'one person in nine in the world is hungry, and one in three is malnourished; 18,000 people a day die because of air pollution; HIV infects 2 million people a year; and every minute an average of 24 people are displaced from their home' (UNDP, 2016: 5).

Global levels of inequality and a widening contagion of conflict, terrorism and sectarianism have contributed to increasing levels of forced displacement both within and between states. The United Nations High Commissioner for Refugees (UNHCR) reported in 2018 that: 68.5 million people were forcibly displaced worldwide; 40 million people were internally displaced; 25.4 million people had fled their countries as refugees and 3.1 million people were seeking asylum (UNHCR, 2018a). Fifty-seven per cent of the world's refugees came from just three countries embroiled in long-running conflicts and social upheaval: Afghanistan (2.6 million); South Sudan (2.4 million) and Syria (6.3 million). This resulted in a spike in migration, particularly from Africa and the Middle East across the Mediterranean to Europe, and peaking at one million migrants in 2015, with an estimated 4,000 people drowning during the journey (UNHCR, 2015).

The migration issue became central to Britain's decision to leave the European Union by referendum on 23 June 2016 and the election of Donald Trump as US President a few months later. It had been ramped up as a threat to local jobs and services by a complicit media which perpetuated stereotypes. A major study of media coverage of migration across Europe found much of it 'reflects political bias and is superficial, simplistic and often ill-informed' (Ethical Journalism Network, 2017). For example, rarely does the media report that the top five refugee hosting countries are in the Global South – Iran (979,400), Lebanon (1 million); Pakistan (1.4 million); Uganda (1.4 million) and Turkey (3.5 million) (UNHCR, 2018a). However, the migration and refugee issue has been seized upon by politically conservative and far-right parties to roll back the rights of migrants, refugees and asylum-seekers, and press for more isolationist and unilateral foreign policies. These political forces narrowly carried the day in the US presidential election and UK EU referendum and have subsequently led to a push for tighter border controls and reduced government spending (McCloskey,

2017). The economist Thomas Piketty has linked growing support for reactionary, populist politics in the US with declining or static incomes in post-industrial regions that feel left behind by Washington elites (Oxfam, 2017: 2).

As the United Nations High Commissioner for Human Rights, Zeid Ra'ad Al Hussein, stated:

> Human rights are sorely under pressure around the world – no longer a priority: a pariah. The legitimacy of human rights principles is attacked. The practice of human rights norms is in retreat. Here in Europe, ethno-populist parties are in the ascendant in many countries – fuelling hatred and scarring their societies with deepening divisions. (UNHCR, 2018b)

Amnesty International's 2017 Annual Report, similarly, described 'a global pushback against human rights' and Human Rights Watch has called for the defending of 'human rights values under attack' (Roth, 2016). While, the post-Cold War period began with much optimism based on the alignment of human development and human rights, the 2008 global financial crisis, economic austerity and resurgence of the political right has squeezed development aid budgets and eroded the human rights building blocks upon which international development is based.

Neoliberalism, austerity and development aid

Although dating back to the 1930s, and despite having the sponsorship of several wealthy supporters, neoliberalism remained on the margins of political power until the early 1970s. Championed principally by Friedrich Hayek, an Austrian economist, and later, famously, by Milton Friedman and his followers in the University of Chicago's Department of Economics, neoliberalism became an all-pervasive influence on political, economic, cultural and social life in societies across the world, thereby profoundly altering the relationship between the state and its citizens. The post-World War II period was characterised on both sides of the Atlantic by a political consensus on the application of Keynesian economics premised upon full employment, high taxation, state-provided social safety nets and government-led development of new public services (Skidelsky, 2009). Neoliberalism represented the antithesis of this vision of development, principally in rolling back the state's role as a welfare and service provider, in its firm belief that the market and competition could 'raise all ships' in a sea of prosperity. It was enthusiastically embraced by the US presidency of Ronald Reagan and British premier Margaret Thatcher in the 1980s, and became central to decision-making in the Atlantic economies. For George Monbiot:

> Neoliberalism sees competition as the defining characteristic of human relations. It redefines citizens as consumers, whose democratic choices are best exercised by buying and selling, a process that rewards merit and punishes inefficiency. It maintains that 'the market' delivers benefits that could never be achieved by planning. (Monbiot, 2016)

From a rights-based and development perspective, the application of neoliberalism has been disastrous, as its first and most comprehensive application suggests. In 1973, General Augusto Pinochet overthrew Chile's democratically elected socialist President, Salvador Allende, in a US-backed coup and imposed a series of sweeping economic 'reforms', or shocks, prescribed by Friedman and the 'Chicago Boys'. The methods have since become a playbook for neoliberalism. Pinochet:

> privatised some, though not all state-owned companies (including several banks); he allowed cutting-edge new forms of speculative finance; he flung open the borders to foreign imports, tearing down the barriers that had long protected Chilean manufacturers; and he cut government spending by 10 percent – except the military, which received a significant increase. (Klein, 2007: 79)

The results of these reforms in Chile were disastrous, with 177,000 industrial jobs lost between 1973 and 1983 and manufacturing dropping to 'levels last seen during the Second World War' (Klein, 2007: 82). According to Amnesty International (2015): 'more than 3,000 people were killed or disappeared and more than 38,000 arbitrarily detained and tortured during the 17 years of military regime that followed' the 1973 coup. Western democracies either turned a blind eye or were complicit in the enforcement of neoliberal reforms and attendant human rights abuses. For example, Margaret Thatcher described Pinochet as a 'true friend' and lobbied against his prosecution for war crimes (Gardner, 2015). On a visit to Pinochet's Chile, Hayek said: 'my personal preference leans toward a liberal dictatorship rather than toward a democratic government devoid of liberalism' (cited by

Monbiot, 2016). Economic and social rights – such as employment, welfare, trade union affiliation and housing – often fall victim to the implementation of neoliberalism, but even more heinous rights abuses, including torture and disappearances, sometimes accompany the 'strong medicine' of neoliberal reform (Klein, 2007).

In *The Shock Doctrine* (2007), Naomi Klein revealed how systemic shocks, such as the Pinochet coup, the military junta coup in Argentina in 1976, the 2003 Iraq war and the natural disaster of Hurricane Katrina in New Orleans in 2005 have been used as cover for the implementation of neoliberal reforms and the curtailment of rights and liberties. The biggest shock of all, however, was to come in 2008 when the global financial system experienced its steepest crash since 1929 as a recklessly deregulated US economy, hopelessly over-extended by a credit bubble caused by high-risk lending by banks and mortgage lenders, went into freefall. *Forbes* estimated the size of the US government's bailout of American banks in the aftermath of the crash as an eye-watering $16.8 trillion (Collins, 2015), thereby completely discrediting the neoliberal model. The economic system that disparaged government interventionism and public ownership found itself dependent on both, but the shock to follow was austerity, imposed on an unprecedented scale. Five years after the crisis, Amnesty International reported that:

> The financial crisis and austerity measures in many EU countries have affected various economic and social rights, including those ensuring access to social security, housing, health, education and food. The measures often disproportionately affect the poorest and most marginalised people. (Amnesty International, 2013)

Amnesty added that when a government is weighing up the impact of cost-cutting austerity measures: 'It is an international obligation to ensure that measures are non-discriminatory, do not disproportionately undermine existing rights, do not hit the most vulnerable and disadvantaged people hardest and do not drive them further into poverty' (Amnesty International, 2013). However, evidence of the impact of austerity in the UK – the country that applied the harshest regime in Europe – suggests that it is the vulnerable who are being hit hardest. The Trussell Trust, which operates a foodbank network across the UK, distributed 1.3 million three-day emergency food supplies to people in crisis between April 2017 and March 2018, a 13 per cent increase on 2017 – with 484,026 of these supplies going to children (The Trussell Trust, 2018). The top four reasons given for referrals to foodbanks were low incomes, benefit delays, benefit changes and debt, suggesting that those dependent on welfare and working in low-paid jobs were most vulnerable to austerity-driven welfare cuts and wage freezes (The Trussell Trust, 2018). The *British Medical Journal* (BMJ) points to a similar situation with housing in the UK, suggesting that 'austerity policies lie at the heart of soaring homelessness and related health harms' with 'an increase in homeless families housed by local authorities in temporary accommodation, rising from 50,000 in 2010 to 78,000 in 2017' (BMJ, 2018).

Almost inevitably, in the wake of the financial crisis in Europe, aid to poor countries dropped as EU member states tightened their budgets and reduced departmental spending (OECD, 2013). Reaching the fiftieth anniversary of the 1970 UN resolution in which donors pledged to commit 0.7 per cent of their Gross National Income (GNI) as Overseas Development Assistance (ODA), only six countries achieved this target – Norway, Sweden, Denmark, Luxembourg, the Netherlands and the UK (Quinn, 2017). Moreover, the total amount donated in aid by the Development Assistance Committee (DAC) of the Organisation for Economic Co-operation and Development (OECD) – the world's wealthiest nations – was $146.6 billion in 2017, which is just 0.31 per cent of their combined GNI. Setting aside the $16.8 trillion committed by the US government for banks in distress post-2008, it appears that the political will is missing to commit to the aid spending needed by the poorest people in the Global South, or to protect the social and economic rights of those hit hardest by austerity in the Global North.

Conclusion

The end of the Cold War and the emergence of the human rights-based approach to development appeared to herald a new era which placed social, cultural and economic rights at the centre of the development process. Human development and human rights became mutually reinforcing components of a new legal framework that drew upon existing – and helped to define new – international conventions, covenants and resolutions. Inspired by Sen's *Development as Freedom*, the United Nations Development Programme commenced publication in 1990 of the *Human Development Report*, which used a Human Development Index to measure the progress of states toward development targets in areas such as education, health and gender equality as well as economic growth. However, the post-Cold War period unleashed unprecedented levels of globalisation driven by a virulent neoliberal economic ideology given its head by the collapse of socialist states in the Eastern bloc and incorporated into the heart of Western governments by the Thatcher and Reagan administrations. The implementation of a 'one size fits all' approach to global development, led by neoliberal institutions that included the International Monetary Fund and World Bank, resulted in the privatisation of public utilities and services, the removal of protections on imports, the stripping away of state supports and welfare, and the emasculation of social and economic rights. In short, the Keynesian consensus was shattered and a competitive individualism came to override collective, community-driven development.

The disastrous deregulation of the banking sector, particularly in the US, was in keeping with neoliberalism's mantra that the market will meet society's needs if stripped of government interference. This directly led to the global financial crisis of 2008, and increasing levels of public disaffection with government and elites. This resulted from static wages, rising prices and the increasing struggle by the low paid to make ends meet. The economist Thomas Piketty found in the US 'that over the last 30 years the growth in the incomes of the bottom 50% has been zero, whereas incomes of the top 1% have grown 300%' (Oxfam, 2017: 2; Piketty, 2014: 25–29). It resulted in a much greater vulnerability for people on low incomes and benefits, undermining their social and economic rights, including the rights to employment, housing, trade unionisation, food, clothing and education. It has created an unstable political environment around the world where migrants are being scapegoated by a resurgent right for political ends.

It remains to be seen if the SDGs can galvanise sufficient resources and political will to roll back the tide of neoliberalism and resist the rising levels of xenophobia. However, a key instrument in achieving these goals is education. SDG target 4.7 calls for all learners to:

> acquire knowledge and skills needed to promote sustainable development, including among others through education for sustainable development and sustainable lifestyles, human rights, gender equality, promotion of a culture of peace and non-violence, global citizenship, and appreciation of cultural diversity and of culture's contribution to sustainable development. (UNDP, 2018)

This target needs to be a rallying call for governments, NGOs and multilateral institutions if we are to ensure the realisation of meaningful development predicated upon international standards and conventions in human rights.

References

Amnesty International (2013) 'Why EU must protect human rights during financial crisis', Public Statement, 3 May. Available from: https://www.amnesty.eu/news/all-0632/

Amnesty International (2014) *Human Rights for Human Dignity*, 2nd edition, London: Amnesty International. Available from: www.amnesty.org/download/Documents/8000/pol340012014en.pdf

Amnesty International (2015) 'Chile: amnesty law keeps Pinochet's legacy alive', 11 September. Available from: www.amnesty.org/en/latest/news/2015/09/chile-amnesty-law-keeps-pinochet-s-legacy-alive/

Amnesty International Annual Report (2017) 'The state of the world: a global pushback against human rights', *Amnesty International Annual Report 2016/17*. Available from: https://www.amnesty.org/en/latest/research/2017/02/amnesty-international-annual-report-201617/

Bello, W. (1998) *Dark Victory: The United States and Global Poverty*, London: Pluto Press.

BMJ (British Medical Journal) (2018) 'Austerity policies lie at heart of soaring homelessness and related health harms'. Available from: www.bmj.com/company/newsroom/austerity-policies-lie-at-heart-of-soaring-homelessness-and-related-health-harms-argue-experts/

Clark, A. (2009) 'US home repossessions rocket to record levels', *The Guardian*, 13 August. Available from: www.theguardian.com/business/2009/aug/13/us-home-repossessions-rise

Collins, M. (2015) 'The big bank bailout', *Forbes*, 14 July. Available from: www.forbes.com/sites/mikecollins/2015/07/14/the-big-bank-bailout/#3a8f07e82d83

Convention on the Elimination of all Forms of Discrimination against Women (CEDAW) (1979) Available from: www.un.org/womenwatch/daw/cedaw/cedaw.htm

Convention on the Rights of the Child (1989) Available from: www.ohchr.org/en/professionalinterest/pages/crc.aspx

DÓCHAS (2003) 'Application of rights based approaches – experiences and challenges'. Report on a Dóchas Seminar on Rights Based Approaches to Development, 12 February, Dublin: Dóchas.

Ethical Journalism Network (2017) 'How does the media on both sides of the Mediterranean report on migration?', Brussels: EUROMED Migration IV. Available from: www.icmpd.org/our-work/migration-dialogues/euromed-migration-iv/migration-narrative-study/

Gardner, S. (2015) 'Tories have forgotten that Thatcher wasn't just a terrorist sympathiser, but close friends with one', *The Independent*, 22 September. Available from: www.independent.co.uk/voices/comment/tories-have-forgotten-that-thatcher-wasnt-just-a-terrorist-sympathiser-but-close-friends-with-one-10507850.html

George, S. (1990) *A Fate Worse than Debt: The World Financial Crisis and the Poor*, New York: Grove Press.

International Covenant on Civil and Political Rights (1976) Available from: www.ohchr.org/en/professionalinterest/pages/ccpr.aspx

Klein, N. (2007) *The Shock Doctrine: The Rise of Disaster Capitalism*, London: Allen Lane.

Isoh, A.A. (2013) 'The human rights based approach', *The Guardian*, 10 June. Available from: www.theguardian.com/global-development-professionals-network/2013/jun/06/human-rights-based-approach

Khoo, S. (2017) 'Engaging development and human rights curriculum in higher education, in the neoliberal twilight zone', *Policy & Practice: A Development Education Review*, 25: 34–58.

McCloskey, S. (2017) 'In the age of Brexit and Trump, we need "development education" more than ever', 27 February, *openDemocracy*. Available from: www.opendemocracy.net/wfd/stephen-mccloskey/in-age-of-brexit-and-trump-we-need-development-education-more-than-ever

Monbiot, G. (2016) 'Neoliberalism: the ideology at the root of all our problems', *The Guardian*, 15 April. Available from: www.theguardian.com/books/2016/apr/15/neoliberalism-ideology-problem-george-monbiot

OECD (Organisation for Economic Co-operation and Development) (2013) 'Aid to poor countries slips further as governments tighten budgets'. Available from: www.oecd.org/dac/stats/aidtopoorcountriesslipsfurtherasgovernmentstightenbudgets.htm

O'Hearn, D. (2009) 'Amartya Sen's development as freedom: ten years later', *Policy & Practice: A Development Education Review*, 8: 9–15. Available from: www.developmenteducationreview.com/issue/issue-8/amartya-sens-development-freedom-ten-years-later

Oxfam (2017) 'An economy for the 99%', January. Available from: www.oxfam.org.au/wp-content/uploads/2017/01/An-economy-for-99-percent.pdf

Piketty, T. (2014) *Capital in the Twenty-first Century*, Cambridge, MA: Belknap Press.

Quinn, B. (2017) 'UK among six countries to hit 0.7% UN aid spending target', *The Guardian*, 4 January. Available from: www.theguardian.com/global-development/2017/jan/04/uk-among-six-countries-hit-un-aid-spending-target-oecd

Roth, K. (2016) 'Defending human rights values under attack', 22 June. Available from: www.hrw.org/news/2016/06/22/defending-human-rights-values-under-attack

Sen, A. (1999) *Development as Freedom*, New York: Alfred A. Knopf.

Skidelsky, R. (2009) *Keynes: The Return of the Master*, London: Penguin Books.

Taylor, A. (2016) 'America's tent cities for the homeless', *The Atlantic*, 11 February. Available from: www.theatlantic.com/photo/2016/02/americas-tent-cities-for-the-homeless/462450/

The Trussell Trust (2018) 'End of year stats'. Available from: www.trusselltrust.org/news-and-blog/latest-stats/end-year-stats/

United Nations (2015) 'The Millennium Development Goals Report 2015', New York: UN. Available from: www.un.org/millenniumgoals/2015_MDG_Report/pdf/MDG%202015%20rev%20(July%201).pdf

UNDP (United Nations Development Programme) (2000) *Human Development Report 2000: Human Rights and Human Development*, New York: Oxford University Press. Available from: http://hdr.undp.org/en/content/human-development-report-2000

UNDP (United Nations Development Programme) (2002) 'A human rights-based approach to development programming in UNDP', 23 May. Available from: www.undp.org/content/undp/en/home/librarypage/democratic-governance/human_rights/a-human-rights-based-approach-to-development-programming-in-undp.html

UNDP (United Nations Development Programme) (2016) *Human Development Report 2016: Human Development for Everyone*, New York: Oxford University Press. Available from: http://hdr.undp.org/en/content/human-development-report-2000

UNDP (United Nations Development Programme) (2018) 'Sustainable Development Goals'. Available from: www.undp.org/content/undp/en/home/sustainable-development-goals.html

UNGA (United Nations General Assembly) (1986) 'Declaration on the Right to Development' (A/RES/41/128), 4 December. Available from: https://www.ohchr.org/EN/ProfessionalInterest/Pages/RightToDevelopment.aspx

UNGA (United Nations General Assembly) (2000) 'United Nations Millennium Declaration', 18 September, New York: UNGA. Available from: https://www.ohchr.org/EN/ProfessionalInterest/Pages/Millennium.aspx

UNHCR (UN High Commissioner for Refugees) (2015) 'Over one million sea arrivals reach Europe in 2015', 30 December. Available from: www.unhcr.org/uk/news/latest/2015/12/5683d0b56/million-sea-arrivals-reach-europe-2015.html

UNHCR (UN High Commissioner for Refugees) (2018a) 'Figures at a glance'. Available from: www.unhcr.org/uk/figures-at-a-glance.html

UNHCR (UN High Commissioner for Refugees) (2018b) 'As Mediterranean sea arrivals decline and death rates rise. UNHCR calls for strengthening of search and rescue', 6 July. Available from: www.unhcr.org/news/briefing/2018/7/5b3f270a4/mediterranean-sea-arrivals-decline-death-rates-rise-unhcr-calls-strengthening.html

20

Conclusion
Human rights in a brave new world: the shape of things to come?

Fred Powell

The metaphysical rebel protests against the human condition in general. (Albert Camus, 1962)

For the sake of the plan, the totality of society – every person, object, and process – must be corralled into the supply chains that feed the machines, which in turn spin the algorithms that animate Big Other to manage and mitigate our frailty. (Shoshanna Zuboff, 2019: 401)

The Little People came suddenly. I don't know who they are. I don't know what it means. I was a prisoner of the story [IQ84]. I had no choice. They came, and I described it. That is my work. (Haruki Murakami, 2011)

This chapter explores the political context of human rights and how it is shaping the future. Hannah Arendt's famous phrase, 'the right to have rights', defines the complex relationship between democracy, human rights and civil society. Human rights are not simply the super-ego (conscience) of politics, but constitute the very substance of democracy by conferring a universal set of rights on the citizen. These rights are the pillars of modern Western civilisation, embracing both individual liberty and social justice. Human rights have been historically contested by tyranny, symbolised by the concentration camp, which created conditions and places where human rights were actually extinguished during the first half of the twentieth century. Guantanamo Bay prison and media reports of the existence of 'rendition centres' remind us that this form of exclusion and detention is also part of contemporary political reality, legitimated by 'the war against terror'. Refugee camps that have emerged in a vast array of internment facilities during the twenty-first century also remind us that the language and practice of human rights is deeply contested in contemporary society. President Trump's wall project is a metaphor for a new medievalism, in which the external world is culturally constructed as 'the enemy' and needy strangers have no right to a place in society.

While Hannah Arendt was understandably concerned about the plight of refugees in post-war Europe, the United Nations Convention on Human Rights (1948) and the welfare state broadened public discourse and understanding of human rights to embrace both individual liberty and social justice. The British sociologist T.H. Marshall linked the abstraction of Hannah Arendt's conceptualisation of human rights to social reality and the institution of the welfare state. According to Marshall's concept of citizenship, it rested on a 'three-legged stool', composed of civil, political and social rights. These are the fundamental pillars of democracy (Marshall, 1973).

Two recent events have captured the essence of our times. First, the re-emergence of civic protest, which began with the global Occupy Movement in 2011 and mutated into the *Gilets Jaunes* (Yellow Vests) in France during 2018–19. Second, the much anticipated Haruki Murakami novel published in 2011, entitled *IQ84*, while clearly inspired by George Orwell's 1984 allegory about Stalinist tyranny, takes the reader into a counter-world of unreality, where surveillance is all-pervasive and the 'Little People' hide from a weirdly unsettling Lewis Carroll wonderland of horrors and the horrifying exercise of power over the mesmerised. Both the civic protest movements and Murakami's *IQ84* illuminate aspects of the world we currently inhabit: the dominance of unaccountable and largely invisible systems of power, but also the willingness of citizens to globally struggle against these dark forces. The 'Little People' have become the 'unsignified signifiers' probing behind the mirror of power (Baxter, 2011: 25). In doing so they are rethinking the nature of modernity as an imaginary act.

Cornelius Castoriadis, in his book *The Imaginary Institution of Society* (1987), redefined modernity as a struggle between a radical democratic project of autonomy (that is, personal freedom to determine one's own future without structural manipulation) and the neo-institutional project of mastery of what Michael Hardt and Antonio Negri (2000: xii), in their book *Empire*, identify as 'a decentered and deteritorializing apparatus of rule that progressively incorporates the entire global realm' under 'a single rule'. The adoption of the austerity project by the European Union has arguably initiated a struggle between the disciplinary agenda of what its critics caricature as the European 'super-state' that is being resisted by the 'Little People' through civic protest. But is this civic protest simply reactive and defensive against change in the form of populism (for example, Brexit) *or* does it represent a new ethical form of democratic engagement from below? It reminds us of Albert Camus' (1962) distinction between rebellion as an act of spontaneous protest as opposed to revolution, which implies the transfer of sovereign power to a new regime. In that sense it is very different in its objectives to the Velvet Revolutions of Central and Eastern Europe and the Maghreb–Mashreq region. The Velvet Revolutions devolved on civil society, populated by active citizens committed to peacefully overthrowing tyranny and its replacement by democracy.

In this discussion Haruki Murakami's literary metaphor of the 'Little People' (civil society) will be developed, probing behind the mirror of power (tyranny) in the context of popular democratic resistance to what Zuboff (2019) calls 'surveillance capitalism'. In the era of artificial intelligence (AI), data as a resource is the new oil in the world economy. In the hierarchy of world ownership of resources, China is replacing Saudi Arabian oil wealth because it has become the most data-rich country on the planet. Data ownership equates with power and profit in 'surveillance capitalism' that has no boundaries or democratic accountability in the eyes of its critics. Zuboff darkly predicts that 'surveillance capitalism' will enable the establishment of a global system of behaviour modification, with the potential to transform human consciousness of what it means to be a human being. That makes it a new Leviathan (Hobbes' tyrannical state), which, by threatening everyday life (for example, social and fiscal), is stimulating popular revolt against political and economic elites in defence of human rights and democracy, as understood by the participants. Elites reframe this form of civic protest as 'lawless' and 'populist', threatening civilisation as we know it at its foundations, by challenging the constitutional conventions that underpin liberal democratic society. The *Gilet Jaunes* in France are widely referenced by media reports as a 'white' rural populist, anti-immigrant, anti-Semitic movement of disgruntled citizens reacting to globalisation (Harding, 2019). On the other hand, civic protest in the twenty-first century could be interpreted as forging a new existentialist narrative in defence of the primordial right to be human, as we currently understand the meaning of being versus nothing, the existential right to consciousness (*cogito ergo sum*), the democratic right to association and the defence of social rights against market freedoms.

Heresy, democracy and the right to associate

In the underground world of public discourse, the first Enlightenment rumblings of a democratic civil and political society emerged during the seventeenth century. The philosopher Benedict Spinoza (1632–77) began to articulate a democratic version of the future, based on the right to associate, in which a benevolent relationship between the citizen and the state became part of the political imaginary. Spinoza imagined a world free from the authoritarian shackles of church and monarchy. Despite censorship and police surveillance, Spinoza became the leader of a radical philosophical movement that began to assert the right to human association (civil society) and democratic freedom (citizenship, liberty and republican governance). He was a 'heretic' (at a point when humans were ready to embrace freedom of thought) but also 'one of the most important and famous philosophers of all time, certainly the most radical of his own' (Nadler, 1999: xi). The discovery of the printing press during the fifteenth century had created a political public that thrived on a diet of pamphlets, newspapers and magazines in what became known as 'Coffee House Society'. But much of civil society remained underground and the realisation of human liberty and republican egalitarian ideals were a century away. After Spinoza's death in 1677 a 'forbidden movement' inspired by his radical ideas spread across Europe despite the constraints of censorship, suppression and hostility.

The publication of Tom Paine's *Rights of Man* in 1791 became the defining statement of modern democracy because it contextualised the meaning of citizenship as human rights. It legitimated the violent French Revolution that had begun in 1789 and was set to transform European society and the world beyond. Paine (1737–1809) was in many respects the founder of modern democracy. Human rights provided a universal set of values to underpin democracy, conferring on the downtrodden masses the equal status of citizenship (Powell, 2010). It was a colossal achievement that constituted a political earthquake. Democracy became the model of popular choice for the modern state. It continued to be challenged by new forms of tyranny in the form of fascism and communism. Human rights are the only legal and moral defence against tyranny and are the alternative to revolutionary violence in democratic societies. Since the foundations of democracy ('the right to have rights') in ancient Greece, it has been involved in an eternal struggle for power with oligarchy based on tyranny. For two and a half millennia democracy disappeared in a world dominated by hierarchy in the form of religious and monarchical tyranny – the divine rights of kings. Indeed, democracy is constantly contested by its opponents, such as Vladimir Putin (political) and Leo Strauss (philosophical). Their opposition to the rights-based agenda of the liberal left is fundamental and highly influential in shaping a Conservative restoration. It has pushed some resistance underground (for example, Anonymous), which is never healthy in a democratic society and suggests a lack of confidence in respect for human rights.

Industrial capitalism produced a flowering of civil society in the modern world among the emergent working class in cities across the planet in the form of mutualist organisations, trade unions, political societies, a vibrant campaigning media world of working-class pamphleteering and a labour press. At the core of this radical civil society was civic protest against an unjust social order. Within the labour movement many activists identified with socialism as their political philosophy. Karl Marx and Friedrich Engels, in their revolutionary pamphlet *The Communist Manifesto* (1848), created the working class as their revolutionary subject. The rise of working-class movements, often led by intellectuals such as Rosa Luxemburg, articulated the felt needs and democratic aspirations of their supporters. In the post-war world, a kaleidoscope of new social movements emerged espousing issues as diverse as feminism, civil rights for ethnic minorities and environmentalism. It was called the New Left.

Steinhoff (2015:103) argues that 'invisible civil society is the by-product of the decline of the late 1960s–early 1970s New Left protest movement'. She contends that the stigmatisation of the New Left, hierarchical organisations and unpleasant confrontations with the police led to the building of newly conceived mini-publics, made up of networks that constitute an invisible civil society (Steinhoff, 2015: 104). Steinhoff is commenting from a Japanese perspective, where the mass demonstration has been significantly replaced by a smaller scale organisational form, known as the *shukai* (gathering), composed of like-minded citizens. Invisible civil society is also a product of the internet, suggesting that the medium of civic protest may have changed but not the message. Jeremy Harding (2019: 3) makes the connection between the past and the present in relation to the *Gilets Jaunes* in France: 'the outings have ritual echoes from a long past of French contestation, but *Gilets Jaunes* are thoroughly twenty-first century citizens, left out in the cold by globalisation. The success of the protest depends on social media'.

The meta-question of democracy: citizenship and human rights

Stéphane Hessel's *Time of Outrage* (2011), calling on citizens to resist alleged state oppression in a similar manner to World War II resistance movements, found its answer on the streets across European cities. France, Greece and Spain became the main theatres of protest against austerity and exclusion. The Brexit debacle, which since 2016 has produced massive street and online protest in the United Kingdom, also needs to be included. At issue is the nature and meaning of governance: 'when those at the top can no longer govern as before and those at the bottom no longer want to be governed as before' (Harding, 2019: 11), paraphrasing Lenin. The lines between civic protest and political revolution are blurred. Human rights offers a form of communicative ethics to democratically negotiate this political impasse.

In Spain *Democracia real ya!* was the slogan of Spanish *indignados* that occupied the Placa del Sol in Madrid and Placa de Catalunya in Barcelona and hundreds of squares across the country from 15 May 2011, calling for changes in social and economic policies and greater participation by citizens in decision-making (della Porta, 2012: 66). In Greece the *Aganaktismenoi* movement occupied Syntagma Square in Athens on 29 June 2011 and engaged in public debate about the consequences of the harsh austerity measures being imposed on the country. The parallels with the classical Athenian *agora*, which met a few hundred metres away, were striking (*The Guardian*, 15 June 2011). The daily occupations of Syntagma Square often drew crowds of 100,000 citizens to protest. In many other European cities similar protests took place organised by outraged citizens. Their sense of injustice was very real. During 2018/19 the *Gilet Jaunes* literally set France on fire, symbolically burning many of the buildings on the Champs Elysee in central Paris. The wanton violence has raised fundamental questions about the democratic credentials of the *Gilets Jaunes* and its political value base, undermining its public credibility as a legitimate form of democratic protest. However, the *Gilets Jaunes* 'Peoples Directives' suggest that its position is more complex, favouring 'zero homelessness', popular referenda and the parliamentary enabling of laws proposed by citizens in a compromise between representative and direct democracy.

The response to globalisation and austerity economics resulting from the 2008 global economic crisis has been threefold. First, the parliamentary Left has mobilised around the management of austerity, including drastic cuts in public expenditure that have downsized the welfare state, wage restraint and the introduction of the gig economy, while supporting commercial banks and financial institutions. Second, the social Left, in the form of the voluntary and community sector (civil society), have responded through community action, including: the provision of food banks, advocacy for the homeless and charitable assistance for the indigent poor on the streets. Third, new social movements have broadened the struggle into a debate about the nature and meaning of democracy – for example, *Democracia Real Ya!* in Spain and the *Gilet Jaunes* in France. This approach seeks not only policy change but greater public participation in the formulation of policy, which digitalisation makes possible. They have put Claus Offe's meta-question of democracy at the centre of the debate by challenging the boundaries of institutional politics (della Porta, 2012: 66). The issue at stake is the quality of individual citizen's personal democratic experiences and the need for political elites to actively engage with citizens' voices and human rights.

Trust in European institutions arguably will not be fully restored until democratic engagement takes place around the question of what it means to be a citizen in the twenty-first century and what human rights it confers. This is the biggest challenge facing European civil society in contemporary reality, since it is existentially founded on the right to associate as the cornerstone of democratic practice (Powell, 2013). That is the meta-question of democracy. Democracy is about humanity's desire to nurture a public sphere for the common good based on a universal set of human rights. But there political contestation about values begins. Truth is shaped by ideology (Pinter, 2005). Because we live in an era when wealth is once again in the ascendant, we should not be blinded by its truths. Thomas Piketty (2014), in his best-selling book *Capital in the Twenty-first Century* based on data from 20 countries and with a historic analysis reaching back to the eighteenth century, has sought to establish long-term economic and social patterns. He adopts a simple and, in social justice terms, pessimistic formula to explain economic inequality: $r>g$ (meaning that return on capital is generally higher than economic growth). The import of Piketty's analysis is that while the apocalyptic predictions by Karl Marx of the gradual immiseration of the population may have been avoided by economic growth and the diffusion of knowledge, inequality is growing. The logic behind Piketty's argument suggests that the optimism that accompanied the welfare state, as a social compromise between capital and labour, was not founded on a solid long-term redistributive base.

Strong democracy and human rights: the shape of the future

John Keane (2009), in his important book *The Life and Death of Democracy*, locates democracy's origins in ancient Athens. The *agora* (a site of political assembly or marketplace) became a metaphor for Greek civil society as Greece evolved into city-states from about 700 BC. Keane (2009:14) concludes: 'through their public encounters in the agora, Athenians could feel their power, their ability to speak to each other, to act with and against their fellow citizens, in pursuit of commonly defined ends'. The *agora* enabled mini-publics to participate in the democratic process. This made it immediate, accountable and transparent.

Benjamin Barber laments the erosion of democracy from within, through the triumph of thin (representative) democracy – which in his view marginalises citizens from the decision-making process and undermines popular sovereignty. He likens this process to 'politics as zookeeping', in which 'democracy is undone by a hundred kinds of activity more profitable than citizenship; by a thousand seductive acquisitions cheaper than liberty' (Barber, 1984: xvii). Thin democracy shifts popular power to distant elite representative institutions, far from communities where citizens live. Instead of participation in decision-making, citizens are reduced to a passive state, like animals in a zoo waiting for their keepers to decide their lives for them. Strong democracy envisages the human right to association and the participation of all of the citizenry in at least some aspects of governance at least some of the time. It is an act of 'democratizing democracy' (Santos, 2006). Human rights opens up the public realm to the possibility of participative democracy because it embraces the mobilisation of the sovereignty of 'the commonwealth' in the form of people power (Hardt and Negri, 2009).

Strong democracy offers society the choice of taking responsibility for the democratic restoration that has the potential to give substance to the somewhat hackneyed slogan 'power to the people'. Prugh and colleagues (2000: 10) have asserted that strong democracy offers immediate advantages over the 'thin democracy' of the representative variety, emphasising: (i) the sociality of the conception of a social 'us' inherent in notions of community; (ii) the dispersal and redistribution of power away from special interests; and (iii) engaging citizens in the challenges and problems of governance. They add: 'we need politics of engagement, not a politics of consignment' (Prugh et al, 2000: 220). Harding has concluded that in France there is no denying that 'the *Gilets Jaunes* have interfered with the clock, slowing down the pace of life and forcing a political hiatus' (Harding, 2019: 11). It has prompted the French government to engage in 'a great national debate', including social justice and fiscal justice as core themes. Over a million citizens have participated in a national questionnaire about the state of society. Thousands have attended town hall meetings, sometimes including President Macron, which has reportedly been very successful (Harding, 2019).

We live in a world where many active citizens are concerned to address the democratic deficits that have arisen in the period of globalisation (Powell, 2012). Participation has become a pivotal concern. Young asserts that: 'beyond membership and voting rights, inclusive democracy enables participation and voice for all those affected by problems and their proposed solutions' (Young, 2000: 9–10). In essence, this is a statement of strong democracy. It promotes participation and inclusion. In contrast, thin democracy leaves it to political elites to speak for us and represent our interests. There is a fundamental issue of political equality and republican respect at issue here. Moreover, there is an issue of trust and toleration that defines pluralistic democracy. The reality is that not everybody is given equal voice in liberal democratic societies. Civic protest gives voice to these discontents with democracy, where citizens may feel they are being treated more like subjects (Powell, 2012). Monarchy survives in its exalted role, a wholly undemocratic institution based on the most extreme form of exclusion – blood lineage. But perhaps more troubling is the role of the oligarchies of power and wealth in manufacturing consensus, through their capacity to monopolise the media and purchase political influence. In this hierarchical world of power, exclusion is rife. As Young puts it: 'perhaps the most pervasive and insidious form of external exclusion in modern democracies is what I referred to as the ability for economically or socially powerful actors also to exercise political domination' (Young, 2000: 54). Brexit is a good example of the manipulation of public discontent with the system of governance. Young asserts that: 'one task of democratic civil society is to explore and criticise exclusions such as these, and doing so sometimes effectively challenges the legitimacy of institutional rules and their decision' (Young, 2000: 55). The above critique of the limits of democratic inclusion begs the question, 'is there any point in participation?' Some commentators suggest that there may not be any value in participation and add that it is unreasonable to push people in that direction (Cooke and Kothari, 2001). They view the postmodern political landscape as barren and civil society as a meaningless concept.

On the other hand, Ramirez (2006: 238) contends that in the task of confronting global hegemonic forces and forging a new grammar of democracy to meet the challenges of the twenty-first century, local and popular movements are opening up new democratic spaces for participation that are effectively counteracting the more extreme forms of exclusion and erosion of citizen's political, social and economic rights. Human rights offer a grammar for politics and an agenda for democracy that will promote peace and prosperity in the future.

Conclusion

There is a rupture in the relationship between the state and civil society, with no clear vision of the future. Austerity alienates citizens from the state. In the circumstances, Benjamin Barber (1984) has advocated to citizens that they have the power to construct their own future by replacing thin (representative model) democracy by strong/thick democracy (participative model). His democratic vision is for a bottom-up renewal of popular sovereignty. Arguably, the best arrangement would be based on a closer alignment between the two models. But there is still need for political substance to underpin this dialogical process. The idea of sovereignty is dependent on rights – human rights that give substance to citizenship. Barber wants citizens to forge their own democratic narrative, in which they once again become sovereign in making history and society through the exercise of human rights. We are invited by Barber to deepen our democracy, think for ourselves, and shape our own destiny. Oddly, this sounds strangely counter-intuitive. Like Benjamin Barber's caged animals, we do not like to leave the comfort of the cage. Somehow, we remain mesmerised like the characters in Haruki Murakami's novel *IQ84*. But there are voices of protest: Extinction Rebellion, the *Akanaktismenoi*, *Los Indignados*, the Occupy movement and the *Gilet Jaunes*. The Occupy movement attracted public support because its members dared to step outside their personal cages and enter the public sphere. The anti-austerity movement resembles those campaigns for the right of association that gave birth to democracy during the seventeenth, eighteenth and nineteenth centuries. That resulted in the twentieth-century welfare state, the purportedly good society that benefited citizens with social rights, even if it failed to stem long-term inequality. It too is being suppressed in the era of 'surveillance capitalism', however successful and compatible with a burgeoning economy. The restoration of a universal welfare state, as the embodiment of human rights in a globalised world, arguably, should be the priority for the future of democracy in the twenty-first century.

References

Barber, B. (1984) *Strong Democracy: Participatory Politics for a New Age*, Berkeley, CA: University of California Press.

Baxter, C. (2011) 'Behind Murakami's mirror', *New York Review of Books*, 8 December, 23–25.

Camus, A. (1962) *The Rebel*, Harmondsworth: Penguin.

Castoriadis, C. (1987) *The Imaginary Institution of Society*, Cambridge, MA: MIT Press.

Cooke, B. and Kothari, U. (eds) (2001) *Participation: The New Tyranny?*, London: Zed Books.

Della Porta, D. (2012) 'The road to Europe: movements and democracy', in M. Kaldor, H. Moore and S. Selchon (eds) *Global Civil Society 2012*, London: Palgrave Macmillan.

Harding, J. (2019) 'Among the Gilet Jaunes', *London Review of Books*, 41(6), 21 March.

Hardt, M. and Negri, A. (2000) *Empire*, Cambridge, MA: Harvard University Press.

Hardt, M. and Negri, A. (2009) *Commonwealth*, Cambridge, MA: Belknap Press.

Hessel, S. (2011) *Time of Outrage*, New York: Twelve.

Keane, J. (2009) *The Life and Death of Democracy*, London: Simon and Schuster.

Marshall, T.H. (1973) *Class, Citizenship and Social Development*, Westport, CT: Greenwood Press.

Murakami, H. (2011) *IQ84*, London: Harvill Secker.

Nadler, S. (1999) *Spinoza: A Life*, Cambridge: Cambridge University Press.

Offe, C. (1985) 'New social movements: challenging the boundaries of institutional politics', *Social Research*, 5(4): 817–868.

Orwell, G. (1949) *1984*, London: Penguin.

O'Toole, F. (2015) 'State puts on rich mouth when dealing with debt', *Irish Times*, 3 February.

Piketty, T. (2014) *Capital in the Twenty-First Century*, Cambridge, MA: Belknap Press.

Pinter, H. (2005) *Art, Truth and Politics*, Nobel Lecture. Available from: https://www.nobelprize.org/prizes/literature/2005/pinter/lecture/

Powell, F. (1992) *The Politics of Irish Social Policy 1600–1992*, New York: Edwin Mellon Press.

Powell, F. (2010) 'Tom Paine', in *International Encyclopaedia of Civil Society*, New York: Springer, pp 438–442.

Powell, F. (2012) 'Citizens or subjects? Civil society and the Republic', in F. O'Toole, *Up The Republic*, London: Faber and Faber, pp 136–168.

Powell, F. (2013) *The Politics of Civil Society*, 2nd edition, Bristol: Policy Press.

Prugh, T., Constanza, R. and Daly, H. (2000) *The Local Politics of Global Sustainability*, Washington, DC: Island Press.

Ramirez, M. (2006) 'The politics of recognition and citizenship', in B. Santos (ed) *Democratizing Democracy*, London: Verso, pp 222–255.

Santos, B. (ed) (2006) *Democratizing Democracy*, London: Verso.

Steinhoff, P. (2015) 'Finding happiness in Japan's invisible society', *Voluntas*, 26: 98–120.

Van Gelder, S. (ed) (2011) *This Changes Everything*, San Francisco: Barret-Koehler.

Young, I.M. (2000) *Inclusion and Democracy*, Oxford: Oxford University Press.

Zuboff, S. (2019) *The Age of Surveillance Capitalism*, London: Profile Books.

Index